DOCTORS' STORIES

DOCTORS' STORIES

THE NARRATIVE STRUCTURE OF MEDICAL KNOWLEDGE

Kathryn Montgomery Hunter

PRINCETON UNIVERSITY PRESS

PRINCETON, NEW JERSEY

LIBRARY OF CONGRESS CATALOGING-IN-PUBLICATION DATA

HUNTER, KATHRYN MONTGOMERY, 1939–
DOCTORS' STORIES : THE NARRATIVE STRUCTURE OF MEDICAL KNOWLEDGE/
KATHRYN MONTGOMERY HUNTER.
P.   CM.
INCLUDES BIBLIOGRAPHICAL REFERENCES (P.   ) AND INDEX.
ISBN 0-691-06888-7
ISBN 0-691-01505-8 (PBK.)
1. MEDICAL EDUCATION—PHILOSOPHY. I. TITLE.
R737.H78   1991   90-9072
610'.1—DC20

THIS BOOK HAS BEEN COMPOSED IN ADOBE SABON

In memory of TSM and LMR

It is a safe rule to have no teaching
without a patient for a text,
and the best teaching is that
taught by the patient himself.
(Sir William Osler)

. . . no ideas but in things—
(William Carlos Williams)

CONTENTS

PREFACE

I STUMBLED on the interpretive nature of medicine through my own need to make sense of the knowledge necessary to practice medicine. Although this study grows out of more than a decade of teaching in three medical schools and observing in several more, I began teaching medical students in the company of biologists. I was an English professor, an outsider, on the faculty of the Morehouse Medical School, a new school designed to grow along with its students by adding a year of instruction each year. We had no hospital, no clinic, and therefore no patients. Except for cardio-pulmonary resuscitation, human behavior, and the medical humanities courses I taught, our curriculum was the traditional one established at Johns Hopkins and confirmed by the Flexner Report at the beginning of the twentieth century.[1] Until quite recently this curriculum prevailed in almost all of the more than 120 American medical schools, and, even after the Association of American Medical Colleges' report on the General Professional Education of the Physician (GPEP),[2] it remains the fundamental pattern. Because there is not much "real doctoring" in these first two years—students do not see patients until their third-year immersion in clinical work—the beginning faculty included few physicians. With the exception of the pathologists, we were Ph.D.'s: anatomists, biochemists, histologists, physiologists, pharmacologists, psychologists, microbiologists, and one literary scholar.

I had taught for ten years at Morehouse College, which courageously had begun this medical school, and, because it was a small liberal arts institution, I had always known scientists. Several years before, the chair of the physics department and I had taught an experimental course in observation and description. More recently in the freshman honors program, I had offered a course called "The Evolution of the Idea of Evolution." A number of my students went to medical school, and soon I was a member of the committee that drafted the faculty's composite letters of recommendation. From there it was a short step to joining my colleagues engaged in planning a medical school. I chaired the committee that studied the inclusion of the humanities and the social sciences in the curriculum.

The humanities were a new part of medical education in the mid-1970s. My assignment was to design and staff the course included in the curriculum in each of the first two years.[3] Drawing on philosophy, literature, anthropology, sociology, religious studies, history, and law, such courses offer first- and second-year students an opportunity to think about and try on the moral and professional lives toward which their education is propelling them. After some initial skepticism—curriculum time is every medical school's scarcest, most valued commodity—most of those whom medical education labels "basic scientists" were relatively comfortable with—and some were stimulated by—the presence of such odd people as philosophers, historians, lawyers, and sociologists teaching about medicine. In its third year, having proven itself successful, the school received permission from the Liaison Committee on Medical Education to admit larger classes and to begin planning for the years of clinical instruction. As it happened, I left just before the physicians arrived.

I went next to the University of Rochester School of Medicine and Dentistry. There I found an older, larger, altogether grander place, recognized for the number of scientific research grants it garners in a highly competitive world and for its curricular attention to the psychosocial aspects of illness. I was presumed to be experienced, but though I knew a great deal about medical education, I knew very little about academic tertiary-care medical centers. I did not expect to be comfortable. Here were physicians, subspecialists, superscientists. The size of the school alone—with classes four times larger than the first classes at Morehouse—seemed to promise a certain degree of alienation. Above all, the two last, clinical years of medical school and the presence of hundreds of interns and residents in the adjacent and affiliated hospitals made this not simply a school but a center for clinical research and highly sophisticated medical care.

My first task there, after my teaching, was to understand this strange territory. An education in English literature and literary theory did not promise to be much help. To remedy my ignorance, I went to seminars that reported on clinical research and to weekly grand rounds that concerned an "interesting" or problematic clinical case. I began with those whose titles I could understand, ones that had a clinical focus. I wanted to know how research into clinical problems was carried out: how were the problems understood and solved? Above all, I hoped to understand how those years of education in the sciences of human biology were preparing students to solve problems in clinical practice.

The research seminars I attended were given by careful investigators who used sound methods and focused on real problems, often with quite important results. Yet the presentations, I noticed, were not quite like a journal article on the same question. Again and again, regardless of clinical discipline—usually near the end of the presentation or early in the question period—I heard an account of the case that had first revealed to the investigator the existence of a clinical problem that was open to research. "There was this one guy . . . ," the speaker might explain, beginning a narrative of the signal case, the instance that had provoked first the investigator's curiosity and then the research. For grand rounds, I realized, the order is reversed: this weekly ritual in each of the clinical disciplines begins with a presentation of a case, considering first the individual patient who poses a difficult question of diagnosis or therapy, and then moves to a discussion of research, often the speaker's own, which has led—or should lead—to a clear, more readily made diagnosis or to a new method of treatment.

Whatever the occasion, whether the case was introduced informally in seminars or presented with routine formality in grand rounds, the method of presenting the data of clinical science was familiar to me. The substance was necessarily new—puzzles made up of reported symptoms and observed and measured signs—but the accounts of a patient's malady and the physician's diagnosis and treatment were the stuff of my own discipline.[4] They were stories, narrative accounts of the action and motives of individual human beings, physicians and patients, who, variously, were frustrated by circumstance, rewarded for effort, and plagued by fate. Stories had been the last things I had expected to find in a medical center. Isn't medicine a science? Aren't such stories mere anecdotes?

I discovered that the theory and methods of understanding that are traditional to the humanities are useful in understanding what it is that clinicians do. In 1983, with a grant from the National Science Foundation, I undertook a project that has itself been an interpretive activity: the understanding of medicine. Daily for two years and in three hospitals I followed willing colleagues on work rounds, to morning report and professors' rounds, to sign-out rounds and problem conferences, to morbidity and mortality conferences, and to grand rounds. During that time (and later when I observed elsewhere or returned to renew my observations) I behaved rather like an ethnographer among a white-coated tribe, observing the clinical education of medical students and house staff in internal medicine and surgery. I attended all teaching occasions repeatedly and then sampled them again in subsequent years while I wrote. For two years I was a regular fixture. I was an outsider, far more observer than participant, but then academic medicine is rife with observers. I was known to faculty and residents as a professor in the medical school located in the same cluster of buildings. I had taught at first a few and ultimately most of the third-year students who joined the hospital units for their clerkships. I did not wear a white coat. On those occasions when I went with a group to the bedside, I was introduced by name and title and task ("She's studying *us*"), and the patient's permission was sought. My project was understood as a study of the way medicine is taught and learned, and it was generally known (and important in a research institution) that, although my field was literature (wasn't it?), I had been funded by the NSF. Few were curious about the study's details or its hypothesis. They assumed (or so it seemed to me) that I was simply around, "backstage," getting a preliminary sense of doctoring before turning to what, given the school's emphasis and the courses I taught, was probably the object of my study: the interaction between patient and physician. They were not entirely wrong.

My focus was on the interaction between physicians teaching and learning to take care of patients, sometimes both at once. I listened for "literary" phenomena: metaphors, absence of metaphor, jargon and its uses, stories in all their variety, narrative themes. I had questions (refined, as I went, into hypotheses) about how knowledge is acquired and how teaching takes place, about the process of professionalization, the effect of the academic hierarchy, and the almost unquestioned assumption that medicine is a science (and the unquestioned uses of that assumption). I took occasional notes, doodling two or three key words on a styrofoam coffee cup. After rounds, I raced back to my office to make a full entry in notebooks that I indexed as I went along. I tape-recorded sessions of morning report. Only one faculty member and two residents were told that I was particularly listening for "stories," and in medicine that word suggests anecdotes rather than routine case presentations. I tried ideas out on these and other informants among faculty, house staff, students. At times the apparently inevitable process of "going native" set in. I would realize that for the past few days I had been listening like one of "them" for the telling fact, waiting to clinch the diagnosis. The antidote was to change location or specialty and become a thorough outsider again. I enjoyed the idea that my research involved much the same interpretive process that I was discovering to be essential to the physicians' understanding of patients.

ACKNOWLEDGMENTS

THE CONSTRUCTION of this account of medical narrative has been enriched by my family and friends and colleagues. Those who know something of the history of attention to patients in American medicine and the investigation of the psychosocial issues that complicate their illnesses and their medical care will recognize the influence of the University of Rochester. While I was still at Morehouse, David Satcher lent me *The Clinical Approach to the Patient*, an influential guide to the patient-physician encounter by Rochesterians William L. Morgan, Jr., and George L. Engel. Once there, I incurred debts that are numerous and great. Throughout the years of my research, my colleagues were unfailingly helpful, subjecting me to little more than a bracing modicum of skepticism about literature's place in understanding medicine. I owe my clinical education especially to Robert L. Berg, Lynn Bickley, Cecile A. Carson, Jules Cohen, Christopher Desch, William R. Drucker, David Goldblatt, William A. Greene, Robert J. Joynt, Rudolph J. Napodano, William L. Morgan, Jr., John Morton, Jr., W. Scott Richardson, John Romano, the late Ernest W. Saward, Olle Jane Sahler, Barbara L. Schuster, Seymour I. Schwartz, and T. Franklin Williams. Craig Hohm, then a third-year resident, was my Aeneas during the first year of clinical observation. Lewis White Beck and Jane Greenlaw were dear and unfailing sources of advice and criticism and encouragement.

At other institutions Howard Brody, Eric J. Cassell, Rita Charon, Julia E. Connelly, Daniel M. Fox, William Frucht, Robert Kellogg, Loretta Kopelman, Joseph Margolis, John Stone, Carolyn Warner, and William Beatty Warner variously argued about ideas, read chapters, or took me on rounds. Anthropologists Joan Cassell, Ayala Gabriel, and Grace Gredys Harris provided essential guidance in the methods of ethnographic research. In the faculty study group on social theory at Rochester I learned much that was useful; I am particularly grateful to William Scott Green, Donald Kelley, and Philip Wexler. I learned, too, from the ideas and observations of those who were then students and residents at Rochester and in the summer humanities seminars for medical students funded by the National Endowment for the Humanities at the Kennedy Institute, Georgetown University; chief among them were Holly Anderson, Emily Finkelstein, Stephen Matchett, Barry Saunders, and Brian Zink.

I am indebted to the Hastings Center, especially to Daniel Callahan, Thomas Murray, Arthur Caplan, and Marna Howarth, for the time I spent there as a visiting scholar near the beginning of this project. A two-year grant from the Ethics and Values in Science and Technology program of the National Science Foundation (RII-8310291) funded my research, and a fellowship from the American Council of Learned Societies and a sabbatical from the University of Rochester in 1986–87 gave me a welcome year to write. Ellen Key Harris, Pelin Aylangan, Elizabeth Gajary, and Jennifer Powell helped with research, and Lucretia McClure, librarian of the Edward G. Miner Library, and Christopher Houlihan, its history of medicine librarian, lightened my work. In Chicago I have benefited from a community of scholars from several institutions, especially James F. Bresnahan, my colleague at Northwestern University Medical School, Christine Cassel, William Donnelly, Leon Kass, and Suzanne Poirier. Charles L. Bosk, Julia Connelly, Ellen Key Harris, J. Paul Hunter, Lisa Hunter, Steven H. Miles, Beth Montgomery, and Francis A. Neelon read many of the chapters in draft and made indispensable suggestions. I have learned from presenting some of its ideas informally to members of the Camellia Grill Literary and Debating Society and, beginning in 1983, at meetings of the Society for Health and Human Values and its Association for Faculty in the Medical Humanities.

Long projects have a way of becoming indistinguishable from one's life, and I am grateful to all those who have shared mine.

INTRODUCTION

INTERPRETING MEDICINE

"Students of criminology will remember the analogous
incidents in Grodno, in Little Russia, in the year '66,
and of course there are the Anderson murders
in North Carolina, but this case possesses
some features which are entirely its own."
(*Sherlock Holmes to Dr. Watson,*
The Hound of the Baskervilles)

THE PRACTICE of medicine is an interpretive activity. It is the art
of adjusting scientific abstractions to the individual case. The
daily life of a practicing physician is made up of observing, testing, interpreting, explaining as well as taking action to restore the patient
to health. Much of this is routine, the exercise of clinical judgment that
has been acquired, first, by a thorough education in human biology and,
then, by participation in the care of a myriad of single cases that are narratively described and studied one by one. The details of individual maladies are made sense of and treatment is undertaken in light of the principles of biological science. Yet medicine's focus on the individual patient,
fitting general principles to the particular case, means that the knowledge
possessed by clinicians is narratively constructed and transmitted. How
else can the individual be known?

Medicine, for all its reliance on esoteric knowledge and sophisticated
technology, is not a science. This ought not to be a controversial or even
a surprising statement, yet many physicians are likely to find it unacceptable. In the twentieth century, science and the ideal of scientific rationality
have played such an important part in medical education and the care of
patients that they are now central to our idea of the profession. Scientific
advances have given us an almost unassailable confidence in medical
efficacy. Epidemiologists and historians of medicine have demonstrated
that it was not medicine that improved health and lengthened life in the
late nineteenth century but a more productive agriculture, pure water
supplies, improved hygiene, and population control.[1] In our own time the
incidence of heart disease in the United States has been lowered not by the
ingenious techniques of cardiac surgery but by a striking alteration of
habits. Yet this epidemiological view of history does not capture our
sense of medicine's importance in our lives. The achievements of public

health and preventive medicine are faceless generalities. Our faith in medical science rests on particular cases, which are far more vivid and compelling. We know people, often close to us, who have been saved by physicians. Even those of us who thus far have been healthy have led lives altered for the better by medicine: antibiotics cure infections; microsurgery repairs a damaged knee; syphilis, polio, and smallpox are rare or extinct; pacemakers, artificial heart valves, laser beams, and birth control pills have given us lives different from those our grandparents lived. Not even medicine's severest critics would be willing to return to the good old days.[2]

A drawback to such progress, however, is that we have unthinkingly assimilated medicine to other intellectual advances of the twentieth century. We have given our faith to science, and medicine's importance to us and its twentieth-century success have led us to believe—physicians as well as patients—that medicine is itself a science. The circumstantial evidence is strong. Physicians have spent years learning the minuscule details of human biology. Some of them conduct scientific research. They use intricate machines designed in accordance with scientific principles to detect and treat disease and physical malfunction. They wear white coats as a sign of their professional objectivity. They prognosticate, knowing truths about our bodies that we ourselves cannot (or have not yet begun to) experience. Above all, they are familiar with death and are fearless and rational in its presence. Most of us will learn from one of them how and approximately when our lives will end. In a culture that shrinks from death and has few ways other than medicine of coming to terms with finitude, physicians are set apart by their education and experience. "Science" serves as the sign of their special knowledge.

Nevertheless, no matter how scientific it may be, medicine is not a science as science is commonly understood: an invariant and predictive account of the physical world.[3] Medicine's goal is to alleviate present suffering. Although it draws on the principles of the biological sciences and owes much of its success to their application, medicine is (as it always has been) a practical body of knowledge brought to bear on the understanding and treatment of particular cases. We seek more from a visit to the doctor than the classification of our malady. We want our condition to be understood and treated. Face to face with a patient, physicians can know disease only indirectly. They depend for its identification on their interpretation of the signs they observe and the story of symptoms the patient tells them. They are barred by ethics and by the chronology of post hoc investigation from many forms of experimental investigation. Instead, like Sherlock Holmes, they must begin with the effects of illness and reason backward to the causes of disease. They cannot offer us a diagnosis, much less cure or palliation, until they have accounted for the symptoms and signs we present to them.[4] Thus, modern medical practice is founded on an arduous scientific education augmented by formidable diagnostic machinery, but interpretive skill is inevitably required for physicians to work even their everyday wonders.

This distinction between interpretive and scientific knowing is not invalidated by the fact that it is given little attention in medical practice and is seldom made explicit in medical education. The limitation of medical knowing is not a new philosophic insight. Two hundred years ago, the necessary retrospection of medicine's knowledge—what Sherlock Holmes describes to Watson as reasoning backward along the chain from effect to cause—was described by David Hume and the Marquis de Condorcet, each in his different way concerned with the legitimacy of knowledge that is based on observation and therefore lacks deductive certainty. In his essay *Du Degré de certitude de la médecine* (1798), Pierre-Jean-George Cabanis, physician and philosopher, recognized that in clinical medicine inductive reasoning is inevitably flawed, but argued nevertheless for the relative, probable, practical certainty that medical therapy might achieve through careful observation, rational classification, and experimental testing.[5] In our time, the immensity of its relative, probable, and practical success has often obscured our understanding of medicine as an intellectual pursuit or as the exercise of practical wisdom in the face of uncertainty.

Despite its success, medicine's identification as a science has had adverse effects on both the education of physicians and the patient-physician relationship: the two are not unrelated. Our misunderstanding has led to mistaken expectations on the part of both physicians and patients and, ultimately, to less than optimal care of the ill and to impoverished lives for physicians. It encourages physicians and patients alike to focus narrowly on the diagnosis of disease rather than attend to what is even more necessary, the care of the person who is ill.

Misplaced expectations of medicine have not been solely responsible for the profession's recent difficulties, of course. Contemporary impediments to the patient-physician relationship have been well described.[6] The proliferation of technology used in the diagnosis and treatment of disease has driven the physician farther and farther from the presence of the patient.[7] The "knowledge explosion" in human biology has meant that a thorough comprehension of any one of its fields could easily occupy a career—and leave little time for the care of patients. The welter of contemporary economic arrangements estranges patient and physician and encourages distrust on both sides; malpractice suits and defensive medicine viciously circle. Underneath it all, however, the mistaken idea of medicine as a body of objective, scientific knowledge that has only to be mastered to bring reliable results impoverishes both medical education and medical practice. It has deprived students of the generative attention of mature practitioners and all physicians of a well founded appreciation of the case-based, skeptical method by which they have achieved so much. About this fundamental misunderstanding, it has seemed to me, something could be done.

What is needed is a conception of medicine, both inside the profession and beyond it, that not only takes account of the physician's daily work of diagnosing and treating illness but also acknowledges its well-developed narrative method of acquiring and conveying its essential knowledge. Medicine is an interpretive activity, a learned inquiry that begins with the understanding of the patient and ends in therapeutic action on the patient's behalf. Far from being objective, a matter of hard facts, medicine is grounded in subjective knowledge—not of the generalized body in textbooks, which is scientific enough—but the physician's understanding of the particular patient. The interpretive task of medicine is made explicit in the language of radiology: "You'll receive a separate bill from the radiologist for the interpretation of the X rays," we are told at the cashier's window of countless American hospitals. There is a palpable text, the roentgenogram, for a physician to read. But the rest of medicine is little different, for the body, too, is palpable—and palpate it physicians do, looking for lumps and swellings, "appreciating" the distance the liver extends beyond the rib cage, detecting suspicious tenderness. The interpretation of the individual patient's physical signs in order to construct a coherent and parsimonious retrospective chronological account of a malady is a methodology that, while thoroughly rational, is distinct from that characteristic of the physical sciences. That physicians are scientifically educated and technologically trained alters not one bit the narrative structure of their practical knowledge. Indeed, the physician's own subjectivity as well as the subjectivity of the patient is controlled by the fixed conventions of medical narrative.

This study advances such an interpretive conception of medicine, describing the use of narratives by physicians to learn and to teach, to record familiar maladies, and to investigate and report unfamiliar ones. It is not a sociology of medicine. I have focused on academic medicine as it is practiced and taught in university medical centers and reported in the *New England Journal of Medicine*. As a consequence, I have not written about the political and economic realities of contemporary practice in the United States, important though I know them to be. American physicians are so varied and under such economic and regulative pressure that such a study would be a formidable task, one I am not qualified to undertake. Instead I have been concerned with medicine as it is taught and as physicians believe they should practice it. I have meant to describe medicine's ways of knowing and its methods of transmitting that knowledge. Clinical medicine is the exercise of practical knowledge, medical education the inculcation of a craft. Despite its reliance on dozens of heavy and expensive textbooks and thousands of scholarly journals, medicine is passed on as a traditional practice: interpretive, diagnostic, concerned with the identification and treatment of disease. The tradition works well in difficult or puzzling cases and is useful in advancing the knowledge of etiology and therapeutics, but it is insufficient for long-term patient care and for the cultivation of interest in the problems of general practice. Scientific advances augment and reinforce the diagnostic tradition; by contrast, chronic illness and dying tend to be "uninteresting" to many physicians because they do not.

My method has been ethnographic, describing the customs and habits and assumptions of medicine's teachers and learners as I have observed them. In the academic medical center, medicine takes its most nearly idealized and scientific form, and its culture influences the rest of medical practice. Absorbed and internalized by every physician as student, intern, and resident, academic medicine remains the "gold standard" of practice no matter how irrelevant it may be rendered by real life in a small-town general practice, an inner-city clinic, or a suburban HMO. There are local variations in custom from one medical center to another and noticeable differences among specialties. But the remarkable thing is the relative uniformity of the culture of academic medicine. Students regularly take residencies at hospitals other than the one associated with their medical school, and their expectation that they will find clinical services much like those where they began their clinical education is seldom challenged. What little variation they find amounts to "local color": whether case presenters may use notes or not, whether the early morning review of new hospital admissions is called "morning report" or "sign-in rounds," whether the professor is told about the case to be presented at professor's rounds ahead of time or truly risks being stumped, whether "humanizing details" are added to the case history or not, whether the "chief complaint" is noted or omitted. The differences—responses to new conditions, the fallings-away, the improvements—are variants of the tradition, an ideology recorded and reinforced by general academic journals. This study focuses on that tradition. In the academic medical center, where it is presumed to be most nearly pure and scientific, clinical medicine must rely on the narration of cases for the preservation and advancement of its practical knowledge.

Understanding medicine as a narrative activity enables us—both physicians and patients—to shift the focus of medicine to the care of what ails the patient and away from the relatively simpler matter of the diagnosis of disease. In the last two decades, calls for physicians to attend to "the whole patient" have not been answered with notable success. There are countless physicians who care deeply about patients and care for them in the context of their lives admirably and effectively. But "holistic medicine" continues to be the object of scorn, especially in academic medicine, designating a practice that would ignore the physical facts for a dangerously narrow attention to the patient's psychological comfort.[8] Physicians who fail to give the patient's circumstances the attention holistic medicine calls for must either dismiss the ideal or find it a source of guilt and dissatisfaction. The accompanying argument that the mind is a part of the body, intimately connected to illness, sometimes to disease and often to treatment, has not taken firm root in academic medicine.

This book draws on the converse proposition—that the body is a part of the mind—with the hope that it will fare better. I argue, first, that the knowledge of a particular sick body is necessarily filtered through the consciousness of the physician-knower and is thus contextual, embodied, and potentially uncertain; and, second, that the narratives medicine has devised and instituted for the representation of bodily knowledge can take account (and make therapeutic use) of some of the human manifestations of that uncertainty. Part One, Medicine and Interpretation, is primarily theoretical. Chapter 1 begins with the medical semiotics basic to clinical knowledge and describes the place of narrative in medical nosology and in the development and exercise of clinical judgment. Chapter 2 concerns the physician's characteristic attitudes and practices—skepticism, the reluctance to generalize, and the reliance on narrative—engendered in response to the radical uncertainty of medicine's case-based knowledge.

Part Two, Narrative in Medicine, describes medical narrative and the conventions of both its oral and written genres. Chapter 3 examines the case presentation, the fundamental oral narrative constructed by a physician from the patient's story and observation of the patient's body, and its part in the medicalization of illness. Chapter 4 attempts to justify the persistence, even in academic medicine, of the despised anecdote, arguing that its identification of the anomalous is essential to patient care, teaching, and research. Chapter 5 describes written case histories in the patient's chart and in published case reports, those controlled and controlling narratives that must serve as data in the science of clinical medicine. Chapter 6 concerns narrative genres peculiar to the *New England Journal of Medicine*, bastion of American (and thus international) scientific medicine: the clinical-pathological conference and the syndrome letter, both straightforward and comic. Chapter 7 contrasts medical narratives and the patient's story of illness, arguing that their incommensurability, given the urgency and power of medicine's therapeutic concern, dehumanizes medical discourse about (and thus the medical attention to) those who are ill. The remedy for this, I believe, lies in physicians' recognition of this incommensurability: first, in their attention to the patient's story during the interview that begins the encounter and, then, in their careful return of the story—not only in understandable terms but with the acknowledgment that it, like the life it relates, belongs to the patient. Chapter 8 makes a case for the physician's familiarity with literary narrative and for a narrative alteration of the medical case. In an age of chronic disease physicians need not only an encyclopedic, Sherlock Holmes-like knowledge of clinical cases but also a sense of the life stories in which illness and medical care take place. Such narrative knowledge will be reflected in a richer awareness of the intersection of their lives with the lives of their patients.

PART ONE

MEDICINE AND INTERPRETATION

ONE

KNOWLEDGE IN MEDICINE

READING THE SIGNS

"All life is a great chain, the nature of which is known
wherever we are shown a single link of it. . . . In solving a
problem of this sort, the grand thing is to be able to
reason backward."
(*Sherlock Holmes*, A Study in Scarlet)

W HAT DO PHYSICIANS DO? Are they scientists identifying the disease at work in the human body, predicting its course and countering it with specific remedies? Or are they practitioners of a more ancient craft, pondering the ways predisposition and circumstance mesh with the laws of nature in a particular case and encouraging the patient toward recovery or to a recognition of death? These visions of exact knowledge and of healing are foremost among the ideals and expectations brought to modern medicine by its beginning students, and they undergo radical revision in the highly technological tertiary-care hospitals where, in the late twentieth century, students of medicine are almost entirely taught. Both scientific investigation and the care of patients are central to medicine's conception of its task. Both activities have fostered medical progress, focusing attention in turn upon the identification and relief of disease syndromes and upon the explanation of the phenomena of illness. Even outside academic medicine, practitioners ordinarily need not choose between the two. They may think of themselves as scientific healers using biomedical knowledge to understand and treat the symptoms the patient brings to medical attention. Years of education and apprenticeship have equipped all physicians, from clinical investigators to general practitioners, with both a practical taxonomy of reified diseases (together with their standard therapies) and a strong skeptical awareness that a patient's illness often evades these strict categories. If either research or the care of patients has been emphasized in an individual physician's career—as, except in rare instances, must be the case—the choice seems to be simply a matter of the number of available hours in a day or the institutional structure of medicine.

Patients share medicine's idealistic double vision, regarding physicians as both scientific wizards who in the near future will eliminate disease from human experience and as intimate, reliable helpers and advisers who can be trusted to take an interest in the subjective experience of illness. As a consequence, medicine and its practitioners suffer from a gap between these expectations and the reality of late twentieth-century medical care. Patients are dissatisfied, students cynical,[1] practitioners unfulfilled.[2] All long for "magic bullets," instant surefire cures, at a time when much of doctoring is occupied with psychosomatic distress and chronic diseases that can be "managed" but not cured. For the majority of practicing primary-care physicians, the somatic manifestations of depression and anxiety and the long-term care of heart disease, hypertension, lung disease, and cancer make up the stuff of medicine. Yet in medical schools curricular innovation is still necessary to teach ambulatory care or psychosocial medicine or geriatrics to medical students and residents. Patients' assertion of self-determination as an ethical and legal principle, the ongoing malpractice crisis, and the rising costs and consequent economic reorganization of medicine have redefined the realities of medical practice, but these matters, too, struggle for a place in the curriculum. All these "special" topics complicate the traditional process of observation, supervised practice, and gradual assumption of responsibility for hospitalized patients that currently gives medical education its apprenticeship character. The modern teaching hospital relies upon residents and students to help care for people suffering the crises of those same chronic diseases, and thus the preponderance of clinical education consists of learning to apply to those crises the diagnostic and therapeutic technology on which medicine has based its twentieth-century success. Are physicians then technicians? Are they "applied scientists" or engineers?

A clear societal perception of the ideals of medicine and the goals and methods of clinical practice might reduce the exorbitant expectations—not only those brought by patients, but also those that physicians have of themselves and their careers. The benefits could be great: plainer communication, increased patient participation in the decisions about care, the possibility of detaching "satisfaction" from "cure" for both doctor and patient. How are we to conceive of medicine? Is the traditional description of a tension between medicine as an art and medicine as a science adequate—or even accurate? Socrates likens physicians to chefs, the wielders of an instrumental art or craft.[3] As patients, we sometimes see them as friendly chemists or technicians of the human body, yet we also ask them to respond to us and our illnesses variously as magicians, priests, parents.[4] To an observer, they resemble Sherlock Holmes, in search of a clue that will unlock the mystery of the patient's illness. They are also highly trained, critical readers of the text that is the patient.

For practicing physicians, the question of the nature of medicine is seldom troubling. Many more immediate, often life-saving or restorative tasks are at hand, and the common understanding that medicine is a science seems entirely satisfactory. If clinical practice still relies on stories as well as observation and numbers yielded by tests, that is surely temporary or local, not an essential part of the discipline. Medicine may be, as Lewis Thomas has called it, the "youngest science,"[5] unfinished and hard at work on persistent problems of disease, but the assumption is that it is a science nonetheless.

Scientific Facts, Narrative Cases

Medicine is fundamentally narrative—especially the scientific medicine practiced in a tertiary-care teaching hospital—and its daily practice is filled with stories. Most important are the opening stories patients tell their physicians. These are not the vivid, repetitive stories told outside the medical encounter—"my operation" or the "war stories" of a missed or delayed diagnosis[6]—but the opening stories of a malady that gain them admission and good standing in the world of the ill. Patients' stories within medicine are more or less pared-down autobiographical accounts that chronicle the events of illness and sketch out a commonsense etiology: "I'd been feeling pretty good, even with the bursitis—I'd been doing some overtime—but then today, almost every step I took, it hurt something awful." Physicians take such a story, interrogate and expand it, all the while transmuting it into medical information. Sooner or later they will return it to the patient as a diagnosis, an interpretive retelling that points toward the story's ending. In this way, much of the central business of caring for patients is transacted by means of narrative.

The patient's account of illness, although it is the first, is far from being the only narrative in medicine. Oddly enough in this scientific endeavor, the physician's own discourse about illness takes the form of a story. The space between the patient's first words to the physician and the physician's closing recommendation to the patient is filled with medicine's narratives. These are not just sociable commentary on work at hand, notes compared at lunch or in the halls. Medical stories are a well established way of sorting through and tackling problems of diagnosis and treatment. Even when a patient comes in with a simple malady, in that brief moment between the patient's telling the story and the physician's making a hypothetical diagnosis, the physician locates its chronological ordering of the details of illness in a narrative taxonomy of similar cases. In such a scientific discipline it is surprising to find this unexpectedly familiar way of making sense of the "facts."

Storytelling events organize the medical day in a teaching hospital: morning report, professor's rounds, attending rounds, weekly departmental grand rounds, and, in a staccato shorthand, evening sign-out rounds.[7] These educational and consultative occasions concern a particular patient's condition, and it is necessary that the condition be described narratively before it can be usefully discussed. Lectures at noontime and conferences on a particular disease or condition are potentially more general, focused on principles and abstractions that can be applied in practice, but more often than not they too begin with an illustrative account of a patient suffering from the condition to be discussed. All in all, it is as if medical educators, having spent a season at the feet of John Dewey, had sworn an oath to ground all discussion of abstract pathophysiological principles and generalized disease entities in the real, everyday experience of patients.

Medical narrative, at first hearing, does not sound very much like storytelling. Its rendition of that real everyday experience does not resemble life as the patient has been living it: "This is the first Memorial Hospital admission," the case presentation begins, "for Lucius Jefferson, a 61-year-old black man, who presented to the emergency room last night complaining of chest pain . . . ." It has the routine sound of all those official and bureaucratic accounts whose narrators are effaced and whose tone is prescribed and objective. The story of distress that prompted Mr. Jefferson's trip to the hospital is pulled and shaped in its medical retelling into a flattened, only distantly recognizable version.[8] What most troubles the patient may be the pain or the disruption of work or family life or simply the fear that this time "it may be serious." The physician inquires about other things, some of them apparently unrelated to the patient's concerns. Pieced together with the patient's story, the answers to these questions are translated into pathophysiological concepts, and this augmented account of the patient's experience is edited and encoded in the chart in order to eliminate the "irrelevancies" and highlight the abnormal physical details. It is all but unreadable to the untutored eye, and the untutored ear fares only slightly better.

The oral recounting of this medical narrative is a central part of clinical education and supervision in a teaching hospital. Residents report to their colleagues and professors on patients in their care, and in this daily oral ritual, the medical narrative is a means of demonstrating the teller's understanding of the illness. The patient's story of subjective experience has become a narrative of education and control. Case presentations are, in fact, highly conventional narratives. They are strictly ordered and their language is meant to be narrowly descriptive and toneless in order to sort out the patient's subjective report of discomfort and abnormality from the physician's more objective view of the case. This flatness aids the emotional detachment felt necessary to the continued and resourceful care of the ill; it also highlights the pattern of the evidence so that the physician can more readily identify the intellectual puzzles posed by the illness. Chillingly unrecognizable and "scientific" as the resulting case may sound, it is a narrative, a story about Mr. Jefferson. Despite its strangeness, it is just what he has come for: to have his story retold as a medical story as a part of the effort to determine the meaning of the events he reports.

But, one may object, these case presentations are actually scientific reports. Certainly their flattened rhetoric and ritual character are attempts to minimize the unconfirmable, and the numbers they report reinforce this objectivity. Nevertheless, they are also narratives. Within medicine their status as (at least) metaphorical stories is clear. Physicians' habits of ordinary speech interchange "case" and "story" so readily that now and then even a grand rounds speaker will say, while signaling for the slides, "I'm going to show you now some stories like Mr. Jefferson's." Narrative orders events in time. "What's the story on Mr. Jefferson?" one resident will ask another. Such an informal inquiry will not elicit a full-blown case history, of course, but the response—if the speaker and listener have not previously discussed the case—will be a brief, informal version of the case presentation: "Oh, he's the man who came in last night with chest pain." If the two have discussed Mr. Jefferson before, or if the inquirer took care of him last night in the emergency department, the answer will be an update, the next episode of the story: "He's gone down to be cathed" or, later in the diagnostic process, a summary, "It was an MI; he's getting a CABG."

The narrative organization of the medical case is still reinforced in many places by the traditional requirement that students and residents memorize its details[9]—the patient's report of symptoms and medical history, the signs of disease or injury revealed in the physical examination, the results of general and routine tests of the body's chemistry and special tests focused on possible causes. Memorizing is not a gratuitous, ritual act of mental exercise despite its ritual nature, nor is it intended to speed up conferences and rounds, although that is a widely appreciated benefit. It is not even an attempt to compel the case presenters to appear to be so brilliantly competent that each patient is indelibly individualized in their memory, although the truth is close to that. The demand that students memorize the details of the case they present is a demand that they master those details and know them as a whole. They must be made to fit together so as to present a recognizable—or recognizably skewed—clinical story. A disease may have a "clinical picture," but ill patients are varied and changing, and their reality can be captured only over time by narrative. "The numbers," the test results, although they are also graphed to show change or stability over time, must be put into the context of the illness and interpreted in its light. Thus a student's or resident's "command of a case" is not simply technological expertise or the prodigious recall of relevant biological and pathological information, but a ritualized storytelling: orally presented evidence that for this speaker, in this instance, the welter of clinical facts about a single patient constitutes a unity that hangs more or less inevitably together.

The Patient as Text

At its source in the academic medical center, medicine is practiced by means of a series of narrative accounts of illness told in a relatively self-enclosed dialect and according to strict rules that define the genre. These stories or case histories are themselves readings and interpretations of events as they have been represented in patients' narratives or as they have left their marks on patients' bodies. As narrative they are capable both of generating and of testing hypotheses about illness and disease. The patients are the texts to be examined and studied and understood by the physician. Sometimes they can be "read like a book," like the text of a newspaper story or a piece of straightforwardly expository prose. In other instances, the "interesting" cases, patients' stories are less straightforward; they resemble novels or poems, those more complicated works that do not always readily yield an easy paraphrase of their meaning.

Physicians are the readers of these texts, and, like all readers, they read by understanding the signs and fitting them together into a recognizable, communicable whole. The rest of us—especially mothers and those of us with a grasp of "body language"—are capable of preliminary and tentative readings of illness. However skilled, we are the ordinary readers, while physicians are more sophisticated interpreters, familiar with the variations and possibilities that a patient may offer. In this, physicians are like literary critics, who (whatever pleasure they may expect from their reading) arrive at the text laden with theory, assumptions, hypotheses. These expectations concern what will be read there, how to read it, and what it will be understood to mean. Every reader has habits and prejudices and expectations, of course. The competence that distinguishes literary critics from ordinary readers is based on their familiarity with a wide range of other similar texts, a knowledge of the genres (or taxonomy) of those texts, and the traditions from which they derive. In addition, literary critics are likely to possess some self-consciousness about their own perceptual equipment and its cultural or personal origins. So it is with the good physician. Here is a reader who not only grasps (and often ferrets out) the patient's story, but one who is also knowledgeable about the habits and expectations of patient-narrators and understands that the way the story is told is a part of its meaning.

Making Sense of Signs

How is the patient to be understood? It is here that the investigative procedures of medicine resemble the act of reading far more closely than they do the laboratory process that has customarily been regarded as scientific. Diagnosis is interpretive; therapeutics is interpretive; and the care of the patient includes the interpretation of what is regarded as brute fact: the symptoms, the test results. "Your pain is bursitis," the doctor says; or, "The biopsy indicates that that lump is malignant." Patients enter the doctor's office sick; they have come for interpretation of their signs and symptoms. They hope to leave mildly diseased—with "a virus that's going around" or, better, a clear-cut infection that will respond to penicillin. In any case, a diagnostic label is the goal, and often the price, of an interpretive understanding in medicine.

There operates in the everyday practice of medicine a "diagnostic circle" very like the "hermeneutic circle," that process of reasoning from part to whole to part again that Wilhelm Dilthey established as the characteristic mode of understanding in the interpretation of texts.[10] Problems of knowing in medicine are little different from problems of knowing in history or literature or anthropology—or criminal detection. "Internal medicine" is the name that we give that enormous summary specialty from which all others except surgery derive, and its name suggests the nature of the epistemological problem and the need for a medical hermeneutics. How are physicians to know what is wrong *inside* the individual, inaccessible, largely invisible human body?

Surgery and radiology may open the body to visual inspection, but even in such cases medicine relies first of all on the patient's report of the subjective manifestations of illness, the symptoms. To corroborate or confound the patient's report, there are also discernible physical signs that the physician discovers upon examination of the patient's body. These are the objective clues, readable signs of the body's malfunction. They point toward what may have most proximately produced the symptoms and toward what, in the medical interpretation of the patient's story, the symptoms mean. In addition to the physical signs, diagnostic tests yield suggestive, often conclusive results. As all clinicians know, it is a mistake to regard test results as invariably hard evidence, for the numbers they yield are not infallible. Each test has its estimated sensitivity and specificity, ready to be put into a Bayesian formula with the patient's own statistics in order to determine the probability of a clinical diagnosis: myocardial infarction, multiple sclerosis, pregnancy.

The physician, like Dilthey's interpreter, takes the presenting details, only a part of the whole picture but ready to hand—the chief complaint, the other symptoms, the clinical signs, and the test results—and sets to work, fitting these pieces to a whole and testing them against a knowledge of their context. Then—the other half of the diagnostic circle—with a grasp of the whole, the physician reasons back to the details (the signs, the test results), asking questions about missing pieces of information that may rule out alternative possibilities and confirm the strongest, most likely hypothesis. Diagnostic tests, although they might seem to short-circuit this sort of circular, interpretive reasoning by establishing conclusive, quantitative, scientific "facts" about the functioning of the patient's body, must themselves be chosen and interpreted. Thus, far from eliminating the diagnostic circle, the tests are readily assimilable into new interpretive loops. Indeed, the decision whether or not to order a test becomes a step in the rational process of the diagnostic circle. It is always possible and often useful in medicine for the physician to isolate the part and study it thoroughly without reference to the whole—the kidney, the liver function tests—but this reductionist procedure, invaluable for the scientific discoveries of clinical research, is not the essence of clinical medicine. That essence is the prompt, attentive care of the patient. Indeed, an isolating, "scientific" approach to a diseased organ or limb cannot of itself include or lead to reliable therapy.[11] To move toward ameliorating the patient's condition, the part must be recontextualized, considered again as a part of the whole. In the process the patient will be reinvested in a narrative, restored to medical discourse, re-storied.

Like a literary critic, the physician has several options in interpreting a text, several ways of making sense of the signs that are read, and different methods may yield differing interpretations. The patient-as-text can be read in terms of its author's past, a reading that is a variety of biographical criticism. Elevated blood pressure may be traced to (among other things) some complication in the patient's life, or carcinoma of the lung to a lifetime of cigarette smoking. These interpretations are most available to those who know the patient well, and as diagnoses they present few problems; they tend to be readily made. They do not present the puzzles that interest those academic physicians who (like postmodern critics) prefer more complex etiologies. Nevertheless, the biographical approach may yield a useful explication of otherwise obscure details that cannot be long ignored, like marital stress, loss of work, a child's illness. Biographical interpretation is gripping for the person who is ill—although the patient may, like many another author faced with a personal interpretation, shrug it off as irrelevant: "Other people smoke and get away with it"; "No, I'm not under any pressure at work. Besides, I can't quit my job, not even if I wanted to."

A fundamental way of making sense of the patient-as-text is a generic reading. The physician-interpreter identifies the kind of illness it is and interprets the fine details in light of it. One kind of illness, like a sonnet, will be recognizably limited and, however deserving of attention, will take a predictable shape no matter where or when it appears. Another illness more nearly resembles a satiric ode, wildly varied and recognizable only after it is well under way and other possibilities have been discarded. This year's flu is a virulent new translation of last year's. A Whitmanesque free-verse sort of upper respiratory infection may be going around—often indiscernible from prose. In another patient, the physician-reader may discern a fatal diagnosis, a reading that may fix a person's fate as surely (and as undependably) as the oracle in a Greek tragedy.

The physical signs of the patient-as-text can be interpreted, too, in their historical and cultural context. Puerto Rican patients employ the Galenic distinction between "hot" and "cold" diseases;[12] the French suffer from liver complaints, Americans from stress. Always, the experienced physician-interpreter will compare the patient-as-text to earlier "works" by the same person, looking for common motifs and themes that will explicate the present malady. Here again (as with the biographical interpreters) there is room for the psychological components of illness; specialists in the connectedness of mind and body and those who study the relation between life and illness may even go so far as to identify a metaphoric relationship between a "broken heart" and cardiac disease,[13] between a desperate refusal of life circumstance and an inability to swallow.[14]

Treatment strategies that follow upon these interpretations may range from the pharmacologic to the metaphoric, but the extremes are not mutually exclusive activities. They are, in fact, in healthy, broad-based methods of medical inquiry, mutually reinforcing interpretive approaches. Although, like critics, physicians have their favorite methods or a soft spot for their area of special expertise, most of them, like good critics in the classroom, will range through all the possibilities, touching on what they believe necessary for the best reading at this moment, in this case.

The Authorship of the Text

Isn't the physician the author of this text that is the patient? It may be objected that, while the comparison of the physician to a literary critic is adequate for a checkup or a limited illness, as a model for the whole doctor-patient relationship it is much too passive. Surely it cannot describe the physician's active, assertive role in a serious or prolonged illness. Moreover, because physicians understand their own centrality in the episodes to follow, they are inclined to feel that they are the authors of the illness narrative. Their duty to reshape the details of the patient's illness into a medical account of disease seems in some sense to create the text as it is interpreted. But physician authorship of the patient-as-text not only ignores the importance of the patient and the patient's story, it is also far too simple. Michael Balint, using the imagery of his psychiatric training, has suggested that physician and patient are coauthors of a single narrative,[15] and this mutual construction of a common story is a useful image of the work of the therapeutic interview. As a model for the relationship between physician and patient, however, co-authorship accords the physician a much too central role in the life drama of the person who is ill.[16] It is interpretive work that the physician is doing, not original composition, nor even (except in rare cases) co-composition. Physicians who attend the funeral of one of their patients have this brought home to them in a striking manner.[17] The discovery that neither the physician nor the disease has been the strongest force in a patient's life comes as a surprise and a relief.

The metaphor of the patient as a text and the physician as a well educated, attentive close reader of that text goes a long way toward capturing the complexities of the emotional and epistemological relation between the physician and the patient. But the medical reading is not a casual or passive one. The idea of physician as reader and interpreter may be pushed a bit farther, for late twentieth-century literary criticism has taught us that the relationship between author and reader is fully as complex as that between patient and physician. Authors create the poem or the novel but cannot control its meaning or its readers; *all* readers, in this view, may be regarded as authors, co-creators of the text. All possess their own version of the text; how to privilege any single reading is a subject of intense debate.[18] Physicians can be understood as the authors of the text-that-is-the-patient in much the same sense. Those who would claim not an equivalent but a preemptive status for their work as critical readers of the patient-as-text strongly resemble, in the perilous silliness and egocentricity of their claim, those literary critics who regard their work as being as creative as—and no less privileged than—the poems and novels they read. They ignore the power of the body and the will to live. Nevertheless, like the tree that falls in the forest unheard, the readerless text has a dubious existence. And so it is with the patient. As a medical construct, the patienthood of the sick person requires a physician-reader for its existence in a way that illness and suffering do not. Indeed, the physician's reading as it is recorded in the patient's chart or presented at morning report transforms the ill, ultimately unknowable person into a knowable, narratable, and thus treatable medical entity. Interpretation is in itself not a method that leads to good or ill. The medical reading ideally does no violence to the person and does not intervene in or alter the illness. Its potential for comfort and amelioration lies in what happens next, the physician's therapeutic acts. The medical interpretation has created a metastory of the illness from the events of the patient's narrative and the observation of physical signs; the history and events of illness have been transformed into a medical narrative so that understanding and treatment may begin.

One Illness, Two Stories

The illness belongs first of all to the person who is ill, and the patient's experience is the ineradicable fact of medicine. The care of someone who presents a malady and an account of its occurrence to medical attention must include a hearing of that account, its transformation into a medical narrative, and the return of that story to the patient. Reinterpreted as a diagnosis, however preliminary, the transformed and medicalized narrative may be alien to the patient: strange, depersonalized, unlived and unlivable, incomprehensible or terrifyingly clear. This transformed account of illness must be reintegrated as an interpretation of events into the patient's ongoing life story—whether that story is one of health or illness, successful treatment, physical limitation, or approaching death. This is not always easy since in its medical translation the patient's account of the experience of illness is distorted and flattened, almost obliterated. Returned to the patient in this alien form (as occasionally it is by a physician who either has forgotten the common language of illness or ignores the need to use it) the medical narrative is all but unrecognizable as a version of the patient's story—and all but useless as an explanation of the patient's experience. A silent tug-of-war over the possession of the story of illness is frequently at the heart of the tension between doctors and patients, for that tension is in part a struggle over who is to be its author and in what language, a struggle for the interpretation of life (and death) events.

Although one story derives from the other and interprets it, it is necessary to distinguish the two narratives. The first, the patient's story, is the original motivating account that the person who is ill (or family or friends) brings to the physician; the second is the medical account constructed by the physician from selected, augmented parts of the patient's story and from the signs of illness in the body. The first concerns the effects of illness in a life, the second the identification and treatment of a disease. Because the physician's story in part derives from the patient's, the two narratives recount many of the same events. This does not prevent their being different stories which, if not quite separable, have nevertheless been constructed from different points of view with different motives and themes. This difference, essential to the care of the patient, is seldom acknowledged in medicine.

The existence of these two narratives is obscured by the adoption of the terms of scientific medicine into the folk beliefs of Western culture. For example, most of us now use "congestive heart failure" as an explanatory term rather than "dropsy" or "heart trouble" or "old age," but our understanding of the malady is scarcely more scientifically informed than it was before. Rather, scientific medicine has pervaded our interpretive community,[19] and, as such, it has given us our modern folk beliefs and our lore about health and disease. The use of the same terms for the same events suggests (especially to those who use them daily) that physician and patient are talking about the same thing, telling the same story. But often only the physical signs and their diagnostic labels are the same; the understanding and the concerns are entirely different. This general use of summary diagnostic terms in ordinary speech is more likely the patient's attempt to reconcile the two versions or to repossess the story of illness altogether—even though its puzzling descriptors remain the property of the physicians. Patients read themselves and their symptoms in the language of the Western folk belief derived from scientific medicine, and this preliminary reading (or a series of them) brings them to the doctor. They are seeking from an expert reader a less subjective interpretation, a more nearly objective understanding of their condition, one informed by a knowledge of the tradition of these matters and a more exact acquaintance with their meaning. Patients often seek in the physician's story the deconstruction of their own interpretation of these symptoms. "Is it serious?" the patient asks. "It's not cancer, is it?"

The creation of the second, medical, story is the immediate goal of the patient-physician encounter. Yet the importance to medicine—and to the patient—of this reinterpretation cannot alter the priority of the patient's experience. Nor should the fact that ordinary people use medical terms to describe themselves obscure our perception that it is the patients (or, properly, the people who become sick) who are the authors of themselves as the primary texts in medicine. It is as if the patient were a poem or novel, composed in the course of a life and intended just for this moment, and we can understand the physician-reader who, failing to distinguish two stories made from one set of events, feels that he or she has brought the patient into being. Nevertheless, the author of the patient-as-text is the person who, last week, felt just fine—perhaps a little tired. The physician's narrative, although it takes on a life and meaning of its own, is secondary, derivative. The patient's account of illness remains the fundamental fact in clinical medicine. The events of illness do not exist for the physician's narrative, even though the physician's narrative, as the process and record of the diagnostic circle, yields us their medical meaning.

The medical narrative, then, is an account of the patient's malady, which is itself a reading of the text that is the patient or, more precisely, a record of that reading. It is not identical with—and sometimes not recognizable as—the original story. The patient's narrative is a simple chronology, with an implicit etiology, of the events of illness. The physician's narrative, constructed from this report and the findings of the physical examination, tells the story of the discovery of the diagnosis. Thus it is not strictly chronological but, beginning with the immediate past, delves into "history" and then, by means of tests, moves on into the not yet known.

Clinical Medicine and "The Discovery of Grounded Theory"

Medicine's narrative, circular way of determining the facts of a case and making sense of them has much in common with the investigative method proper to anthropology or history and described by Barney Glaser and Anselm Strauss (who take no note of its applicability to medical practice) as the "discovery of grounded theory."[20] Used in those disciplines where experimental possibilities are limited or manipulation of variables is undesirable or unethical, this method relies upon the investigator as the principal research instrument and employs a "constant comparative method" of analysis in which "all statements, explanations, and views of phenomena are regarded as data themselves." Challenging the view that ethnographic research, like research in the physical sciences, ought to consist of the objective verification of hypotheses, Glaser and Strauss maintain that in the social sciences the theories under investigation are substantive rather than formal: a matter of what-is-going-on-here? rather than abstractions concerning, for instance, the action of enzymes. Theory, therefore, is drawn from the data as they are collected, and the emerging hypothesis directs the further collection of data. Such "grounded theory," according to Glaser and Strauss, is tested by four criteria: its fitness and adequacy in explaining all the data, its acceptability as an explanation to the people studied, its generalizability to other instances, and its usefulness for application and change.

The parallel with clinical medicine is striking. Not only are hospital and clinic fields of investigation where, for ethical or chronological reasons, the variables can seldom be manipulated, but also the physician's method of generating and testing a list of possible diagnoses involves a very similar process. Beginning with the preliminary data, the physician assembles a list of possible hypotheses—the differential diagnosis—that could account for the signs and symptoms. Then he or she sets about gathering more data, not at random, but along lines indicated by the differential diagnosis. Using the new information, the physician then can rule out or discard those diseases on the list that do not account adequately for all that is now known. This may leave one highly probable diagnosis or it may narrow the possibilities so that additional and more narrowly focused data must be gathered in search of a determining fact that will enable the physician to distinguish between the remaining possibilities by the criterion of adequacy.

Medicine's diagnostic method also shares the criteria Glaser and Strauss set out for establishing the validity of its hypotheses. A diagnosis must be adequate to the facts and seem plausible to the patient it describes; it must be generalizable to other cases of the same kind and useful when applied to the cure or relief of the patient's malady. As in ethnography, quantitative techniques are a valuable part of the discovery of data, but scientific measurement is not the goal of the investigation. Instead, the investigator is in search of a narrative explanation of the situation at hand, an understanding of what is going on. Early in this process of ratiocination, with luck and modern technology, the physician's data gathering may include a test result that will quickly confirm one of the diagnostic possibilities. But what if such a test does not exist or, if it does, is dangerous or painful or prohibitively expensive? What if its results are ambiguous or mistaken? Tests are useful shortcuts to diagnostic conclusions that often can be reached by other means, but they are not, even now, the basis for diagnostic methodology. Because in medicine data gathering is not separated from hypothesis formation or from hypothesis testing,[21] the method of reasoning embodied in the differential diagnosis (as in the discovery of grounded theory) operates as a check on both the adequacy of the hypotheses and the reliability of the technology. The clinical dictum, "If a test result doesn't fit an otherwise satisfactory hypothesis, throw out the test and get a new one," echoes the master, Sherlock Holmes, who observed that "when a fact appears to be opposed to a long train of deductions, it invariably proves to be capable of bearing some other interpretation."[22]

However familiar this method is to those who puzzle out what is wrong with patients, it seems heretically "backward" to those who hold that knowledge is produced only by the methodology of the classical natural sciences. There the investigator is believed to be a detached observer, and the generation of theory (albeit a much more abstract and lawlike theory) is rigidly separated from the collection of data. Validity lies in the replicability of the quantitative measurements that constitute the observational data. What then are we to make of a cognitive method for medicine that grounds both theory and its verification in the search for additional phenomena? That medicine operates this way is a matter of record. Even Alvan R. Feinstein, foremost among those who would rationalize medical practice, stakes out rational therapy as the domain of clinical science and yields diagnosis to clinical experience.[23] A methodology of medicine as it is practiced thus would seem to have as much in common with interpretive disciplines like anthropology, history, and literature as with biochemistry and molecular biology, the sciences which it calls "basic."

The defense and explication of medicine's way of knowing is part of a wider movement which has called into question the logical-positivist scientific model as a useful or exclusive paradigm for knowledge outside the classical natural sciences. Not only have the behavioral and social sciences (with their less passive, more humanly constructed, and therefore more value-laden subjects) sought a method that is adequate to their data, but something like the discovery of grounded theory has been well practiced and defended as a historiographical and literary critical method as well. History, as Arthur Danto has argued, "is all of a piece" since in its narratives description and explanation are inextricably one.[24] Substantive hypotheses emerge from the primary material and are tested with further discovery. Unless it is laid out as a disjointed list of quantitative "facts" (and even this is doubtful), there can be no "value-free," nonexplanatory history. George Steiner's apt description of the method of the French historians of the *Annales* school applies to history generally: "The document breeds intuition and the archive is made witness."[25]

Medicine and Science

The logical-positivist concept of science as value-free and uninterpretable, an ideal of science which medicine still accepts without question, has not gone unchallenged in its own domain. For all its rigor, scientific knowledge itself is not entirely a matter of demonstrative deduction or tight geometrical proof. Nor will observation alone, even of the most meticulous kind, suffice. All that we know about perception suggests that scientific observation (like the clinical observation of patients) is necessarily hypothesis-laden. E. H. Gombrich has taught us that painting in the Western representational tradition is based on common cultural property, the visual schemata that artists acquire and reproduce in their work. No one ever simply "paints reality," he maintains; there is no "innocent eye."[26]

The perceiver's dependence upon expectation is consistent with what we now understand about knowledge in the physical sciences. Thomas

Kuhn, in his revolutionary *The Structure of Scientific Revolutions,*[27] observed that the ordinary scientist in any given field operates within the received paradigm, which experimental activity in that field works to round out and substantiate. In the ordinary work of science, scientists already know what there is to be seen and this enables them to see it, just as physicians must already know what the signs of a malady, taken together and in context, may mean. Experiments are intended to elaborate the way details fit the received theory and thereby confirm it. The capacity to perceive anomalous details, "facts" that do not fit, that elude established pigeonholes even as they thrust themselves upon the attention, is for Kuhn the common genesis of all scientific revolutions.

In clinical medicine the proportion of "ordinary" and "revolutionary" activity differs from that in physical science. Aberrant details and odd observations are far more frequent in the practice of medicine than in physics or chemistry or even biology. If Kuhn's model of "ordinary science" as working within a paradigm were applied to clinical nosology, the description and classification of disease, the result would be biennial revolution as "new" diseases are identified and old ones subdivided or combined. Applied microcosmically to the diagnosis of patients, the idea of paradigmatic work is frustrated by the frequent alteration and revision of hypotheses about individual patients. For each patient is potentially abnormal, an anomalous instance of disease. "Normal" science in medicine is like "normal rhythm" in Shakespeare's blank verse: the meter, we know, is iambic pentameter, but we are often hard pressed to find a classic invariant line. Still, it is the nature of poetry's music to assert its normative pattern in the face of a potentially bewildering number of variants. Likewise in medicine the variants are reconciled to a generalized sense of pattern. The *Washington Manual* lists the clinical signs necessary to make a diagnosis; there is for most diseases a range of possibility, a Wittgensteinian "family" of definition. Rheumatic fever, to take the example Feinstein uses, may be diagnosed from "arthritis, chorea, carditis, erythema marginatum or subcutaneous nodules."[28] There is no conclusive test. Students and residents learn to temper the concretion of the textbook description with the probability that a particular patient fits the pattern. Lesions and signs do not always match, nor do signs and test results. Even lesions and test results sometimes may not correspond. As Otto Guttentag pointed out in 1947, the "clinical entity," mocked by eighteenth-century German physiologists, is not the "naked truth" that the triumph of the germ theory has made it seem. It is instead only a preliminary typology.[29] Clinicians and clinical researchers work to perfect the maps of illness, but each patient, each instance of illness, is uncharted territory.

One might argue that there is properly no "received paradigm" for a patient whom the physician has never before encountered, but much of the time physicians have their expectations. Even if they have not seen the patient before, they have had experience with "people like this" or are told that the patient has been in a car accident. These are predisposing facts and, given the nature of the practice within a certain specialty in a familiar locale, these "facts" create an expectation of the maladies the physician will encounter. Years of experience or the epidemiological fact of a current influenza epidemic further shorten the distance between a clue—malaise, muscle aches, fatigue, headache, cough—and the diagnosis: "It looks like you have the flu." These clinical expectations are shifted by new diseases, new drugs, new practices like wearing seatbelts, but the daily care of patients would be impossible without them. Trained in hospitals, physicians are conditioned from the start to resist their lure. "Think TB!" "Think tertiary syphilis!" students and residents are enjoined, although syphilis now seldom goes untreated so long, and tuberculosis (still shamefully present among the poor) is not common. Then, once the rarities habitually spring to mind, the corrective aphorism is uttered: "When you hear hoofbeats, don't think zebras."

In practice, physicians must recognize the normal, the expected malady, yet be prepared for the anomalous detail that will confound their working hypothesis. Indeed, they are obliged to look actively for disproof. When an ill-fitting, "revolutionary" detail is found, a more nearly adequate hypothesis must be generated to account for it. An inordinate thirst and frequent urination will transform a patient's suspicion of "flu" to a diagnosis of diabetes. A low-pitched inspiratory rubbing noise in the chest that is not exactly an "ordinary" pleural rub will lead to the discovery of an otherwise unsuspected case of scleroderma.[30] When no paradigm can be found in textbooks and journals or in the clinician's memory to account for an anomaly, a new syndrome, perhaps a new disease, has been discovered. Legionnaires' disease in the seriously ill, hospitalized elderly, for example, was not detected earlier because all bacteria were believed to be known and such deaths fit readily into the ordinary "pneumonia paradigm."[31] But an epidemic among the relatively healthy gathered in a hotel was irregular and led to the investigation that established the existence of a bacterium previously unknown. Such redefinitions of the evidence are far more frequent in clinical medicine than in science. In part this is because medicine is the "youngest science." In part it is because in medicine scientific experiment follows the clinical discovery of disease. Advances in clinical medicine are shaped by the need to take care of the ill—people with AIDS, for instance—while disinterested experiments, like those in genetics, often have little effect on practice or the mindset of clinicians until years later.

Recently, philosophers and historians of science have argued that the interpretive or hermeneutic methodology is characteristic of science as well. They maintain that physics and chemistry are far more context-dependent than logical-positivists recognize and that these fields of study have more in common with anthropology, history, and literature than is customarily acknowledged. Mary Hesse, who has long held that, in the absence of ideal natural categories, theory in science is a matter of choice among competing metaphors, argues that science is not essentially predictive but explanatory—a humanist activity.[32] Likewise, the line between the "pure" and "applied" sciences has been blurred. Louis Pasteur, in denying the independent existence of applied sciences, imagined an organic connection between them: "There are science and the applications of science, linked together as fruit is to the tree that has borne it."[33] Currently, however, the distinction itself is denied. Edwin T. Layton, a historian of engineering, maintains that the criteria of theoretical priority and "purity" will not serve to distinguish between science and engineering. No one doubts the importance of scientific research, but given the degree of generalization in scientific theory necessary to obtain clean, linear solutions, technology must generate its own body of knowledge to address the context-laden nonlinearity of actual situations.[34] Certainly the results of research in fields like cancer therapy and cardiovascular disease bear this out. As Layton observes, "Complexities of practice transcend theory. The result has been the evolution of a substantial body of esoteric knowledge associated with practice."

The blurring of the distinction between theory and the world of practice, whether owing to the metaphors of quantum mechanics or to application-driven research, leaves comfortably unchallenged the assumption that medicine is a science. For many of its practitioners (and a great proportion of the public) "science" is simplistically understood as knowledge that is necessarily detached and noncontextual, essentially mathematical, and replicable. The goal of science, in this view, is an unmediated truth about its objects. For others, what is known of the philosophy of modern physics—relativity, the "uncertainty principle"—seems to normalize and thus leave unexamined the uncertainty that is characteristic of medicine.

Far more relevant to medicine is the life science on which it is based. Biology, Stephen Toulmin points out—especially as conceived by C. H. Waddington and J.B.S. Haldane—is a science that requires interpretation of its subject matter on four levels—the biochemical, the physiological, the developmental, and the evolutionary—none of which is entirely adequate.[35] A comparison with medicine is instructive. Kenneth F. Schaffner has described medicine as "an interlevel science of particulars."[36] Like biology, it gathers data for its theories from several levels of specificity and generates theories that are sufficiently variable to make no simple universal generalization possible. Medicine is, if anything, more complex and multilevel than biology. This multilevel character is the central feature of the "biopsychosocial model" of medicine propounded by George L. Engel, which is based on the systems theory of Ludwig von Bertallanfy.[37] Engel's model extends the medically relevant variables well beyond the molecular and organic levels recognized by medicine's constituent "basic" sciences. Without neglecting these, he proposes widening the focus of the "biomedical model" to psychological and social interaction that may affect the onset of illness and the response to treatment. The reception of Engel's potentially revolutionary position in medicine has been distinctly odd; no one disagrees, yet little changes. This is in part because the concept of the "biomedical model" points to what scarcely exists in practice.[38] Indeed, it is difficult to imagine clinical medicine attempting to proceed as if it were a laboratory science, for its "material" is not passive, nor is it made up of comprehensible or invariant objects. Michael Alan Schwartz and Osborne Wiggins have observed that "the biomedical model exists . . . more at the level of mythical views of medicine than at the level of real medical practice."[39] The idea of medicine as a science remains splendidly useful for its reification of disease and thus for the encouragement of greater precision in diagnosis and treatment; but as an exclusive guide to the care of patients, clinicians for the most part have understood that it is more honored in the breach than in the observance. As myth, it goes on serving as an ideal of medical-scientific rigor which physicians hope to approximate but do not put into practice because of its potential harm to patients.

Medicine and Narrative

To explain what medicine is and to define the nature of its rationality, literature supplies a methodological analog more apt than either the natural or the social sciences. For not only is the metaphor of reading as it is used for the interpretation of the patient's condition a fundamentally literary metaphor, but, more important, medicine already has something in common with literature and literary study through its figurative language and its narrative organization of the facts of illness. The medical case, the central narrative account of the study and diagnosis of disease in an individual patient, developed along with that most modern of Western literary forms, the detective story. The ratiocination of Edgar Allan Poe's Dupin in the 1830s was shared by the early pathological anatomists. Sherlock Holmes's methodology is also enshrined in Richard Cabot's clinical-pathological conference, still the model for all written and oral narratives of medical investigation. The nineteenth century was the most narrative of centuries, and the connection between epistemology and storytelling, which produced very long works of both history and fiction, was so strong and thoroughgoing that it was taken entirely for granted. Following Michel Riffaterre, who describes the literary text as the "actualization of cultural presupposition," Lawrence Rothfield has argued that the connection between realistic fiction, which came to the fore in the nineteenth century, and medical inquiry is in fact a radical one:[40] fictional realism is medicalized in its techniques and seeks for its characters and events the concretion of fact and etiology that medicine offers for illness.

For Sherlock Holmes, the particular relation between fiction and medicine has been very well documented. Arthur Conan Doyle, his creator, was himself a physician, and as a student at Edinburgh he attended the lectures of Dr. Joe Bell, a wizard of "deduction" whose feats of clinical reasoning were legendary. According to Harold E. Jones, another student of Bell's, the professor urged his students to use The Method. "What is the matter with this man, eh?" he would ask. And when at last a student ventured that it was hip-joint disease, Bell is reported to have answered:

> Hip—nothing! The man's limp is not from his hip but from his foot. Were you to observe closely, you would see there are slits, cut by a knife, in those parts of the shoes where the pressure of the shoe is greatest against the foot. The man is a sufferer from corns, gentlemen, and has no hip trouble at all. But he has not come here to be treated for corns, gentlemen. His trouble is of a much more serious nature. This is a case of chronic alcoholism, gentlemen. The rubicund nose, the puffed, bloated face, the bloodshot eyes, the tremulous hands and twitching face muscles, with the quick, pulsating temporal arteries, all show this. These deductions, gentlemen, must however be confirmed by absolute and concrete evidence. In this instance my diagnosis is confirmed by the fact of my seeing the neck of a whisky bottle protruding from the patient's right hand coat pocket. . . . Never neglect to ratify your deductions.[41]

If Bell is the model for Holmes, it is the steadier, rather obtuse Watson who is Conan Doyle's "medical man" and, as narrator, our representative in the stories. Holmes himself is not a physician nor, in our modern sense, a scientist. Although he is at home in the laboratory and prizes exactitude of detail, most of his "work" is done by snooping about and by brooding on the concatenation of clues. Like an anthropologist or a literary critic or a clinician, he is an expert reader. Every event is presumed to have left its legible trace in the physical world. Never before have crushed blades of grass beside a footpath or heelmarks of varied pressure received such scrutiny. Holmes, like Dr. Bell, relies upon his keen observation of detail to generate hypotheses, which then must be confirmed by further details of physical evidence. At the scene of the crime he loses contact with his companions and immerses himself in the phenomena, like a reader in a book—indeed, like Conan Doyle's readers immersed in a book about Holmes. In *A Study in Scarlet*, the novella that is the first-published of Dr. Watson's Holmesian "case histories," we learn before we meet him that in the laboratory Holmes has a "passion for definite and exact knowledge."[42] But all his science, as evinced by his monograph on cigar ash, is in the service of his "fieldwork." There can be no failure or imprecision of observation, for immediately and ultimately, his hypothesis will depend upon it.

Nor does Holmes theorize prematurely. On the way to the scene of this first crime, he asserts the necessity of keeping an open mind. "No data yet," he explains to Dr. Watson, who (like us) is struggling to grasp his method. "It is a capital mistake to theorize before you have all the evidence. It biases the judgment" (p. 27). The injunction is a means of staying alert to new data, something the physician attempts with the conscious formation of competing hypotheses in the differential diagnosis. But for both Holmes and the clinician, such scientific strictness applies only to the first observation of the scene of the crime, to evidence a physician would call the "presenting symptoms." Only a few hours later, as he assembles corroboratory details, he declares to Watson, "There is nothing like first-hand evidence. . . . As a matter of fact my mind is entirely made up upon the case, but we still may as well learn all that is to be learned" (p. 32).

If interpreters cannot begin from theory, neither can they lack theoretical knowledge once the process has begun. In Holmes's odd line of work what constitutes theoretical knowledge is narrative. His stock in trade is a thoroughgoing knowledge of human nature manifested in its criminal acts. Coupled with his eye for evidence, this information enables him to move rapidly from clue to conclusion. His memory is stocked with stories of crime, and his ability to reconstruct a probable sequence of events has been honed on these anecdotes of the possible. He volunteers stories of relevant cases at the drop of a clue, shaming rival Scotland Yard men, showing up their ignorance of the general principles of their profession. "You seem to be a walking calendar of crime," observes the mutual acquaintance who introduces Holmes and Watson. "You might start a paper on those lines. Call it the 'Police News of the Past'" (p. 18). Dr. Watson, cataloging his friend's strange store of knowledge, records, "Knowledge of Literature—Nil. . . . Knowledge of Sensational Literature—Immense. He appears to know every detail of every horror perpetrated in the century" (pp. 21–22). An atrocity that provokes Watson to exclaim, "This is terrible," draws from Holmes the exactly measured analysis that we may mistake for mere delightful Holmesian understatement: "It does seem to be a little out of the common" (p. 26). "I have a lot of special knowledge which I apply to the problem, and which facilitates matters wonderfully," he remarks modestly. "There is a strong family resemblance about misdeeds, and if you have all the details of a thousand at your finger ends, it is odd if you can't unravel the thousand and first" (p. 24).

Sherlock Holmes is equally at work whether poking about the scene of the crime, performing arcane experiments in his laboratory, or thinking: brooding in his "digs," smoking his pipe, playing his violin. All these activities are essential to his interlevel analytical task. Immersed in the clues, with his theories grounded in the phenomena, he works diagnostically, interpretively. His hypothesis in this first case, as in all those that follow, is an imagined story. His method requires the retrospective construction of a hypothetical narrative in order to work out the relation of the clues to one another within an acceptable chronology. Within the published story written by Arthur Conan Doyle and told by Watson, the action ends with Holmes telling the story he has constructed.[43] Holmes's story is diagnostic, a narrative reconstruction that aims to recapture lost time and unobserved deeds, and it closes Conan Doyle's story (and the mystery within his narrative) with a restoration of clarity to the events that occasioned its opening. Besides us—Conan Doyle's readers to whom Watson tells the story[44]—Holmes's conclusive story typically has for its audience not only Dr. Watson but the guilty party or the victim, and the details of the crime are unfolded in triumph with the story's plot. The discovery is, as Peter Brooks has unriddled it, the plot of both crime and story.[45]

The diagnostic skill that is the focus of a physician's education bears striking similarities. Like Sherlock Holmes's narrative reconstruction of the crime, the physician's medical version of a patient's story is the narrative embodiment of a diagnostic hypothesis, the reconstruction of what has gone wrong. Nowhere is this more evident than in the case presentation. Ordered according to its unstated conclusion and proceeding with a report of "denials" and "unremarkable" details,[46] it leads its audience inexorably past possibilities that have been ruled out to focus on the signs of the logically concluding diagnosis. Experiment is forbidden to both detective and diagnostician, for theirs are observational sciences exercised after the fact. The clues must be dealt with as given. Although more evidence may be sought from tests, the originating situation cannot be experimentally replicated.[47] Only the narrative can be manipulated to account for the evidence and then matched with narrative paradigms conveniently stored in diagnostic manuals or the memories of expert practitioners. Medical diagnosis, much like Sherlock Holmes's detection,[48] is an interlevel activity that combines attention to a range of detail from the molecular to the environmental and cultural. Like the master, the physician uses narrative first as a means of organizing the details that with luck and careful thought will flower into a testable generalization and then to demonstrate the accuracy of that generalization in the chronological chain of its details.

Medicine as Interpretation

Medicine is not a science. Instead, it is a rational, science-using, inter-level, interpretive activity undertaken for the care of a sick person. As an interpretive activity turned toward an endless succession of individuals, it takes the patient as its text and seeks to understand his or her malady in the light of current biological, epidemiological, and psychological knowledge.

Medicine's claim to science, like the white coat that manifests that claim, is a part of its magic and serves as its rational, disinterested ideal. In a secular age that can summon to its aid almost as little religion as sorcery, "science" is the locus of what there is of the unexpected and miraculous in our lives, and the miraculous (or some faith in it) may be equally necessary for patients and for physicians in an imperfect, uncertain, death-defying field. Why then should we not take medicine's claims to scientific status at face value? If the idea of medicine as a rigorous, objective science, a beacon for many physicians, is in fact inoperative in practice, why should we disturb it? The trouble is that it is not invariably harmless—either to patient or to physician. What Stanley Tambiah has called the "imperialism of the term 'science' as it moves from a paradigm for rationality to its synonym"[49] closes the mind to other possibilities, to the appreciation of more appropriate, Holmesian ways of making sense of human beings. In addition to the psychic and occasional physical harm to patients that accompanies their reification under an exclusively scientific regard, the idealization of medicine as science offers physicians preparation and support for only a part of their task. This is certainly not to say that there are no caring physicians who are psychologically perceptive, skilled in human interaction, and committed to health education and the prevention of illness. There are many. But for the most part these traits were theirs before their medical education. Methods for fostering these traits and skills and for integrating them earlier and more firmly into a professional life have been a matter of haphazard attention in American medical education.

Medicine absorbs many of our best minds, and, as Michel Foucault has observed, in the absence of a general religious belief it has taken a central place in twentieth-century discussions of the philosophical status of humankind.[50] What we are, the nature of human beings, is a question raised persistently in our encounters with illness, disability, and death. Medicine is ill equipped to answer this question directly. As a human enterprise, medicine speaks primarily through the narratives its practitioners construct as hypotheses about a patient's malady, the stories that convey the medical meaning they have discerned in the text that is the patient.

TWO

A SCIENCE OF INDIVIDUALS:

MEDICINE AND UNCERTAINTY

"While the individual man is an insoluble puzzle, in the
aggregate he becomes a mathematical certainty. You can, for
example, never foretell what any one man will do, but you can
say with precision what an average number will be up to."
(*Sherlock Holmes to Dr. Watson*, The Sign of Four)

I T IS A SAFE RULE," wrote Sir William Osler, "to have no teaching
without a patient for a text, and the best teaching is that taught by the
patient himself." This pronouncement, from the 1904 essay "On the
Need of a Radical Reform in Our Methods of Teaching Medical Students,"[1] was a part of his campaign to move students of medicine in that
newly scientific era away from their books and to the bedside. Not merely
an anticipation of John Dewey's advice about the enrichment of learning
through experience,[2] Osler's rule declares that medical knowledge is essentially, unavoidably clinical. It is phronesis—practical and applied
knowledge—and not a matter of scientific principle alone.

Osler's assertion of the centrality of clinical experience was intended to
counterbalance the effect that the scientific rationalization of medicine in
the previous century had had on medical education. In nineteenth-century
France and Germany, the biological sciences—anatomy, pathology,
physiology—were brought to bear on clinical practice, altering nosology
and drawing medical education into the university.[3] Then as now, vision-
aries imagined that medicine would soon be an exact science. William
Thayer, one of Osler's successors as professor of medicine at the Johns
Hopkins University, proclaimed, "The method of authority has given
way to the method of observation and inquiry."[4] Yet in the decades since,
scientific advance has continually relocated but not diminished the tension between knowledge of biological principles and their application to
the understanding of disease in patients. Science is medicine's foundation,
but the qualities of intellect and character cultivated in clinical education
differ from those inculcated in the classroom and laboratory. Only with
the examined and reflective care of patients do well educated students of
human biology become physicians.

Clinical action, guided by science and imbued with rationality, at once embodies and refutes medicine's understanding of itself as a science. Foremost among those who extended scientific method to clinical observation, Osler reminded his contemporaries, as he reminds us still, that in the care of human illness, a body of general principles must somehow be applied to individual instances of illnesses that may not always follow the received pattern of their kind. Far from being an exact science, medicine is more aptly described as a science of individuals. It is a rational undertaking that uses science in the care of the ill. Its principal characteristics— a strict hierarchy, a quest for scientific advance, its skepticism and its dogma, the drive toward subspecialization, physicians' reluctance to generalize, and, above all, the epistemological importance of narrative—are medicine's responses to the uncertainty inherent in its predicament as a science of individuals. Because the uncertainties of diagnosis and prognosis are fundamental to medicine, the methods physicians have devised to meet them are a fundamental part of medicine as well. In this enterprise, it is the very strategy of observing and reporting the individual case that bridges the inevitable gap between principles and their application.

Science, as Aristotle described it, seeks to establish general truths, universal laws of nature.[5] But medicine differs from physics or biology in its concern with general rules that must at once be true and still apply usefully to the individual and variant case, often as that case is in the process of changing. Physicians cannot control the variables of illness or disease, and their duty to act on behalf of the patient often makes sustained scientific observation impossible. Analysis in medicine, as in meteorology, does not always produce a firm description of fact.[6] Variations are fine, and the object of investigation changes as it is studied; prediction, however reliable in the aggregate, is notoriously uncertain at the local or individual level.[7] Thus, medicine practices a clinical casuistry, reasoning, as the moral casuists did, from the concrete instance. The individual case is the touchstone of knowledge in medicine.

Medicine's casuistry is particularly evident in clinicians' habitual skepticism, in their refusal to generalize, and, above all, in their pedagogical and mnemonic use of single, particular, chronological accounts of illness. These methods govern how new knowledge is acquired by experienced practitioners as well as how established information is acquired by first-time learners. For the understanding of the patient's malady is a problem in medical explanation; in philosophic terms it is a problem of reconciling general biological laws, knowledge that is abstract or nomothetic, with accounts of illness which are idiographic, presented singly and chronologically in the context of the life of the person who is ill. This difficulty not only affects medical pedagogy but also conditions the habits of mind and manner that are regarded as characteristic of physicians.

Medicine is freighted with book learning. Enormous compendia of biological and clinical knowledge are supplemented weekly by experimental data reported in an avalanche of journals. How is this knowledge, the science of medicine, to be applied to the particular case? And how is new knowledge to be acquired? The sick person remains the locus of the fundamental problem of medical knowledge: how objective information and scientific explanation based on abstraction and generality are to apply to the particular human case. Medicine offers no firm answer to this epistemological problem. Instead, as Renée Fox argued in her early work, the lengthy scientific education and a rigorous clinical training in diagnostic and therapeutic methodology are aimed at limiting and learning to tolerate its inevitable uncertainty.[8]

In the study of medicine this problem—the distance between theory and practice—is posed most sharply at the juncture of biological education and clinical training. Each of the two "halves" of traditional medical education is intended to address one side of the epistemological gap. Scientific education in the first two years supplies the general pathophysiological principles that explain illness abstractly, nomothetically. Thereafter, clinical training focuses on the individuals who are ill, narrating the varied courses of illness and treatment until paths of action are well worn in the memories of tired practitioners-to-be. How is one half to be related to the other? Third-year medical students who have absorbed the basic sciences are faced abruptly in their first clinical clerkship with the problem of applying the principles they have learned to one particular patient. All the rigorous courses in biochemistry and physiology and microbiology and histology and pathology are of uncertain and hypothetical relevance to this one sick individual. The body must be watched; the numbers that the tests produce must be studied for clues to what might be wrong. Bodies differ. Etiology is seldom simple. The ills that flesh is heir to do not come singly but overlap, offer false clues, subordinate or omit their principal signs. If their elaborate, detailed education has rendered third-year students merely informed, intelligent observers of disease and treatment, this is only different in degree from their elders. However scientific the post hoc assessments of therapeutic measures, physicians must always act on incomplete knowledge of the patient who is before them, and they are still, therefore, necessarily empirical. The consequent uncertainty is medicine's fascination: it is a science not in the laboratory but in the arena of a living body. It is biology applied with that oldest of interpretive skills, clinical judgment.

This gap between theory and practice is more than a disjunction between knowledge and the need to act. Nor is it merely a pedagogical stenosis preserved in conservative medical curricula that are divided into "basic science" and "clinical" halves. Although it may seem the exclusive property of new learners, a gap that more information will surely close, it is also a thoroughgoing epistemological problem that perseveres in clinical practice. The same awkward imprecision that troubles clinical students haunts all physicians to some degree—and their response to it is a hallmark of the physician's character. For how is even the experienced physician to apply pathophysiological principles to the understanding of the individual patient? Despite an enormous number of reliable, well worn diagnostic and therapeutic paths, there is never enough certitude. Rules of thumb are useful, and the long residency training is meant to inculcate them: "Whenever people like this start looking sick," a resident will instruct an intern, "you push a cc of cortisone." The local connotation of the descriptor "sick" constitutes a rule for applying a rule of thumb to "people like this." But what rules govern the application of this rule?

The Single Case

Only now, and with particular reference to medical ethics, are contemporary philosophers discussing the problem of reconciling the single, difficult, necessarily circumstantial case to the general rules.[9] The casuistry that Albert Jonsen and Stephen Toulmin have rehabilitated for use in problems of bioethics is in fact a methodology characteristic of clinical medicine itself. Clinical casuistry, like the casuistry of early modern theology and that of our legal system, is the comparative analysis of a particular case with all its special circumstances in an effort to relate that case reliably to a system of received principles. The body of wisdom that results from the scrutiny of many individual instances—moral theology, case law, clinical experience—is not a matter of theoretical principles but the tested accumulation of generalizations: practical guidelines, clinical dogma, rules of thumb.

Medicine's status as an idiographic science of individuals is evident in its beginnings. Until the nineteenth century it was a body of knowledge and a system of therapeutic practice taught chiefly by apprenticeship. The learning codified in the Hippocratic writings and in the oldest surviving medical text, the *Edwin Smith Surgical Papyrus*, consists not of scientific principles but clinical observation and procedural rules, diagnostic and prognostic, therapeutic and professional. "One having a dislocation in the vertebra of his neck while he is unconscious of his two legs and his two arms and his urine drips," Egyptian surgeons were advised, suffers from "an ailment not to be treated."[10] This general rule is a "clinical picture," although it resembles a still from a movie rather than a static portrait. Drawn from the observations of skilled practitioners, it is a composite of their experience in innumerable single cases. Modern biomedicine has complicated the explanation of spinal-cord injuries and enables us to save the lives of quadraplegics, but it has not created covering laws with any more force than those recorded five thousand years ago.

The single case remains the basis for much of medical education and for the identification of problems to which research methodology will be applied.[11] When a professor of medicine asserts in conversation, "The anecdotes of an expert have scientific status," he knows a physicist could not make the same assertion, but his tone is three-quarters serious and his position is sound. With the advent of "expert" programming, one of the productive way stations on the road to artificial intelligence (AI), the knowledge possessed by a single mortal authority can be preserved to supply algorithms for future education and consultation. Experts, like a soon-to-retire cardiologist who can tell precisely when to take patients with endocarditis to surgery, are studied as they exercise the subtleties of their diagnostic and prognostic skill on series of single cases. Even when surgical risks are high but delay is fatal, clinical judgment is based on the same skeptical question that must be asked by a physician who has tentatively categorized a sore throat as a viral infection: How is this one different?

Surgical Clinics of North America illustrates the "scientific" status of an expert's stories. These compendia of case studies demonstrating the state of recent surgical art began in 1912 at Mercy Hospital in Chicago with *The Surgical Clinics of John B. Murphy*.[12] They are collections of what have become traditional case presentations together with Dr. Murphy's lucid, colloquial, but learned commentary. They are not essays in a formal sense nor straightforward textbook discussions of the clinical facts, but instead direct transcriptions of surgical grand rounds. Diagnosis, operative technique, prognosis, and etiology are recorded together—along with the clinician's wise observations about the plight of the patient. After an account of the diagnosis and treatment of a patient with vasculitis, for example, Dr. Murphy comments that surgeons will receive more thanks for remedying an ingrown toenail than for performing life-saving surgery for this condition; despite its mortal danger, vasculitis is not frighteningly painful. Like generations of clinical teachers who have followed him, he illustrates the perils of confounding the disease possibilities considered in a differential diagnosis with a story of his own error: "I had a case once . . ." (II, 819). The purpose of this annual collection of cases was the perfection of the art of surgery, and attention to the single case was the means by which knowledge in surgery was established and broadcast. These early *Surgical Clinics* added—as the numerous specialty

Clinics continue today to add—to the individual practitioner's inductive chain of cases observed and reported and discussed. The creation of a store of single instances, seeded with skepticism about their generalizability, remains a fundamental method in all clinical learning.

Medicine somehow has managed rather well in the face of these difficulties. Stimulating the sciences of human biology, studying their application to the maladies presented by patients, it has become the epitome of our control over nature. Indeed, few physicians are troubled by the fragility of their knowledge. Much of the uncertainty individual physicians feel is believed to be reducible by further reading or further advances in research. Nevertheless, the radical uncertainty in medicine is a constant. Scientific progress, advanced training, subspecialization—all distract attention from this corollary of medicine's status as an inexact and seldom replicable science. Traditionally, physicians in their demeanor are anything but uncertain. They survive the appalling moment at the beginning of clinical training when they are compelled to realize that, despite their years of successful study in the basic sciences, they know almost nothing that would be of any help to a patient. Once immersed in the life of the hospital, physicians take for granted the disjunction between biological science and clinical experience, between theory and practice. Overcoming it is precisely what has confirmed them as physicians.

Hierarchy

How is this epistemological gap overcome? Medicine's structural solution to the problem of its radical uncertainty is an elaborate academic hierarchy of learning and responsibility that extends from the medical student up the steps of the residency and subspecialty fellowships past the attending physician to the professor and chief of service. Like all hierarchies, the medical one expresses gradations of authority and power, but it focuses on the acquisition of knowledge. Residency programs are its justification or, as residents see it, its base. These recent medical graduates are young physicians who once would have been out in the world, already in practice, but who since World War II have spent increasingly long periods of time in postgraduate clinical training. Today a physician cannot receive a license to practice without a year's internship, and most complete a three-year residency; surgical specialties and subspecialty medicine require additional time. Thus, counting the third and fourth years of medical school, a five-year minimum spent in clinical training in the academic hierarchy is one of the medical profession's antidotes to uncertainty, a necessity in the face of the immense range of clinical knowledge in every field.

Beyond residency, subspecialty fellows and the ranks of the professoriate work to advance clinical knowledge and to refine clinical practice. Medicine's inexact knowledge motivates the habit of peer consultation and, along with the obligation to teach, lies behind the rounds and conferences that are part of the life of the academic medical center. One chief of surgery, a man with an excellent research record, setting aside for the moment his lifetime of laboratory experiments, explains the need for his department's morbidity and mortality conferences: "What we do in surgery is terribly empirical. All we can do is re-examine the empirical choices." His inclusive "we" extends the need for reflection beyond students and residents, indicating a need felt by practitioners and clinical teachers as well as by new learners. Such conferences serve as ongoing exercises in continuing education and peer review because the re-examination of empirical choices, like the choices themselves, takes place in a hierarchy that slowly rewards those who develop their clinical skill and judgment and, equally slowly, discourages and deflects those who do not.

This hierarchy is an academic one. Physicians wholly in private practice are for the most part outside it. Having chosen to spend their professional lives primarily caring for patients, they customarily play little part in medical education or clinical research. They will not be the ones who first adopt new therapies or develop new diagnostic strategies. Physicians in private practice who retain a foothold in the academic hierarchy as members of an adjunct faculty are in a halfway position: halfway up the ladder, halfway in, halfway free of the academic world. In most institutions they are the attending physicians, the source of private patients for the teaching hospital, the role models for students and residents who look forward to an office practice, and, often incidentally, the teachers of clinical medicine. It is clinical management the attendings teach, while relying on the residents' constant availability and their freshly acquired information to assist in the care of their hospitalized patients. Indeed, the give and take between the usually conservative habits of attending physicians and the residents' up-to-the-minute knowledge is a source of education (as well as irritation) for both parties. Here, too, general knowledge and practical experience meet abruptly.

The academic hierarchy enforces the means by which physicians learn to negotiate the gap between theory and practice. Gradually the student's knowledge of general principles of uncertain relevance becomes the clinician's informed willingness to act for a particular patient. This transition is accomplished by means of the habits and rituals that are part of every physician's clinical training. Charles L. Bosk has identified eight strategies for dealing with uncertainty in patient care: hedged assertions, probability reasoning, a focus on uncertainty as a research problem, requests for consultation, Socratic teaching, deciding not to decide, gallows humor, and "hyperrealism."[13] In addition, new rituals, such as "uncertainty rounds"[14] and a "Greek chorus" for hopelessly ill patients,[15] have been proposed as ways of accommodating situations with no right answer. In the daily interaction of rounds and conferences in an academic medical center, students and residents learn as much about accommodating uncertainty in the care of patients as about therapy itself.

Scientific Advance

The physician's awareness of advances in clinical science remains the foremost means of controlling uncertainty in medicine. Improved information moves whole clinical topics from what Richard Rorty has described as "abnormal discourse" about the not-yet-understood requiring a recursive interpretation to the realm of "normal discourse," where a positivist epistemology works quite well.[16] This is true at the level of both the individual physician's knowledge and the community of practice represented by a hospital or university service. Uncertainty provokes many of the resident's trips to the library—and the frequency and the pressing nature of such scholarly curiosity are reflected in the long hours that hospital libraries are known to keep. There, peer- (and rival-) reviewed studies contain the latest emendations and correctives to the resident's textbooks and summary pocket manuals. Survey articles digest and evaluate recent research on particular clinical problems. For students and residents (and clinicians who have not kept up with recent research) the information to be found in the journals will seem an adequate antidote for uncertainty. The problem of action in regard to a particular patient will very likely be solved by a consensus article or a report of a clinical trial that gives a slight edge to one treatment over another. Interpretation, however, is still necessary to determine by which rules the patient fits into the categories that the article describes. The fit of the present patient to reported cases is always approximate, and physicians look to the account of illness embedded in the patient's chart (and in the case of students and interns retold to their teachers as a case presentation) for a likeness sufficient to authorize a choice of therapy.

The scientific advances embodied in these journals seem to promise an ultimate reduction in uncertainty. Lewis Thomas has argued that biomedical research is our only way out of the morass of "halfway technology" for diseases treated with very high technology, great expense, and limited efficacy.[17] Yet, even at its best, scientific progress is a matter of halving the distance: the steps from our present state to a complete and exact knowledge may become infinitesimally small, but the gap never closes. Moreover, in medicine the gap is perpetually widened by our cultural redefinition of disease and by new tasks, new conditions about which something now can be done. Meanwhile, physicians experience a need to know that is held in balance, often just short of Faustian excess, by a carefully inculcated skepticism.

Skepticism—and Clinical Dogma

Accounts of individual cases may alter standard diagnostic and therapeutic practice, for the accumulated wisdom of clinical experience is subject to constant testing and occasional revision. Although the academic hierarchy embodies an authority regularly appealed to in the casuistical discussion of individual cases, neither this authority nor that lodged in journal reports of the most recent research ever goes unchallenged—except by the inexperienced. On rounds, a surgery professor who has been quizzing a group of residents on their test-ordering habits asks almost querulously, "How much diagnostic information do you need in order to operate?" It is the perennial question about therapeutic action, present daily in the most ordinary patient encounter, but raised most powerfully in a situation on the edge of crisis. In conditions of uncertainty, what is the proper balance of knowledge and action? A senior resident replies, "It's a matter of judgment, of course. But you don't do things just because other people say to."

Shaping that judgment to accommodate the individual case is the task of residency education—and of the physician's own lifelong attention and self-correction. Physicians learn that one must have knowledge enough to act, but be willing to make decisions even in its absence. One must know what are regarded in each particular instance as the diagnostic and therapeutic procedures "of choice." (The use of the phrase implies that among the wide variety of possibilities, for the well informed there is little choice at all.) But everyone is aware that authorities are rapidly superseded. Indeed, advances in clinical practice and, therefore, clinical reputation depend upon a skepticism of authoritative views that will lead to new knowledge. Skepticism in this way, as in others, forms an essential part of medicine's ethos. If there is no absolutely right way, a better way may always be found.

Clinicians must also be skeptical of the new. The early 1980s saw the publication of several books (noteworthy in a profession that prefers the short form) on how to read and assess reported research that almost inevitably is of uneven quality.[18] A professor of family medicine, a specialty taunted by other academic medical specialties for having no identifiable research of its own, declares only half in jest that a useful study could be done of the rates of iatrogenic illness among those whose physicians read research journals within a week of their publication and, as a result, practice only the very latest medicine. His hypothesis is that these physicians' very currency can lead to harm. Thalidomide, Zomax, and a long list of false diagnostic and therapeutic hopes such as the L-dopa challenge for Huntington's disease and hyperbaric oxygen therapy for multiple sclerosis bear him out. A professor of gastroenterology in a conference on idiopathic (i.e., nonalcoholic) cirrhosis in an 80-year-old woman describes a new treatment for the bleeding esophageal varices that are threatening the patient's life: "This is what I do. Whether is is right or not, I don't know, but it is logical." He pauses. "We don't have an answer. In two years I will come back and say 'do not do esophageal sclerosis for varices.'" But, of course, in two years the people around the table will be gone. It is necessary to equip them for the certainty of change. In a conference on Crohn's disease, another professor mentions a recent summary article by several experts that has compared the various treatment algorithms for the disease. In general, he says, he agrees with its conclusion, but in the case under discussion he recommends the treatment ranked second. "We know we get good results with it," he explains, "and I believe the data aren't all in" on the newly preferred therapy.

These conferences are described on the daily department schedule by their subspecialty labels—"10 A.M.: Gastroenterology Conference, 5th Floor Conf. Rm."—and are known to students and residents by disease labels: conferences "on Crohn's disease," "on idiopathic cirrhosis." Nevertheless, they teach much more, including a vital if unacknowledged lesson in skepticism. As with all else in medicine, students learn it, residents practice it, their elders reinforce it. Skepticism is the mark of their profession. With each case they are taught the tentativeness of their knowledge and the uncertainty of their practice. They also learn how these difficulties are accommodated in the daily life of medicine.

In practice this skepticism is often modified because physicians, who cannot risk being paralyzed by doubt or failure of memory, need a clear procedural path. Rules of thumb are often conveyed dogmatically, codifying the knowledge a resident needs to possess as a habit of practice: "Always use an n.g. tube," a senior resident tells an intern in the emergency department, conveying the fruits of his experience with dozens of similar cases. The uncertainty that provokes such dogmatic assertion may be individual and remediable (as with a resident or rusty practitioner), professionwide but temporary (until research provides an answer), or ultimately ineradicable (as with the unknowability of patients or the exceptions that stand between us and the infallibility of tests). Whichever the case, physicians have a low tolerance for uncertainty. Their need for certainty may come to rest with the force of conviction: opinion among physicians is often expressed as strong belief. Such declarations are at first glance distinctly odd in a scientific discipline, yet recommendations are frequently conveyed in this way. "In a case like this, Dr. Levine doesn't believe in cortisone," a resident reports of a subspecialty consultant. Or a professor says dismissively, "I have no faith at all in a stapled anastomosis." As their language suggests, these are dogmatic statements, possessed of a factual base but expressed as belief. Such a custom is finally not surprising in a profession that calls the advice of an expert an "opinion." In tension with the dogmatic force of the assertions of which they are a part, the regular use of belief-words is a semantic reservation, a perhaps unintended admission of the fragility of knowledge. Often in medicine the evidence is equivocal, equally impressive—or unimpressive—on either side of the question. The next case will have to be judged on its own merits. As a senior professor once concluded in a bleak but firm voice, "You have to proceed with the guidance of the information you trust."

The Flight to Certainty

Another way physicians control their exposure to the radical uncertainty of medicine is to seek the narrower ground of subspecialty medicine. There are other reasons for this contemporary trend, of course. Economic factors are strongly persuasive, and subspecialization may also be the manifestation of a character structure unwilling to stop until the last exam has been taken. At the same time, both those motives are consistent with a flight from uncertainty. Discomfort may lead physicians to narrow their field of knowledge and practice until their personal uncertainty quotient reaches a bearable level.

The drive for certainty also contributes to the physician's reassuring professional demeanor. "In the face of the uncontrollable," the traditional clinical manner declares, "we are doing everything that can be done." This implicit claim, verbalized, remains a physician's best defense against death and the feeling of failure: "We did everything we could." The statement itself is a defiant paradox. An acknowledgment of humankind's inability to prevent death, it nevertheless asserts the profession's perceived duty to defeat death or postpone it as long as possible. The drive for certainty, for control of the confounding variables, leads also to clinical situations that express the extremes of physicians' need to "do everything." There are legions of us who are grateful to this medical defiance, but in the past twenty years medical technology has rendered excessive and immoral an unthinking automatic response to uncertainty. The need for reassurance in the face of uncertainty can lead to an excessive use of medical technology that is blind to the needs of patients.

The Refusal to Generalize

Medicine's clinical casuistry is also evident in physicians' characteristic refusal to generalize. Because this refusal informs the traditional case-by-case method of clinical instruction, it is the principal lesson of the long residency. The daily conferences and rounds appear to teach the efficient diagnosis and preferred therapy for this or that disease. But many diagnostic tools and most therapies will change in the course of one practitioner's career, often more than once. As a consequence, the pedagogical method—one of Oslerian observation and case study rather than the study of textbooks—conveys the true lesson of clinical training. Beyond pragmatic lessons in how to diagnose and treat a sudden fever or shortness of breath, residents have it brought home to them again and again that, despite well worn diagnostic and therapeutic paths mapped by biomedical science and established by clinical experience, each case may differ from other cases of the same kind. The potential variability of the individual case underlies the professionwide reluctance to comment upon the treatment of another physician's patient. This reluctance is not simply the protection of the herd. "I don't know all the facts," a physician is likely to say, and the demurral is well founded. Even if the physical phenomena remain the same from one patient to another with the same disease, the perception and interpretation of what is regarded as "fact" as well as the ramifying circumstances affecting the patient will be subtly, sometimes markedly, different. The decision to offer only medical treatment to one man with angina, for example, while another will be led toward coronary artery bypass surgery may have to do with the patient's response to therapy, his reliability as a manager of his own medication, or his attitude toward risk. These circumstances can be understood and reliably assessed only as part of the physician's ongoing understanding of the patient. Likewise, whether a surgeon staples or sews one piece of tissue to another can be a matter of style, of strongly held belief, or of individual skill. No matter how readily one physician says that he or she would not take care of a patient as another physician has chosen to do, there is always a reluctance to take the next step—indeed it is not seen as a next step—to say that the other method is therefore wrong. The first physician knows all too well that circumstances—the resources available, the experience of assistants, the pressure of time, the emphases and prejudices of training, even pure luck—may have influenced the other physician's choice of treatment strategy.

This refusal to judge is manifest in the profession's use of the word "appropriate." It is a judgmental word, yet its frequent use as a term of approbation is remarkable for its reserve. It implies that something not now seen may yet go wrong. Its opposite, "inappropriate," condemns a course of action or a therapeutic choice of which the speaker disapproves. But as substitutes for "right" and "wrong," these are more nearly situational words. They appear to emphasize the relation of the act to the circumstance rather than appealing to an absolute, objective standard. Devoid of reference to fact or truth, they avoid the categories of good and bad, assessing first the efficacy of an act and only secondarily and by implication its correctness or morality. No matter how authoritatively "appropriate" and "inappropriate" may be uttered, they carry the unexpressed reservation of the speaker's subjectivity. The case may have been different in ways the speaker does not know.

This ingrained awareness of the potential variability of the individual case is also related to what philosophers on occasion have described as physicians' unwillingness—some have said their inability—to generalize about ethical issues. Pressed for a solution to a moral dilemma, a physician is likely to answer, "It depends—." This is not necessarily a caution engendered by lawsuits, for it existed long before defensive medicine became a force in medical practice. It is rather an unwillingness to generalize that is grounded in the knowledge of human illness and its circumstances. What is "appropriate" in one instance may be "inappropriate" in another, even though a preliminary view suggests that the instances are very similar. Consequently the unwillingness to generalize characterizes all of medicine, its ethics as well as its epistemology and for the sound reason that medicine deals with complex and variable human beings one by one.

The ungeneralizability of moral decisions has been argued by Peter Winch, in an eloquent essay on Herman Melville's *Billy Budd*.[19] In that novella, Captain Vere, a naval officer during wartime, must pass judgment on a naive young sailor who has accidentally killed his tormentor, the evil Claggett. Billy Budd is an innocent man; yet the law states unequivocally that homicide in the ranks in time of war must be punished by death. There is no right answer. Captain Vere's predicament resembles not only the "quandary ethics"[20] that has characterized most of the early work in biomedical ethics but many of the everyday medical decisions about matters that are entirely clinical. No sure answer is to be found in even the clearest principles. Those who decide must match a clear general principle to a particular case whose features are not accounted for in, and may indeed contradict, the prevailing rule. The particularities of human illness, the very phenomena that medicine takes for its own, if they are to be fully comprehended, inevitably resist satisfyingly complete abstraction, and thus a physician's decision in the many matters about which there is no consensus does not have a binding effect on the next such decision of its kind.

Clinical Judgment

In the absence of answers that are invariably right, medical education focuses on the formation and exercise of clinical judgment. Whether viewed as an acquired skill or a personal quality—no doubt it is both—judgment is the bridge from knowledge to clinical action. The difficulty of reconciling science and praxis, knowledge and action, is illustrated by the status of the term. No one doubts that clinical judgment has a central role in medicine: its development is the goal of clinical education, and a physician who is said to possess good clinical judgment has received medicine's highest tribute. Yet at its most manipulative, clinical judgment may oppose investigation and constitute an unsubstantiated claim to authority—as when a curmudgeonly clinician harrumphs, "I don't care what McGillicuddy's article says, in my clinical judgment . . .." Despite the cynicism with which it is occasionally regarded, particularly by the young, clinical judgment is never without honor. For everyone knows of theoretical experts who have made mistakes in applying their knowledge, and residents who are chock full of fresh new up-to-date information are well aware that they are not yet accomplished practitioners.

Medical education cultivates and clinical practice refines clinical judgment. It is a kind of tact that grows out of the memory of experience, both real and vicarious,[21] a matter of sensing when to act and when to subject received knowledge to skeptical scrutiny. On those occasions when clinicians are in full possession of the necessary information, the hard scientific facts, they still must allow for their own subjectivity, the fallibility of the tests' technology, and the uncontrolled, uncontrollable variable that is the patient. Black polar bears, the bêtes noirs of inductive reasoning, prowl constantly through the thickets of medical knowledge: this patient may confound the rules, requiring the special exercise of clinical judgment, may even provoke the clinical insight that will eventuate in new knowledge.

Because of this particularity, clinical judgment is traditionally acquired and exercised idiographically, honed and extended with "historical controls"[22] and the narrative representation of single cases. This was the method of medical education before the biological sciences rationalized diagnosis and therapy. Today, even with the refinements of clinical epidemiology and the study of decision making, narration of the single case remains the basis of learning in medicine, whether it is the advancement of knowledge by clinical researchers or the acquisition of established knowledge by new learners.

The Computer and the Single Case

The physician's inductive chain of single cases is subject to analysis and correction, of course, and, since Alvan Feinstein's pioneering 1967 study, *Clinical Judgment*,[23] clinical epidemiology has called physicians' attention to the problem of the statistical reliability of their diagnostic and therapeutic decisions. Clinical signs are fallible; despite improvements, tests are far from being perfectly accurate; and very few treatments are without side effect. Given these impediments to certainty, impediments that medical science is not likely to remove, "clinimetrics" asks how likely it is that a single case follows the general rule for its kind.[24] Information about the conditions of human choice and advances in computer science (to say nothing of pressure for quantitative research in the "generalist" subspecialties of medicine and pediatrics) have led to the rapid growth of medical decision analysis, generating since the late 1970s a scholarly association, an annual meeting, and a journal. Valuable for its study of the complexity of human choice in conditions of uncertainty,[25] and for encouraging recognition of social and psychological factors that affect medical decisions, including patients' preferences,[26] decision analysis nevertheless does not enable physicians or their patients to choose infallibly. In arming them with information about the sensitivity and specificity of tests and with estimates of diagnostic probability for patients of a particular description, decision analysis describes—and indeed is predicated upon—that very fallibility. As a consequence, physicians now are able to be more precise about the nature of their imprecision.

The value of decision analysis in clarifying choices and limiting mistakes—like the value of an individual physician's judgment—depends on the stock of cases upon which its statistics are based, and in the last two decades the statistical analysis of diagnostic and therapeutic alternatives has yielded useful studies of threshold conditions and predictive symptoms. A study of acute upper gastrointestinal bleeding by Donald Bordley and his colleagues, for example, now enables physicians to sort the patients whose bleeding will recur from those who may be sent home from the emergency room.[27] Susanna Bedell and her colleagues have identified the conditions for which cardio-pulmonary resuscitation is futile and, in effect, an assault that prolongs dying.[28] Knaus's APACHE classification scheme attempts to codify knowledge that will designate patients whose clinical conditions will be most likely to benefit from the Intensive Care Unit—and those who will be excluded.[29] Studies like these reestablish for our incomparably more complex medicine a level of generalization that approximates that of the Egyptian surgeons and promise to serve as guides through the thickets of therapeutic choice. They are more comprehensive and highly refined rules of practice rather than scientific principles, and the extent to which they represent a genuine shift of these topics from abnormal to normal discourse will be tested by their resistance to challenge by exceptional cases.

With this success in establishing general rules of thumb for well defined therapeutic situations, can computers be put to further—and earlier—use in the diagnosis of a particular patient? The prospect of AI in medicine is a kind of litmus test of physicians' beliefs about the wholly scientific nature of their discipline. For no matter how scientific they hold medicine to be, most physicians find it all but impossible to entertain the notion that what they do is so entirely a matter of objective, replicable knowledge as to be captured by computer programming. A computerized stock of medical diagnoses can augment and improve medical care. Learning can be simplified; experience can be acquired quickly (and without risk) in fictive situations; new information can be added rapidly to the store. But clinical judgment, separable from particular instances and transferable to the understanding of new problems, remains to be encoded.

Where one stands on the question of encoding clinical judgment depends in part on how one understands disease. The controversy goes back to the first half of the nineteenth century, when the pathophysiological studies of the German "phenomenologists" like Carl Wunderlich and Ludwig Traube attacked the study in Britain and France of "clinical pictures" and "specifics" as an insufficiently scientific "ontologism."[30] Is a disease a thing in itself, as the "ontologists" seemed to think, an entity that follows its own course and must be counteracted by specific remedies? Or is it rather, as Virchow held, "life under altered conditions?" The apparent triumph of ontology, following the development of the germ theory later in the century and abetted by the practical demands of medical education and daily practice, is rather like the persistence of Newtonian physics in daily life: except in special cases, the old generalizations work. Whether patients or physicians, we tend to ignore much that our reified concept of disease does not account for, and, although the cultural determinants of disease are well known,[31] we live—and physicians practice—as if diseases were objects in nature. Thus there can be protocols for the diagnosis and treatment of disease, clinical rules of thumb, expert systems, and competent and sophisticated practice by barefoot doctors, nurse practitioners, and physician's assistants. The value of such generalizations for medical as well as paramedical decision makers depends wholly upon the individual's ability to know when he or she is in the presence of a phenomenon not accounted for in the system.

Computers can replicate whatever we can specify, and clinical science moves slowly to expand the specification of human maladies. But variables in the clinical encounter (as elsewhere) approach the infinite, and signs shade into the absence of signs. Even with a working agreement about what constitutes disease, the interpretation of these subtleties involves a process of selective inattention and recognition that is now unimaginably difficult to specify and is obscurely linked to the unassessed diagnostic and therapeutic value of knowing human contact. The clinical judgment required to sift medical "facts" from the patient's presentation and to direct inquiry toward a probable meaning resembles the work on narrative "scripts" done by Roger C. Schank and his associates. Their Script Applier Mechanisms (SAM),[32] a "top-down" system that ignores the generative rules of language in favor of collections of "episodes" with turning points, uses information about context to "read" news stories and reliably answer questions about them. Like a physician plotting a patient's illness, SAM is capable not only of skipping over diversionary details but also of recognizing clues to what may be missing or suppressed. It is ponderously slow, however, and its limited diet of daily news is a mere speck compared with the universe of illness that can present itself at the physician's door. These perhaps insuperable limitations suggest that physicians are more likely to gain admiration for their diagnostic reasoning from AI than they are to be replaced by it.

More immediately promising are diagnostic and therapeutic programs that do what physicians do more quickly and immeasurably more completely. Given a set of symptoms, diagnostic programs are capable of slowly generating a differential diagnosis. They function not as consultants but as prompters, capable of reminding physicians at an early stage of their investigation of the possibilities that they may not yet have thought of. Clinical judgment is still required to apply the information gained to the patient's condition. Only CADUCEUS (originally INTERNIST)[33] attempts to pinpoint the diagnosis and this from a "short" list of five hundred diseases.

The new field of medical informatics struggles incessantly with the problem of the level of generalization that can be achieved concerning diagnosis and treatment, a problem fundamental to medicine as a science of individuals. Rules of clinical practice exist, but they suffer from the same limitations as laws in history or economics: those of sufficient generality run the risk of ignoring the specific instance, while those that take into account all the possibilities are of little help in guiding action.[34] The narrative solution devised by James F. Fries and his colleagues is suggestive. In the absence of a sufficiently large number of cases and a satisfactory etiology to account for variants (conditions shared by all programs when confronting one particular patient), their time-oriented program for the American Rheumatological Association Medical Information System (ARAMIS)[35] specifies "conceptual [diagnostic] units" rather than using a rule-based system. Like an experienced clinician, it matches the chronological account of a newly diagnosed patient's illness with similar cases in order to suggest prognosis and map treatment strategies. Physicians, even as they enrich their knowledge of the diagnostic possibilities or simplify the calculation of therapeutic choice with computer programs, themselves remain their first and best clinical instrument.

Narrative and the Education of Clinical Judgment

Despite the refinements of clinical epidemiology and the study of decision making, the careful construction and interpretation of the individual case remains essential to learning and remembering in clinical medicine. The task of knowing for the physician remains one of rejecting information, sorting through detail, knowing what to ignore, and applying general rules while retaining the skepticism generated by an awareness of the single exception. The well informed, experienced human being attends to these subjective minutiae rather well, and much of this skill we fail to recognize and understand even as we rely upon it. Even if clinical judgment is an innate ability, it can nevertheless be enriched and improved. An internist, questioned by residents in attending rounds about how he knows whether to hospitalize a patient, observes, "You get a feel sitting down and looking at them. Are they really sick? That's where clinical judgment comes in. You develop a sense—. Second-year residents develop it rapidly in the emergency department." He contrasts this time-bound, emergency-room judgment with the ability to use time as a diagnostic tool in ambulatory medicine (although not, he points out, in a suburban practice, where patients are busy and willing to pay for a quick diagnosis). In an office practice, diseases listed as possibilities in the physician's differential diagnosis can be ruled out, he says, "on the basis of elapsed time. It's a matter of balance: part of sound clinical judgment is ignoring information you don't want."

Like Sherlock Holmes with his fund of information about the odd or important crimes that he has solved himself or studied carefully, physicians acquire a collection of cases that they have either treated themselves or observed directly, and they augment these with others reported in journals. Continually refined and reorganized as its possessor reads reports of clinical research and engages in the exercise of clinical judgment, this practical knowledge informs the interpretation of each new case as the clinician goes about fitting it to the clinical taxonomy of diagnosis and therapy. The idiosyncrasies of individual experience are to be eliminated by "keeping up with the journals," articles reporting clinical studies that represent large numbers of cases selected and observed so as to control the variables. These studies in turn are subjected to the test of the clinician's own experience.

As the comparison with Schank's SAM suggests, clinical judgment is not so much a mathematical or logical ability of determining causes as a fundamentally interpretive one, a capacity for identifying and understanding the significant elements of multifactorial situations in the process of change. In narrative terms it is the ability to discern a plot. Like the Egyptian account of spinal-cord injury, the "plots" of clinical cases are formulated and refined as case narratives by practitioners, and they constitute a body of medicine's general rules. They are recorded in diagnostic handbooks and committed to memory as clinical pictures. Physicians know the plots of these already constructed cases and the many variants that both cluster them in a differential diagnosis and ultimately distinguish among them. In their light, the patient's story of puzzling or worrisome illness is reinterpreted as an identifiable malady.

In medicine as in moral theology, jurisprudence, and Sherlock Holmes's detective work—all fields in thrall to the case—the particulars are narrated in sufficient detail to provide clues that will enable the casuist to measure and match them against the yardstick of the worldview under consideration: disease, salvation, legality, crime. In all these fields the idiographic, chronological account of the particulars bridges the gap between general principle and isolated case. For physicians it is not merely the existence of certain signs and symptoms that determines the diagnosis. As Perri Klass has observed with only a little irony, "all written descriptions of all clinical presentations of all diseases are similar: if you list every possible presenting symptom, eventually they all overlap."[36] The physician's understanding also depends on the chronology of their development over time, their narrative emplotment. The patient's story of illness, augmented with the results of the physical examination, is interpreted and shaped into a medically plotted version by the light of the physician's store of clinical information and then compared not only with standardized, textbook plots of the most probable diseases (those in the differential diagnosis) but also with plots of comparable cases in the physician's experience.

If, as Osler maintained, there is no teaching without a patient for a text, there is no medicine either. For the single patient provides the text that medicine must read and make sense of and explain. Physicians begin by hearing the story of the illness and then "read" the body, interpreting, sorting, matching all the while. As expert readers they use both scientific knowledge and a familiarity with the plots of similar cases to make sense of a welter of detail, sorting through a differential diagnosis, testing hypothetical accounts of disease against the details of this particular one. The diagnosis that emerges is the physician's interpretation of the events and signs of illness, and it places the patient in the midst of a recognizable story of disease. Narrative thus bridges the gap between rule and case.

As a method of addressing the uncertainties of medicine, narrative is more exploratory and flexible—and therefore more useful—than general laws, which become trivial as they approach the reliably applicable. It enables the physician both to know and treat the patient, and to organize and revise medicine's knowledge of human possibility. This narrative construction is one of the principal ways of knowing in medicine, and it situates medical knowing somewhere between the positions taken by the ontologists and the physiological phenomenologists. In this view disease is not so much an entity as an identifiable chronological organization of events. At this level of generalization, the "plot" of disease encapsulates the "clinical picture" but allows for variants, exceptions that prove the rule. The descriptive precision and chronologicality of narrative make it possible to fit the phenomena to a useful rule or, if they do not fit, to form the basis for proposing a useful class of exceptions.

Narratives of variants, such as toxic shock syndrome or Legionnaires' disease, eventually place the confusing particularity of the ill-fitting case in a revised clinical nosology. They are new clinical entities. Accounts of anomalous conditions, like many of the AIDS-related disorders in the early 1980s, postulate exceptions to the received schemata of textbooks. They constitute new knowledge, which is assimilated to the rules of thumb by which those schemata are interpreted. These accounts of new phenomena existing at the forefront of discovery move toward an elaboration of the biomedical order. Indeed, in the case of "new diseases" they may provoke the dismantling of a part of the old scheme and reconstruction of a new order in the science of pathophysiology.

Medicine is practiced somewhere between the forest of textbooks and a thicket of potential algorithmal trees. Narrative plays a major role in the dialogue that continues between latter-day phenomenologists and ontologists—the former at their benches and computers, chipping away at uncertainties, the latter in their clinics ignoring epistemological problems in favor of efficacious generalizations. By means of the temporal organization of detail, governed by the "plots" of disease, physicians are able to negotiate between theory and practice, sustaining medicine as an interlevel activity that must account for both scientific principle and the specificity of the human beings who are their patients. Narrative is the ultimate device of casuistry in medicine (as in theology and law), which enables practitioners who share its diagnostic and therapeutic worldview to fit general principles to the single case and to achieve a degree of generalization that is both practicable and open to change.

Medicine as a Human Science

Medicine, then, is a science-using, judgment-based practice committed to the knowledge and care of human illness and characterized by its varied and ingenious defenses against uncertainty. Because disease is culturally defined and not simply "out there" in nature and because human beings are ultimately unknowable, medicine's knowledge is fundamentally, ineradicably uncertain. As a consequence, those sources of uncertainty that to some degree can be controlled—the individual physician's lack of information or skill and the incomplete state of biological knowledge that informs medical practice—are regarded as the objects of constant improvement. Indeed, medicine's claim to be a science and only a science very probably has its roots in physicians' awareness of this uncertainty, especially in the face of their patients' often critical need for accuracy. Yet the radical uncertainty remains, inherent in medicine's status as a science of individuals. Medicine shares something with disciplines like history and cultural anthropology, which must make sense of data that are less sought after than created by the questions investigators pose. It shares even more with disciplines like political science and economics, which must study, statistically and after the fact, human situations over which they have little control. In this complex epistemological situation, the strict positivism of medicine's outdated view of "hard" science is of limited use.

Medicine manages to negotiate its predicament as a science of individuals rather well, and its steadfast ignorance of its epistemological paradox may be part of its success. Its peculiar mix of science and belief, dogma and skepticism, authority and scrupulous attention to the unexpected enables physicians to move between abstractions and particularities, intepreting cases in light of rules, revising the rules in light of cases. Human biology and clinical epidemiology continue to refine the knowledge of the circumstances in which this interpretive work goes on, moving specific medical conditions from the realm of "abnormal discourse" to the established truths of normal science. All the while narrative, however unacknowledged, remains medicine's principal way of applying its abstract knowledge to the care of the individual patient.

There are signs that both physicians and patients have been oversold on medicine as a science. In place of an unexamined assertion of its scientific character, medicine—and society—would be better served by a broader understanding that, retaining rationality as an ideal, acknowledged its reliance upon idiographic as well as nomothetic explanation. A recognition of medicine's fundamental uncertainty and the well developed tradition of narrative that is central to its epistemology might help to moderate our society's unrealistic expectations of medicine's work. Currently, even physicians' own expectations for their careers and abilities are distorted by our narrow understanding of medicine as a realm of knowledge that is or can become as certain as chemistry or physics. A more comprehensive understanding of medicine might attract to the profession people more tolerant of uncertainty, and, once there, they might demand an education that challenged them not only to reduce uncertainty wherever possible but also to integrate an awareness of it into their engagements with patients. Above all, a broader understanding of medicine might serve to lessen our outrageous expectations as patients and public of what is at its best an imperfect human activity. In the late twentieth century we have transferred from theology to medicine our concerns with frailty and perfectibility, death and life, and the meaning we attach to well-being and suffering. It seems quite enough to ask that medicine provide us with an understanding of human illness and an ameliorating care.

PART TWO

NARRATIVE IN MEDICINE

THREE

THE REPRESENTATION OF THE PATIENT

*"At least I have a grip of the essential facts of the case.
I shall enumerate them to you, for nothing clears up a case
so much as stating it to another person, and I can hardly
expect you to co-operate if I do not show you
the position from which we start."*
(Sherlock Holmes to Dr. Watson, "Silver Blaze")

IN MEDICINE the case is the basic unit of thought and discourse, for clinical knowledge, however scientific it may be, is narratively organized and communicated. As the medical account of a malady constructed from the patient's words and body, the case is a doubled narrative: the patient's story is encapsulated and retold in the physician's account of the process of disease in this one individual. The act of telling the medical story is likewise a redaction of the patient's own earlier presentation. The physician's presentation of the case to the medical audience represents (and re-presents) the patient's initiating presentation of body and self to medical attention. As a fundamental ritual of academic medicine, the narrative act of case presentation is at the center of medical education and, indeed, at the center of all medical communication about patients. As a narrative genre, the case has acquired a conventional structure and language that have become a central tradition in scientific medicine. The case presentation conveys the physician's observations, thought process, and conclusions about the illness of a sick person who has asked for help. Even more important, it guides the proper acquisition of knowledge in a scientific discipline that often must act upon incomplete and subjectively reported information.

Case Presentation

"Dr. Sanders, do you have a case to present us this morning?" The chief resident has assumed a formal manner. It is seven-thirty. Residents who were on call last night and those now coming on duty have filled styrofoam cups with coffee and grabbed a doughnut. Joking a little, trading follow-ups and "war stories" from the day before, they have seated themselves around two long tables placed end to end. This is the beginning of sign-in rounds or, where the military metaphor is still used, "morning report."

Dr. Sanders, a second-year resident, gestures with a folder of X rays. "Right here," she replies.

"Okay, let's have it."

"This is the first Memorial Hospital admission for Hope Ferrier, a 56-year-old white woman who presented to the emergency department last night about 11:30 complaining of nausea, vomiting, and right upper quadrant pain. She said she 'felt queasy after dinner and then got a terrible stomach ache that doubled her up and she vomited several times.' After three or four hours of increasing pain, her husband brought her on in. Her past medical history is significant for . . .."

The discourse of academic medicine takes place in a mind-boggling sea of detail and under circumstances that assault the human being's ordinary sense of denial, threatening the self. Here at its most scientific, at its self-consciously most objective, physicians' communication about patients strives to be plain and flat and dry. Physicians rely upon the fixed form of the case presentation to order the potentially confusing accumulation of information concerning the dozens of patients they see daily. The aim of medical discourse is always to eliminate or control the purely personal and subjective, whether its source be patient or physician, so that the physical anomalies that characterize illness can receive the attention their successful treatment requires. Illness is a subjective experience, and the examining physician faces the task of translating it, locating the malady in the medical universe and conveying its characteristics and their meaning to others who know the medical language well but this particular patient not at all. As a means of accomplishing this, the case presentation is strongly conventional in its form and style. There are no fixed rules on record, but local variants are minor compared to the fundamental uniformity that has evolved. All case presentations seek to turn an individual physician's interpretation of the patient's subjective and private experience of illness into an objective, scientific—or, from another viewpoint, a reliably intersubjective and medically recognizable—account of disease.

In a teaching hospital, the presentation of the case comes at the end of the opening movement of the work of medical care. Patients begin this movement by presenting themselves to medical attention: calling for an appointment and arriving at the office or, if suddenly ill or injured, by being brought to the emergency room by family or friends, or strangers. Although none of us can know the illness experienced by another person, we are not entirely barred from an approximate understanding. We have our own experience or the stories of our acquaintances, and—increasingly important in an age when few people are seriously ill until quite late in life—we have fictional representations in novels, short stories, and plays, including those for movies and television.

Medicine, however, focuses on the measurable abnormalities of body and behavior that, by appearing regularly in cases of illness, are the indices of identifiable disease or injury. When the ill person appears, asking for medical attention, the nurse or the physician begins with "the facts" of the experience, asking first what the trouble is and then recording as accurately as possible the details of the onset of the illness, its intensity and duration. This taking of "the history" is precisely where the medical construction of the medical story begins. Question follows question, reconstructing the patient's story and extending it along logical lines of inquiry. The questions concern not only areas of the body and organ systems but travel, occupational exposure, diet, habits, medication, change in weight, disability, and the patient's own interpretation of what is wrong. Those questions that yield no information—or, rather, yield the information that nothing is awry in an area of inquiry—seal off whole avenues of investigation. History taking is an interactive process, the first step in the care of the person who is ill. It goes on even in the direst emergency, the caretaker asking the person who is now a patient (or in the case of children or the incompetent, the person speaking for the patient): What is the matter? Tell me about it. What is it like? When did it begin? What were you doing at the time? Has it changed? Does anything you do make it better? Worse? What remedies have you tried? What do you think is the matter?

The account of illness that the physician is putting together is not the patient's story, although it depends upon and in part reconstructs it. Instead, it is the beginning of the medical story, a narrative that will be tested against the physical findings and amplified and refined by the physician's physical examination and the results of tests. It will be recorded in the patient's chart, and, depending on the circumstances, may be recounted at rounds or in a conference. If the malady is unusual and therefore instructive, the case may ultimately be written up for publication. But for the moment, the physician's concern is to translate the subjective experience of illness into the recognizable discourse of medicine and to record its details, codelike, in the patient's medical record.

The case presentation, if it follows, will be the physician's performative telling of this medical story. Beginning with the patient's presentation to medical attention and the retelling of his or her account of illness, the resident's presentation of the case reconstructs for its medical audience the otherwise unobserved acquisition of knowledge in the interview and examination. In that reconstruction, the resident retells the patient's story as a part of the medical story, which also includes the observation of the body and the extension of that observation, the results of preliminary tests. The difference between the two stories is more than one of arcane language. Reorganized according to a biomedical schema and the long-standing medical convention of the case presentation, the patient's story is transformed into a narrative that scarcely would be recognizable to the person whom it most concerns. Indeed, physicians traditionally have been reluctant to let patients read their charts, and in recent years they have become more sensitive to the possibility of offending or alarming patients with the presentation of their case at the bedside.[1] Nevertheless, the medical narrative's "translation" and replotting of the patient's experience is a major step in providing the help patients seek: a diagnosis and a plan for care.

The order and content of the case presentation are rigidly conventional, and the physician presenting a case is bound to its communally established narrative form. Scientific expectation or the conventions of expository writing might have it begin with a diagnostic hypothesis and then set about proving it. But that is wholly contrary to custom. Nor does it begin at the beginning with the onset of disease. The case opens, as Horace two thousand years ago advised that dramatic narrative should, *in medias res,* with the patient's initiatory request for care. In a single opening sentence we are given, along with a brief identification of the patient by age and sex and race or ethnic group, the time and circumstances of the patient's presentation to medical attention and a statement of the nature of the malady that occasioned the request for help. Ms. Ferrier, for example, reports that she "felt queasy after dinner and then I got a terrible stomach ache that doubled me up and I kept wanting to throw up." This is her "chief complaint," the single symptom or cluster of symptoms given in answer to the physician's opening question: "What seems to be the trouble?" Traditionally the answer has been recorded and reported in the patient's own words.[2]

In the opening sentence of her presentation, Dr. Sanders has established a narrative present at the point of clinical beginning; she has briefly introduced the principal character and hinted at the action to follow. Then she turns back in time to report the history of the present illness, a narrative constructed from the patient's story and answers to the physician's questions.[3] Next come more truly historical matters: what is called without any sense of redundancy the patient's "past medical history," an account of the patient's health in previous years, and the medical history of family members. After this double step into the past, the case presentation then turns toward the narrative present with the social history, a brief survey of the patient's family and work and habits up to the present time. It ends with a report of the physician's methodical inquiry into present symptoms, the "review of systems," beginning with the head and proceeding in fixed succession through the body to the extremities. Whether the information was gathered with a history-taking questionnaire or in an open-ended interview, the order of the entire "history" is more or less inviolable. Individual practice varies and no therapeutic encounter is ever quite like another, but as nearly as possible, the medical audience is provided a narrative representation of the observational situation.

The results of the physical examination are related next: the patient's general appearance and condition, the vital signs, and then the more particular observations made by sight and sound and touch. The order of these findings is that of the review of systems so that, although the examination very likely was conducted by areas of the body, the signs—or lack of them—follow the same order as the symptoms that the patient reported. Then come the results of tests ordered upon entry to care.

Up to this point, the physician has scrupulously avoided an interpretation of this abundance of information in either the actual patient encounter or the case presentation that relates it. The probable diagnosis is held suspended although the experienced listener can discern thematic clues: the hypothesis implicit in the presenter's line of questioning and the narrative inclusion of normal findings for systems that listeners might reasonably expect to be involved in the malady. "No fever, no rigors; bowel sounds were normal." This is medicine's peculiar rhetoric of denial, a list of noninvolvement that might put a Congressional witness to shame. The negatives represent narrative connections that were attempted and could not be made; they deflect listeners' attention from the myriad of possibilities and direct it toward a sustainable hypothesis. Taken all together—chief complaint, the patient's story, physical findings and nonfindings—these are "the facts." What they may mean has been delayed until all the available information has been reported.

Then comes the differential diagnosis, a reasoned consideration, in order of likelihood, of several maladies from which a patient with these signs and symptoms might be suffering. Just as the case presentation replicates the physician's investigative process, so it also replicates (and thus acts as a guide for) the thought process that accompanies inquiry: evidence both for and against each diagnostic possibility is considered, and logical steps are taken to confirm or rule out each one. The goal is, first, an accurate diagnosis with a minimum of tests and, then, prompt treatment leading to recovery with the fewest side effects. Last in the case presentation, as in the rational process, come the patient's prognosis, including the severity and probable duration of the malady and the expected results of treatment, and the plans for further tests, if necessary, and for the care of the patient.

In this highly conventional form, every medical student learns to investigate and narrate the events surrounding a patient's most recent entry into the medical world. As medicine's investigative pattern, the case pres-

entation arranges those events to highlight the pattern of disease, to translate the patient's subjective report of the physical problem into the physician's more objective and abstract account, and to sort out the intellectual
puzzles posed by the illness which the physician must address. So standardized is the case presentation that with local variants—such "rehu-
manizing" details as "man" for "male" or the inclusion of the patient's
occupation and family role, "an accountant living at home with her husband and teenaged son"—the pattern prevails wherever Western scientific medicine is taught. Students and residents have traditionally been
expected to memorize the details of the cases they present to enforce their
sense of the wholeness of the story—not only the coherence of the clinical
picture but its embodiment in one particular sick person. The information
is soon forgotten, replaced in a lifelong series of subsequent cases, but the
habits of thought and the order of the telling become second nature to
physicians. This is how they think and know. Years after residency, a
physician who has left academic medicine can still present a case almost
automatically, flawlessly. The case presentation is the coin of the medical
realm, the medium of clinical thought and communication. Even in a foreign country, with only a rudimentary grasp of the language, a physician
will be able follow the presentation of a case.

In its fully detailed form, the case presentation appears weekly in the
clinical-pathological conferences of the Massachusetts General and (occasionally) the Beth Israel hospitals, a genre of medical narration that has
been published weekly for more than seventy-five years in the *New England Journal of Medicine*. The "invention" of the clinical-pathological
conference has been attributed to Richard Cabot, who instituted it at
Massachusetts General in 1910.[4] But at least as early as 1832 in Paris,
something very like it was the weekly custom of Pierre Louis, famed for
bringing pathological anatomy to bear on clinical problems.[5] At each
meeting of the Society for Medical Observation formed by his students,
one of the group submitted for collective scrutiny a single puzzling, instructive case.[6] Shortly thereafter, in 1846, Erasmus Darwin Fenner, dean
of the New Orleans Medical School, not only organized a similar group
but required students enrolled in what was the first clinical clerkship to
write "a connected narrative" to be read to the professor on rounds.[7]

Whatever its precise historical origins, the case presentation is central to the discourse of medicine. In addition to morning report, almost
all other hospital conferences—even informal conversations about patients—follow its pattern at a greater or lesser distance: first the presenting symptoms and the history of the illness, then the findings of the
physical examination and the preliminary test results, followed by a differential diagnosis in order of likelihood. Students, residents, and experienced physicians listening to the same case presentation are to some ex-

tent hearing different things, attending to different aspects, acquiring, testing, and refining their increasingly sophisticated knowledge. In addition to learning how cases are presented, students are comparing the lists of symptoms and differential diagnoses they learned in their pathophysiology course with their manifestation in the real world of patients. In their first postgraduate year, interns listen for the process of diagnosis and treatment. Residents, refining their knowledge of the variation in disease, listen for diagnostic "red herrings" and clues to the unexpected. Professors attend to the competence of the residents, offering advice and comment, and fill out their own store of information from the presenting resident's early morning forays into "the literature"; pet theories are tested and ideas for clinical investigation may be generated. At every level of knowledge and experience, the listeners are enlarging their experience of medicine. The presentation of the case provokes them to think about an instance of a general rule—or an exception to it—that they otherwise might not have seen. After the clinical observation of patients, the presentation of cases is the principal teaching method in clinical medicine.

"To Present"

The goal of the case presentation is a precise, scientifically accurate account of the patient's condition, and thus it is not surprising that its language is plain and unmetaphoric. The resident may occasionally use a bare descriptive simile, speaking of a "water-bottle heart" or a "bullseye erythema," but otherwise the figurative language that livens medical discourse is all but banished. Certainly in the discussion that customarily follows the presentation, metaphors will flourish again. But for the moment, in this ritual performance, the most striking use of language is the word "present" itself.

"To present" and "presentation" have two meanings in medicine, and they are used without confusion in close proximity for both the patient's introduction to medical care and the resident's subsequent performative narration of that event. "Ms. Ferrier presented to the emergency department . . .." Given the number of linguistic oddities medical language has to offer, the word would scarcely seem to merit notice. Yet in its all but unmetaphorical use for the patient and her case, "present" is one of the most revelatory of medical words. In the teaching hospital the word means exactly what it means in ordinary speech: "Sarah presented a case like that Tuesday," a student may say later in the week. This unsurprising use for an introduction or demonstration derives from the conventions of etiquette—"May I present Mr. Morgan?"— or the rituals of the theater—"Joseph Papp presents . . .." But why, on a formal and "objective" occasion in a discipline that strives for scientific precision, does a word have a double reference to both an act and a narrative of that act?

The doubleness of "present" tells something about the nature of case presentation and about its importance for medicine as both an intellectual discipline and a transmissible body of practical experience. Not only does Dr. Sanders present the case (and thereby, metonymically, the patient), but the narrative she presents includes an account of that other "presentation," the patient's entry into the bright light of medical attention. "Ms. Ferrier is a 56-year-old white woman who *presented* to the emergency department last night . . .." Thus in the first sentence of a case presentation, the verb "present" is used not for the presentation Dr. Sanders is now making but for the patient's initial request for care. Ms. Ferrier's earlier act, that earlier presentation upon which the resident's narrative account of the case depends, is of a very different sort. It is primarily an action (which includes her telling the story of her illness), and in this event is the germ of the second presentation, the physician's performative telling that marks and confirms the medical existence of the patient.

The resident who saw Ms. Ferrier last night and tells about her at morning report is invariably said to "present" the case. The formal, somewhat theatrical sense of the word suggests the special place of the case in modern scientific medicine. The patient is presented; she is not "described" or "introduced." "Describe" is imprecise for a narrative, and the patient is both less and more important than "introduce" would imply. Her case will not take up all the time and attention in the conference or rounds or morning report, for these are also occasions for instruction. The authority—professor or chief resident—must move on from the particular case to general principles, or at least to guidelines or rules of thumb. Nor, unless the conference is rigged for a visiting expert, is the case merely the pretext for a scientific discussion. The patient in the resident's case presentation has become the text itself, and the case presentation a narrative interpretation that itself will be subject to explication and revision.

But who was Ms. Ferrier before she presented to the emergency room? How has she become the text for this conference? When did she become a "case"? Last night she was simply "Ms. Ferrier," a woman who was wheeled into the emergency room and who registered at the desk asking for help. She "presented," becoming a patient by that act. Although she will be the object of the verb "to present" when Dr. Sanders presents her case at morning report ("I'll present Ms. Ferrier"), in that narrative account of her presentation to the emergency department she is herself the subject of the verb: "She presented with nausea and vomiting and . . .." This self-presentation is not at all the same sort of presentation as the resident's subsequent narrative of the case. "Present" when used for

Ms. Ferrier's act of seeking medical care is a reflexive verb; no object follows.[8] It is never said that she "was presented," for instance, by ambulance or by her husband; the usage which has the patient as its subject has no passive form. Probably we were originally to hear the unexpressed reflexive, "herself." But by now, in its well established medical use for newly arrived patients, the verb is intransitive. It differs from the passive form used for sponsored exhibitions such as debutantes or theatrical productions—or medical cases—all of which "are presented." By means not yet specified from a life not yet described, a woman has actively entered the present tense of medical attention. Her body with its material qualities and quantities and its particular history is to become the object of examination.

The patient's arrival in the office or emergency department is thus a dividing line. Life before the moment of presentation, including the onset of illness, which those gathered at morning report are soon to hear about, is her "history." Her life thereafter in the medical present—or the physical manifestations of that life—will be meticulously recorded and analyzed. In the compilation of information—symptoms, signs, test results—her illness has been opened to investigation and interpretation. She has become a case. Although her condition may not have altered at all, the moment of her presentation marks the distinction between all that is "soft" and uncertain in the case history on the one hand, and, on the other, the diagnostic method and its technology.

Case presentations begin with this distinction between "history" and the medical present. It grounds the investigator's discovery of information about the patient by acknowledging its singular and subjective source, and it shapes a reliable narrative of what is known about the illness. The patient's story straddles this line between history and scientific investigation and as a consequence is regarded both with careful attention and with a skepticism that sometimes amounts to disdain and suspicion. On the one hand, "the history" is an important piece of medical information, and medical tradition places it in high regard. It is said that perhaps 70 to 90 percent of the time a good clinician makes the diagnosis from the history.[9] Cognitive science confirms its importance. Marsden S. Blois has described the predictive power of the patient's history as far more powerful than any diagnostic technology or artificial intelligence we possess.[10] The physical examination and the tests that follow are used to confirm and delineate the history. The telling of this history takes place in the present tense of medical observation, and many times the patient's story is the only source of knowledge about events that characterize the development of a malady. Therefore, physicians are taught to record it with careful attention to detail and to append an estimate of the teller's reliability: "In spite of her discomfort, Ms. Ferrier is a good historian." The "data" in the history of the present illness belong to the patient. Like the opening moments of the patient-physician encounter with which the case begins, the patient's history is not scientific. Subjective, often incompletely or badly reported, sometimes unreliable or outright diversionary, it concerns events that may not have happened—not in the way they are perceived and reported or, sometimes, not at all. The events of the patient's past enter the medical arena already interpreted— by other physicians, by family members, by the patient herself. Chances are that it was one of these prepresentational interpretations—"This is something serious!" or "Oh, but I've had a pain like this before and it's gone away"—that has brought the patient to seek (or delay seeking) medical care. Hence the physician's high regard for history coexists with strong skepticism. That something so subjective and potentially unreliable as the patient's account of illness is so powerful can be, for the good physician, a perpetual source of uneasiness. As with all history, there is no way to go behind the interpretation to bare uninterpreted "facts." The patient's narrative must be deconstructed, resolved into its elements again, and their traces sought in the present. Physicians do not really know—and *know* they don't know with any reliability—until the patient's history is confirmed.

The patient's presentation to doctor's office or emergency department, then, is not simply her presence at the registration desk, but the initiatory movement into the arena of scientific medicine: "Ms. Ferrier presented . . .." That moment marks the division between her history—what must be reported by her and, with some skepticism, relied upon by a resident who does not know her—and the scientific domain of medical investigation which that resident presently brings to bear upon her case. Why, then, after a long night on call are they so careless as to use one word in two ways?

"Anyone have an interesting case?" the chief resident asks. "Sarah?"

"I'll present Ms. Ferrier."

Representation

Far from a source of confusion, the double use of "present" is an implicit claim to representation. A discourse striving for accuracy and precision might be expected to avoid two distinct uses of a single word. But, in this instance, misunderstanding seems to be courted. The two presentations often occur only a few hours apart, and both involve the puzzle of how to care for a patient whose illness must first be understood. To those not directly involved in the patient's care, the first presentation, the patient's act of self-presentation, comes to be known only as a part of the second (and narrative) presentation. The double use passes unnoticed by physicians; there is no effort and apparently no perceived need to prevent confusion. The two are in some sense one.

For its medical audience, the case presentation re-presents and represents the patient's presentation—including her own story of her illness and her medical and social history. The two presentations are bound to one another and in the medical view seem to be two mutually dependent aspects of a whole. Certainly they have an inviolable temporal order: the patient's case (or, taking the whole for the part, "the patient") can be presented by the resident only after the patient herself has presented to the emergency department. Her presentation is narratively embedded in the resident's presentation, and then, in its first sentence, the narrator presents the patient to a medical audience just as the patient herself presented for care the evening before. The resident would have nothing to present had not the patient presented to the emergency department. Likewise, the patient, however real her illness and her presence in the emergency department, depends for her medical existence upon a ritual of investigation that makes of her the text of a case that can be narratively presented. Thus the two acts, by patient and by physician, are firmly connected: the case, which embodies the patient's medical existence, is a narrative version of the inaccessible, time-bound beginning of medical care.

Yet representation is not identity. Despite the claim to iconicity implicit in the use of the same word for both act and narration, the narratives associated with those presentations are not the same—not even the same story told by different people. Nevertheless, by a bit of metaphoric shorthand—"Sarah's presenting Ms. Ferrier"—the case often comes to stand for the patient and her history. The ease of this substitution suggests a reason for physicians' lack of anxiety about the linguistic doubleness: in medicine there is no working perception of a difference in their referents. The two uses of "present" are not confused or often noticed because the two presentations readily collapse into one: the patient becomes the medical presentation, a case. Such metonymic imperialism is a hazard of the act of representing another person in a narrative of one's own construction, and it contributes to the professional shortsightedness that sees maladies rather than people as the objects of medical attention.[11] A measure of self-consciousness in a physician's use of language is required to guard against it, remembering that the case and the ill person are not the same. Although the case presentation originates from the story of illness the patient has told and although the two narratives concern the same malady in the same person, the case presentation is a representation and not a replication (nor, except in very practical metonymic figure of speech, a replacement) of the patient and her story.

In literary terms and from a medical point of view, the clinical narrative bears much the same relation to the patient's narrative as plot bears to story. The distinction in narrative theory between "story" and "plot" points to the difference between events and the order of their telling. The story of *Oedipus the King*, for example, encompasses the years from the oracle concerning the hero's birth until his blinding; its plot, on the other hand, is the order of events during a single day of discovery. This distinction between plot and story at first might seem overly sophisticated for a medical narrative that aims only to present the plain unvarnished truth. Indeed, its tellers often fail to recognize it as a narrative at all. So transparent and wholly representational does the case presentation seem that its tellers and audience are scarcely aware of it as a form; one physician-writer, reacting to its impersonality, recently characterized its opening lines as "banter."[12] Yet the medical narrative is created as surely as a work of fiction. The physician not only adds observations from the physical examination and test results to the patient's story, but also selects among the details presented by even the most reliable patient. Moreover, the medical narrative alters the straightforward chronology of events in the patient's life.

Narrative representation is always, inevitably, an interpretation of the events it relates. The two stories have different authors, different narrative modes, different themes. The patient's story of illness, although it may serve as source material for the physician's account, is not simply "raw data." The patient has constructed it in an effort to make sense of life-altering events. But different tellers alone do not explain the differences between the patient's story and the medical narrative. Each is told for a different purpose, and, as a consequence, different events are selected and organized in quite different plots. They have much in common: a set of events connected with an illness in the life of a single person. Near their beginnings, if the physician records the chief complaint in the patient's words, the two will even contain a common sentence: "I felt queasy after dinner and then I got a terrible stomach ache that doubled me up and I kept wanting to throw up." Beyond this, however, the two narratives diverge radically. First of all, their narrators differ entirely in their involvement with the events they relate. The patient is speaking of what is often quite intimate experience, drawing upon a sense of self, while the physician, however empathic, is objectively engaged in solving a problem. The content and theme of the two narratives differ as well. The patient's story includes history, circumstantial etiology and leaps to meaning; the ways of answering the question "What seems to be the matter?" are as variable as patients themselves. In contrast to this subjective story of illness, the physician's traditional, highly patterned version is shaped by strict criteria of inclusion and exclusion. Its problem is illness and its goal the recognition and treatment of disease. In pursuit of diagnostic and therapeutic goals, the medical narrative orders not just the patient's account but all the details of the physician-patient encounter, rendering it observable and intersubjective, open to critique. The patient is the subject of the first narrative, the object of the second. The patient's story is framed—some might claim it is appropriated and devalued—by the medical version that represents it in the medical world. Two narratives would seem to require two tellers and (at least) two listeners, but in this sequence of double presentation three people suffice. The physician-listener turns from the patient-narrator to become a medical narrator, altering the story in order to tell it to a medical audience in a medical way.

The Physician's Narrative

Medical narrative has an order so regular and fixed that a case presentation seems to be an undistorted representation of the events as they happened. But rather than a transparent account of "reality," its highly organized, conventional structure imposes meaning upon the events it sets in order. "Here is another sick person," the case implies, "in the long line of people who ask for our help. This is what she has told me, this is what she looks like; here are my observations and the preliminary sense I have made of the information I have gathered. This is what I have done for her so far; here is what I plan to do." The "I" that is the subject of these actions is never spoken, however, for the physician-narrator (who may need the case presentation's soothing abstraction most of all) is all but effaced from the case presentation. Only Dr. Sanders's presence and her public act of narrating assert her responsibility as actor in the plot. The rigor and sameness of all such presentations effaces the observing, narrating speaker just as they obscure the organization or plottedness of the narration. Yet, no matter how carefully constructed and clearly presented, the case remains a version of events which themselves cannot be directly known. The achievement of the regular, patterned, self-effacing plot of medical narrative is to control insofar as possible the subjectivity of its observer-narrator and the variables of its actual telling. The physician-narrator's purposeful arrangement of the events and the subjectivity of her act of narrating are taken for granted by everyone in medicine. Fixed and communal, the constructedness of the case presentation is ignored and forgotten.

As a part of this plottedness, the order of events related in the case departs from the strict chronology of the illness. A case presentation may be extended or brief, but its structure is always the same. Beginning in the midst of the patient's story, at the dividing line between the subjective and the objective drawn by the patient's act of presentation, it then pursues the account of the patient's history until it returns to the extended present, which is taken up with the medical events that have transpired between the patient's and the resident's presentations. Beginning at the moment of the patient's presentation is a sound choice from both a narrative and a scientific standpoint. It is as if James Boswell had begun at a point one-fifth of the way through *The Life of Johnson*[13] on the evening he met Dr. Johnson rather than writing about Dr. Johnson's parentage, birth, and early career—all the years that Boswell, thirty-one years younger, did not witness. More precisely, it is as if on the first page of the biography Boswell had mentioned the middle-aged Johnson's entrance into Davies's bookshop and then, with only a bare identification of the man, had outlined the circumstances of Johnson's fifty-four years that had led on that particular evening to his stopping in.

The patient's entry into medical care, like Dr. Johnson's arrival in Boswell's life (and *Life*), is the point at which the narrator's reliable knowledge based on his or her own observation begins. Although biography and the medical case might be thought to have goals equally plain and representational (biography is, after all, something of a case study in human behavior), that is not the case. Biographers traditionally begin at the beginning; Horace contrasted its narration *ab ovo* with drama's beginning *in medias res*. Biographical narratives aim to be representational, historical; seldom, except in a general sense, are they meant to influence the world of action. The traditional medical narrative, on the other hand, is not a life history but an account of a particular set of events worth relating for reasons other than the biographical. It must formulate an implicit argument for action. Although its creation of historical record is valuable (or may some day be), the case aims first to make coherent, narrative sense of symptoms and signs, discovering their immediate causes and intervening to change the course of disease. Thus it subordinates all that has gone before, even much that is medically relevant, to the presentation of the immediate situation. An earlier condition may have nothing to do with the present one; or if it does, there is always a possibility that it was misinterpreted and misunderstood. The case presentation takes a new look.[14] Its theme is the quest for a diagnosis, and therefore, with perfect scientific soundness, medical narrative begins at the beginning of medical observation, *in medias res* with the first observations of one clinically trained, reliable narrator.

The life events narrated in the patient's story and their interpretation as medical events in the case presentation thus take part in two different plots. The patient's presentation to medical attention occurs in the middle of an ongoing life. That moment is not the beginning of either Ms. Ferrier or her life story. At most it begins a new chapter; it is the pivotal event in the chronological chain of events from the onset of illness through diagnosis and treatment. But in the medical plot, that chronological chain is caught up by its initiatory medical event, and past and future are subordinated to it. The represented time in the medical narrative is not the lived time of the illness but the plotted time of medical discovery, from the patient's entry to care until shortly before the case presentation begins. Beginning in this way with the patient's act of presentation is both reliable and effective. The narrator implicitly acknowledges the identity of the person who has become a patient—"Ms. Ferrier is a 56-year-old white woman who . . ."—and the sources of the information that is being regarded as fact. "Here is what I saw or had immediately reported to me by other health-care professionals," the structure of the resident's narrative asserts. "And here also—for its undeniable but still suspect value as our best information on important matters such as the onset of illness and the nature of the symptoms—is the patient's account." The subjective experience represented in the patient's presentation, particularly the troubling symptoms, is rightfully the point at which the medical plot begins, for it constitutes the problem for both patient and physician. More important, that experience of illness sets out the problem the case presentation must begin to solve: what is the meaning of this presentation for this patient? The motivating, narratable departure from the norm makes the story worth plotting, indeed makes it a story in the first place. The puzzle constituted by these originating symptoms must be solved, and that solution will be the narrative's end.

Narrative Knowledge

The medical plot, the narrative organization of the case, is shaped by the physician's quest for an understanding of the patient's illness: a diagnosis. Its organizing principle is the desire for an answer to the question of what best can be done for this particular patient. In contemporary literary criticism and in the theory of the human sciences, narrative is understood as a way of knowing.[15] Georg Lukács, for example, in finding inadequate both the arbitrary, author-imposed, representational plots characteristic of nineteenth-century fiction and the refusal to plot that is the modern reaction against them, likens the function of plot to that of theory in more linear, less discursive disciplines. Like theory, he maintains, plot is the mediating force in "the dialectical movement from concrete reality to abstract representation and back to conscious participation in [reality]."[16] This is an apt description of the medical case and the rational process it embodies, in which both the investigation of the malady and the plot of the narrative that reports it are shaped by the diagnostic hypothesis. Given the constraints on the physician's information and investigative method, neither the diagnostic quest nor the plot it shapes and motivates proceeds in a linear fashion. The tentative hypotheses of the differential diagnosis that emerge from the patient's initial account of illness are tested and refined against data gathered from the patient's history and physical examination. Possibilities must be ruled out, often by further testing. Circling between the available clues (including pertinent negatives and normal findings) and the general rules that define diseases, the medical reasoner generates a full and plausible set of possibilities, discards those that are not borne out by the "facts," and thus, even in the absence of a confirming test, arrives at the best hypothesis for the case at hand.

Like a Sherlock Holmes story, the case presentation is a narrative of interpretation, one whose investigation is replicated in its narrative. As in a detective story, the plot not only reveals to its audience the meaning of the puzzling events it recounts but also is the narrative of the discovery of that meaning. Both genres are concerned with the way knowledge is acquired as well as with the nature of the "facts" and their communication. The narration in both stories at once relates and records an interpretation of the information at hand and reproduces and enacts the process through which it was interpreted. Like the criminal in the Sherlock Holmes story, the disease in the case presentation is discovered in a double sense: it is determined by the investigating physician and revealed by the same person, now become the narrator. In both senses—its determination by the investigator and its disclosure to the audience—discovery proceeds from the careful arrangement of the data which the physician, like Sherlock Holmes, has gathered from the words and the body presented for scrutiny.

For readers or the audience at morning report, such a plot of discovery reveals both the meaning of events and the means of their interpretation. The resident must at once be both Holmes and Watson. Part of the genius of Arthur Conan Doyle's stories is his choice of an innocent everyman as narrator. Dr. Watson is our surrogate, representing to us our ignorance and our fascination with a method we are able to follow, for the most part, only after the fact. For him as for us, Holmes's "deductions"—both the process and the achievement—are a source of wonder. But in medicine the physician-detective often must also narrate the case, and in an academic hospital the resident works furiously to construct both narrative and solution before presenting the case at morning report. It is presented as a puzzle by someone who, like Watson, knows its solution, but, unlike him, has also directed the investigative process. This does not mean that the case presentation is simply a pedagogical device and not a heuristic one. Its traditional structure has been useful in thinking about the case from the beginning. The knowledge of the medical plots of countless other cases has guided the acquisition of knowledge about the patient and shaped the application of general principles of human biology and clinical medicine. A command of the form enables the resident-detective to seek advice by making an abbreviated presentation to a more experienced physician. The delineation of a recognizable pattern of illness—recognizable in part because of its patterned telling—enables a consultant to understand the case and make useful suggestions. The conventional plot of the case presentation sets out the problem, suspends judgment until the facts are told, organizes the available information in orderly and familiar patterns, guides its testing against "clinical pictures," and, with luck, leads to a diagnosis.

The representation of the patient's now inaccessible act of presentation—including her presentation of her past—returns its teller and its listeners to that moment when Ms. Ferrier entered the hospital: minds were fresh then and devoid of assumptions about her malady. Although Dr. Sanders's first act on Ms. Ferrier's behalf depended upon the patient's own subjective account of her predicament—"I felt queasy after dinner . . ."—by the time of morning report she has put the patient's story in the context of her physical appearance and the signs of her condition. The case presentation reconstructs Dr. Sanders's acquisition of information about Ms. Ferrier—history, physical findings, test results—followed by the rational process of determining what might be wrong and the first steps to alleviate her pain. The case is both a narrative representation of what happened to the patient in the emergency room and an account of the resident's process of reasoning.

Like detective-narrators, the narrators of medical cases tell us not only "who done it" but how the crime was solved. And, like the readers of detective stories, the auditors of a case presentation listen at varying levels of comprehension and experience different sorts of suspense. Some are learning what happened, some how the diagnosis was made, others are listening for the aesthetic (and the pedagogical) pleasure of hearing a case well solved. All are testing their grasp of the case against the application of knowledge and experience that led to action for this particular patient. Like Sherlock Holmes himself, physicians require clues; they are unable to begin their work merely from general knowledge. But, equally important, they cannot lack the general and theoretical knowledge that enables their leaps from particular clue to conclusion. Like Sherlock Holmes, the good physician acquires a store of index cases. These narratives, with their purposeful organization of events, mediate the application of generalities—pathophysiological principles, the textbook descriptions of disease, rules of thumb—to the signs and symptoms of the individual case. The case presentation not so much proves as narratively demonstrates the diagnosis. The progress of the illness recounted by the patient and its traces in the body are matched against the abstract order of detail in the diagnostic handbook even as the process of interpreting these "clues" is replicated in the narrative unfolding of the case.

Because clinical reasoning, like Sherlock Holmes's ratiocination, is a comparative process operating through time, this dialectical process of discovery and understanding is well suited to narrative representation. Like Holmes, the physician relies on clues for the generation of a theory, a plot which must then be corrected and confirmed by the details of the physical evidence. Under the circumstances, it is the most rational way, the most scientific way, to proceed. In the absence of controls available to those sciences that are not also practices, the narrative case presentation demonstrates a method of reasoning that is adequate both to the variability of a single case and to the development of a pathological condition over time.

The case presentation is the fundamental medium of clinical thought and discourse. Guiding the methodical acquisition of information about the patient's malady and the consideration of its hypothetical interpretation, the narrative representation of the patient's plight is the opening summary in the process of medical care. It constitutes the foundation of medical attention, the goal of which is the recognition and treatment of the disease that is the source of its narratability. If a case illustrates problems of diagnosis or therapy—or, much less frequently, if it demonstrates their solution especially well—it might be presented more than once. But for the most part, unless the malady is rare, the diagnosis and the existence of a therapy of choice mean the end of the case. The mystery is solved; the medical narrative then exists only in its rudimentary form in the patient's chart. "Happy families are all alike," begins Tolstoy's *Anna Karenina*, a novel of (among other things) family unhappiness. It is the principle of medical storytelling as well. Uncomplicated cures make very short tales, and although their endings are happy, their plots tend to be simple and boring. We must look elsewhere than to the traditional case presentation for a narrative that will lead, as the adage has it, to "cure sometimes, care often, but comfort always." Nevertheless, the case is supremely useful in shaping the record for subsequent interpreters of the facts as they are now understood and for communicating the present understanding of the patient's plight. The plot of the case presentation is a heuristic pattern that facilitates that understanding and models the means by which it has been reached. The physician's act of constructing the case has ordered the evidence both for teller and for listener. As Sherlock Holmes observes as he begins to present "the essential facts" to an open-minded but clueless Watson, "I shall enumerate them to you, for nothing clears up a case so much as stating it to another person."[17]

FOUR

"THERE WAS THIS ONE GUY . . .":

ANECDOTES IN MEDICINE

"Well, Mr. Holmes, what are we to do with this fact?"
"To remember it—to docket it. We may come on something
later which will bear upon it."
(Sherlock Holmes to Mr. Lestrade,
"The Adventure of the Six Napoleons")

T HE OPENING LINE of Leo Tolstoy's *Anna Karenina* has the sound of folk wisdom: "Happy families are all alike; each unhappy family is unhappy in its own way." A wise perception about painful human situations, the aphorism is also a cornerstone principle of narrative and narrativity. Good news is no news—unless it is unexpected. The maxim is as true of novels as of newspapers.[1] Tales, those worth the listening, are told about what is different, surprising, unpredictable.

Medicine is filled with stories. The imperfect fit between biological knowledge and the expression and treatment of disease in the individual leaves room for variants, surprises, anomalies. These are events, noteworthy occurrences, and every event in medicine, potentially at least, has both oral and written narratives. The most ordinary and unsurprising are minimally recorded. A falling temperature in response to an antibiotic in the midst of a relatively unremarkable course of medical care, for example, is noted in the patient's chart. But it does not qualify the case for presentation, even though therapy has been a success. Where success is expected it is not a criterion of narratability—as teenagers doing well in school and society often complain. At the other end of the spectrum of surprise, however, narratives abound. Unexpected clinical phenomena are brought to grand rounds for the edification of experienced clinicians and then written up for publication. The oddity may appear as a case report, a clinical-pathological conference, or a letter to a journal. In the hands of a physician-writer it may form the substrate of an extramedical essay on its origins or the issues it poses.

In addition to the cases formally presented to colleagues and professors during the clinical years of a physician's education, informal stories of difficult cases, solved and unsolved, are the stuff of professional and quasi-social interaction. Yet "anecdotal" would stand very near the top of a list of pejorative words in medicine—and for good reason. The number and variety of signs and symptoms observed and reported by the ill render the single case a deceptive guide to understanding disease in another human being, even the same disease in a second patient. Diseases described in textbooks are hypothetical abstractions, "classic cases," and their most common variants. But how are particular instances of illness in individual patients made to fit these abstractions? As with the formal case presentation to which, like a poor relation, it is allied, the anecdote enables physicians to bridge this epistemological gap between the general rules of disease and the particular facts of an illness.

In the midst of a highly technologized, scientific profession, the anecdote is a clear reminder of the fundamental nature of medicine's "raw material," the exigencies of the particular illness. Yet if sentiment were its purpose, an occasional story would be sufficient, a nod in the direction of the human object as a reminder of its subjectivity and variety. Anecdotes are much more frequently told than sentiment alone would warrant or the profession's sense of time's pressure would tolerate. Something so pervasive and so contrary to medicine's scientific ideal as the anecdote must have a function in the everyday business of medicine. Its very taken-for-grantedness suggests that the anecdote is of a piece with modern scientific medicine and will reveal something of its nature and philosophy.[2] Playing a part in medical education, in clinical research, and in the daily care of patients, this oral narrative is actually a neglected, interstitial medium for the transmission of medical knowledge.

Knowledge in medicine is focused first and last on the diagnosis of the patient. In the simplest cases, a disease will be easily recognizable when its major symptom is readily apparent and all but synonymous with the disorder. In many other cases the diagnosis is far more complex. That is, while a sudden squeezing chest pain *is* angina, most illnesses are known and labeled at a level other than their symptoms. Instead, they are identified either with an etiological agent anterior to the symptoms or as a syndrome of which the single symptom is but one part. For the former, diagnosis may be a matter of a positive test for bacteria or antibodies; the latter are the more difficult to diagnose because their symptoms and signs and test results could be attributed to a number of conditions. In the absence of a pathognomonic sign or a test result that will confirm the presence of a particular disease, diagnostic criteria have been established for a number of problematic diseases in order to standardize their recognition by the general medical population. Based on the statistical study of numerous instances of the disease or condition, these criteria constitute a definition by "families" of attributes. The American Rheumatological Association, for example, has identified eleven physical findings or test results that are characteristic of rheumatoid arthritis, none of which is exactly specific to the disease. Because none of these eleven characteristics is a necessary consequence of the disease and all of them may occur in patients without rheumatoid arthritis, the diagnosis of "classic" rheumatoid arthritis, it has been decided, depends upon the presence of seven of the eleven. Any five of the eleven justifies a diagnosis of "definite" rheumatoid arthritis; the presence of any three a "probable" diagnosis. For this disease, prognosis and response to therapy are equally varied. It is not quite true that no two cases are alike, but they can be categorized only in retrospect. In prospect, every case is different.

In the quest for a broad-based, scientific understanding of disease and the efficacy of its surgical and pharmacologic treatment, clinical studies are based on a large number of cases, and the medical investigator has the obligation, common to all scientific research, to report accurately the negative results as well as the positive ones and to specify the variables that may have contributed to the outcome. Practitioners rely upon these statistical abstractions—as do medical students and residents in the process of learning to take care of patients. Physicians form their habits and throughout their careers modify their customary practice to take account of the refinements in diagnostic knowledge and the advancements in therapy that have been established and reported in this way. Such careful description of diagnostic criteria and reliable studies of treatment is the foundation of modern scientific medicine. In this understanding of medicine, there seems to be no place for the single, untested case.

Stories in medicine, however, like stories everywhere, are inevitably concerned with single instances. Thus, insofar as they purport to convey knowledge, they are regarded as antiscientific in themselves, and late twentieth-century physicians are likely to associate them with unenlightened, prescientific practice. The deceptive power of the single case is the bane of scientific medicine. The imprinting of the isolated bits of experience or of hearsay may skew the clinician's judgment in subsequent cases. The physician who leaps to a mistaken diagnostic conclusion on the basis of limited personal experience, like the surgeon who refuses to use a particular instrument because one of them went bad in the middle of an operation, or the internist who employs a marginally effective therapy because it once had good results, swims against the tide of a statistical medicine based on scientific principle.

Stories, clinical accounts of single cases, were once the primary medium of medical knowledge. Sir Thomas Sydenham's careful observations in the seventeenth century were an important advance over a practice so tied to theory that physical examination was rarely undertaken and diagnosis by mail was widespread.[3] Yet his classification of disease was based on a series of witnessed accounts of single cases. In the late eighteenth and nineteenth centuries physiological studies and pathological correlations took the place of single accounts and ultimately enabled physicians to correct and extend their understanding of disease and its treatment. The disrepute in which anecdotes are held is thus historically rooted in the shift to a scientific, specifically pathophysiological, explanation of disease. The vehemence with which they are condemned suggests the collective pain of those moments in medical progress when the old understanding stood in the path of the new. Today anecdotal evidence is believed to be only marginally better than no evidence at all. Like clinical judgment itself—the skill or quality that these stories are often meant to illustrate—anecdotes may represent (as a resident once put it) "what's left after the facts are forgotten." They are seen as snares and traps for their unwary auditors, who may mistake them for "real" knowledge. As the time elapsed since residency grows, physicians are urged to "keep up with the journals" as a means of preventing terminal anecdotalism.

Nevertheless, medicine is filled with stories. Indeed, among the disciplines of human knowledge, medicine can be characterized by its dependence upon narrative. The care of a patient begins with the patient telling a story while the physician listens. The case presentation, the study and review of a single patient's clinical course, is the narrative center of medicine as a discipline, providing clinical education not only for students and residents during their hospital training but for physicians throughout their medical careers. Stories illustrate the limits of available knowledge in a field that experiences constant change in information and technique. Particular cases, not statistical abstractions, are the almost unvarying focus of conferences with colleagues. Above all—and essential to the healing encounter—the physician provides patients with the narrative translation of their own stories, explaining the maladies that have occasioned their visit. Some of these uses of storytelling are scientific, some are professional, some both at once. All are an inalienable part of medicine.

In their own clinical variant of Tolstoy's maxim, physicians, like writers, are alert to the minutely different. The inevitable consequence of this focusing of attention is the anecdote. Beyond the formal case presentation, medical anecdotes abound. Throughout medical practice, informal accounts of cases past and present hover at every point, always present to the memory, often brought forth as illustration. "There was this one guy . . .," the anecdote may begin. Or: "We had a case last year that . . .." These anecdotes are precedents and variants that form the experiential context for the case at hand. They are available for instructive comparison or illustrative contrast, for wonder or for comfort. These casual, "unofficial" stories are despised by clinical purists. Told by physicians to their colleagues or their juniors (students, residents, or less experienced clinicians), anecdotes are incidental, believed to be peripheral to good medical practice, a source of embarrassment to the profession. Yet they are most often told when for some reason the case under consideration does not fit the textbook description and the physician needs to puzzle out why and, even in the absence of an answer, decide what must be done. It is this use, the anecdote as a tool of medical thinking, that is most interesting because its value is unacknowledged. Anecdotes also intrude into teaching rounds; they are included as asides in research seminars. In both formal and informal encounters they frequently identify the anomalous "fact" that must be explained, and thus, as we will see, they have a defensible function in scientific investigation.

Regardless of the anecdote's content, the act of storytelling itself is useful in the education and professionalization of medical students and in the ongoing education and professional life of out-of-school physicians. Exempla are told as cautionary tales, not only to warn against particular mistakes but simply to identify the terrain as treacherous. A physician meeting a group of interns early in the year begins his professor's rounds with a story from his own apprenticeship: "I remember how it is," he says. "When I was an intern at St. Joseph's once, going into my second day on call, I mistook a mycoplasma pneumonia for pulmonary edema." There is grudging laughter. The anecdote bears no information about either malady, but he has begun to establish his character and his awareness of the nature of medical practice.

Occasionally stories are used to set out points of procedure or etiquette. "You'd better call him," a third-year resident will advise a resident one year her junior about an attending physician, "With most of them you can go right ahead and do what you think is best. They might be annoyed if you called. But last year Sam had a patient who was one day post op and spiked a fever in the middle of the night. Dr. Yancy read him the riot act for not letting him know."

Clinicians may actually be invited to tell a story as a gesture of hospitality, an invitation to share in the teaching. In a conference attended by a respected but seldom seen clinical professor from another hospital, the chief of a service calls on that relative stranger to relate his experience with cases like the one under discussion, drawing him in with a request not for the latest news of research from the journals but for an anecdote: "Anybody had any experience with this?" he asks. "How about you, Bob?"

Because storytelling is an "in group" activity conducted within a hierarchical group of physicians, it tends to be specialty-specific. In their small, regular departmental or unit conferences physicians both teach and learn, reviewing the state of knowledge in their discipline. There they are at liberty to air their views of competing therapies, different procedures, other specialties. On these informal although quite serious occasions anecdotes flourish. By contrast, combined rounds between, for example, medicine and surgery seldom include anecdotes, for that is a far more formal proceeding, "scientific" and objective in tone. A resident from one service will present the case; a resident from the other will take up the account at the point when the patient was transferred from the first service. Subspecialty consultants from, for example, infectious disease or pathology will supply commentary. Questions flow not from elders to the residents on their service but from one service to another. A united front, even in the face of a mutually perplexing problem, is maintained, and informal stories will not breach the tone of detailed, rational inquiry.

Anecdotes also may be culture-specific in a larger sense, for physicians who are not native speakers of English tend to conduct professor's rounds without illustrative anecdotes, relying instead entirely on published studies. This may indicate that medical cultures other than ours are less narrative or rather, as I suspect, that the foreign-born physician is less "at home" and may also feel a need to demonstrate a command of the technical literature.

In general, it seems that the smaller and more regular the group and the more its members are engaged in the same clinical activities, the more anecdotes will be told. Yet even in relatively formal situations the pedagogical power of storytelling is recognized. Near the close of a large regular departmental conference, a professor, one of the elders present, addresses himself to broader issues than the case at hand. Others might have begun, "I had a patient last winter with this same diagnosis," or "Some of you may remember Ms. Maxwell, who was a patient we took care of last year."[4] This time, however, with a ritual apology that shows a more than ordinary self-consciousness, yet without any hesitation or any expectation that his question would meet a negative, the professor asks, "May I tell an anecdote?" The chief of service replies almost genially, "By all means; it makes the information stick."

Beyond this mnemonic effect and the more general social value of storytelling in the professionalization of the young and in the communal life of all physicians, anecdotes have a vital function in the acquisition and organization of knowledge.[5] They play an important, intellectually respectable part not only in introducing established information to new learners but also in advancing the new knowledge of experienced learners. They have a use in the scientific investigation of disease. They suggest where research attention needs to be turned next, functioning as a preliminary critique of current therapy, and they stake out new knowledge, new subgroups in the clinical spectrum of disease. Anecdotes serve as critical commentary on such things as the published criteria for a diagnosis or for the stages of a disease. They are useful not only in locating research problems but also in keeping alive a skepticism about new knowledge claims in a hierarchical, authoritarian discipline. As rough accounts of the unexpected and occasionally the improbable, they are frequently the as-yet-unorganized evidence at the forefront of clinical medicine.

It is, after all, the aberrations that become physicians' stories. While classic "textbook" cases occasionally may be presented in rounds as good teaching cases, a reassertion of the familiar pattern of disease, or as an introduction to the discussion of a new diagnostic test or therapy, most narrative and almost all anecdotes are about the variant or anomalous. Only if ill with a fatal disease would a patient want to provide material for a medical story. Sick with an ordinary illness—appendicitis, pneumonia, a broken bone—a patient ideally will provoke no anecdotes at all, but instead be an uneventful textbook case passing unnoted from illness to recovery. If the patient presents a minor variation on the textbook description, he or she may be a story told in passing (an anonymous one, of course) tossed out to convey the difficulty of the day or the competence of the speaker. Or the case may become the subject of a brief informal consultation with a colleague. If the case is "interesting"—that is, if it is either seldom seen or presents instructive difficulties of diagnosis or treatment, it will be presented at morning report or at teaching rounds. The story may be brought as a case to a weekly conference in a specialized service for its instructive value so that residents may mull and reinterpret it. In extreme instances, the puzzling, aberrant patient becomes a story at weekly departmental grand rounds or at a clinical-pathological conference.

Some events are too puzzling to fit the prevailing general principles. If there seems to be no place in the intellectual scheme of medicine for the anomaly the story represents, then the story may simply be told and retold over lunch or in the locker room until enough colleagues have replied, more in sympathy than with much practical help: "I've seen that"; "You get 'em like that"; or "We had somebody like that a couple of years ago who . . .." Then, with its strangeness reabsorbed, familiarized, the story disappears, replaced by others, all but forgotten.

Such a story, apparently forgotten, may reemerge when a second improbable instance occurs: when another baby is born with flippered arms, for example, or another patient in the emergency room dies after taking a new "wonder drug" like Zomax.[6] In the early days of the AIDS epidemic, a young New Yorker presented with a condition that looked like deep vein thrombophlebitis or Baker's cyst, but was instead something new and as yet undescribed. What ensued is not uncommon in clinical medicine. As Gerald Weissmann tells the story, he heard at lunch one day of a puzzling case very like the one that had stumped his chief resident. Within a short time he and his colleagues had turned up three more cases of what they at first called AIDS-related non-Baker's-cyst hyperalgesic pseudothrombophlebitis. In due course it was documented in the *American Journal of Medicine* in a five-case report with, significantly, five authors.[7] In instances like this, what has been forgotten as a useless datum, a bit of noninformation, may be recalled when a similar case is reported by a resident or a colleague. This can be the beginning of a "series" that will grow into a study and thence make its way into a textbook.[8] It is possible now to turn up early instances of recent "new diseases" like toxic shock syndrome or Legionnaires' disease, cases that puzzled their observers but went unreported because the physicians were too busy to write them up or felt they had failed to get to the bottom of them. For those physicians, the case remained an anecdote. Although the few cases he had seen were sufficient evidence, the Australian physician who discovered the teratogenic properties of the drug thalidomide introduced the matter at a public meeting with an epidemiologically naive yet characteristic apology: "As a scientist," he said, "I have no grounds for speaking. As a human being I cannot keep silent."[9]

Anecdotes are told about the anomalous details that fail to fit the current patterns of disease description. They often concern new drugs, new therapies, or an odd postsurgical course. Some are about a broad category of anomalies that are sometimes called management problems: noncompliant patients, patients who have refused treatment, patients for whom families wanted useless treatment, dying patients who have arranged their deaths. Many tell of occupational or environmental maladies, "accidents" that befall their victims because of identifiable circumstance. Anecdotes thus have a function in the advancement of knowledge and practice. While biomedical science elaborates the mechanism of disease and clinical epidemiology studies the prevalence of disease and the effectiveness of therapy in order to refine diagnosis and treatment choice, narrative constitutes a third way of knowing in medicine.

Anecdotes are an informal extension, however unlicensed, of the case presentation. Like that more formal, conventionally patterned narrative, the anecdote is intended to improve clinical judgment, the hallmark of the expert physician. Clinical judgment is an intellectual virtue that depends not only on knowledge and skill but also on an innate thoughtfulness and decision-making ability that may be improved with exercise. Clinical judgment ripens with experience. Because in medicine, as in the rest of life, no one person can experience everything (nor would anyone choose to experience the bad), every physician stores up cases from his or her own practice as well as journal articles and accounts of other physicians' cases. In an advancing discipline, good physicians never stop acquiring and discarding these examples, which serve as guideposts in the assessment of illness. Neither biology nor information science has improved upon the story as a means of ordering and storing the experience of human and clinical complexity. Neither is likely to. Narrative as a human activity is in part intended to provide its listeners with a widened, vicarious experience; and that experience is memorable precisely because it is necessarily enmeshed with past and future, cause and consequence. The story is not a collection of fact but an exploration of the possibilities of individual variation and its meaning in relation to the whole of human experience. It is not surprising that it serves this function in medicine. The claim of a highly regarded professor of medicine, "The anecdotes of an expert have scientific status," would seem to return medicine to Sydenham's day, if it did not apply equally well to the *New England Journal of Medicine*'s clinical-pathological conferences, and if there were not a iconoclastic twinkle in his eye.

Narrative in medicine ranges in size from full case presentations at one extreme to the barest half sentences at the other, mere acknowledgments that other instances exist of the sort that is presently under discussion. "I've seen that," an attending physician will say, confirming the existence—in his or her experience—of the phenomenon just described. This affirmative "witnessing" is one of the most common functions of the anecdote. It confirms the validity of some odd detail in the patient's history or physical exam, something unexpected and unaccounted for in the textbook descriptions of the malady that is suspected to be at the root of the trouble. Lest the younger and less experienced physician be lured by the oddity from the investigative path, an elder will offer confirmation, and, depending on the occasion, this may be a full-blown story or as brief as a nod. "It can happen," the elder will say. Peers may offer affirmative witness, too. When the intern on his team presents a case with an unusual physical finding and meets with a silence that seems like skepticism or bafflement, a second-year resident turns to another and says, "Like that guy you had who was . . .." The second resident nods and the intern proceeds with the presentation.

The real stories, the anecdotes proper, come later in a discussion of a case. Like the brief affirmative witnessing, they may be intended to confirm, on the basis of the speaker's own experience, that such phenomena as a colleague or junior—seldom a senior—has just described are indeed in the world. Responding to the presentation of a patient with an unlikely brain tumor, probably metastasized from an unknown primary site, a resident tells of a comparable case: "Mr. Lopez, a patient I had last fall, presented with cancer of the brain. It turned out to be from the bowel, but that was asymptomatic." A second adds, "Mr. Johnson—the man with the poorly differentiated lympocytic leukemia last spring?—came in with nothing [wrong] but a swollen tongue." The resident who had prompted these brief stories by doubting the likelihood of such misleading symptoms ends the exchange by granting, "Oh well, it can happen, but it's pretty rare."

Affirmative anecdotes also emerge as justification for including what seems to be an unlikely diagnosis in the differential list or for undertaking a less than obvious therapy. As justification, they are never offered by the physician presenting the case. He or she is operating then in a stricter mode. Instead they are supplied by a listener, almost always a superior—partly because the presenters are residents but partly, too, because to offer advice or even affirmation to one's senior is an act of arrogation. Young assistant professors, back from conferences at other medical centers, will begin to supply an anecdote or two—first from their experience in a place not recently known to those who are their elders, but then, slowly, if all goes well, an occasional one or two from their everyday experience. By such small acts do the young rise and measure their progress and begin to enjoy a place among the experienced.

Equally often anecdotes supply comparative examples, cases by which a rule is proved. Late in a session, whether attending rounds or a morbidity and mortality conference, when the case under discussion has been clearly laid out and is all but solved, accounts of similar cases or worse instances of the same general type will emerge. Old hands will describe how difficult it once was to make the same diagnosis or treat the same malady, and clinch the point with an example. These are not idle yarns. They are told to those who in the future may not always have a CT scanner, Mast trousers, or the other resources of an academic center available; they are how-to instructions for practice in an emergency or in the time warp of a small hospital.

Comparative anecdotes also have a function in discussions of the differential diagnosis. Once the probable diagnosis is settled upon, the alternative possibilities must be eliminated. At this point, before the case is entirely solved, when the need for further tests is still not quite settled, a review of the differential diagnosis will often generate comparative anecdotes. These cautionary stories emphasize the seriousness of these alternate possibilities by illustrating the existence of an outcome different from the one now regarded as all but certain. It is not that these accounts replace rational analysis; they extend it, apply it to experience, take up where the textbooks and statistical studies leave off. For example, anecdotes are almost never told when infectious mononucleosis is the likely diagnosis because the test for that malady is comparatively reliable and its therapy—avoidance of strenuous exercise—is without side effect. Instead, stories are told when the tests are less clear or the stakes are higher. At such times, despite logic, a further test is sometimes undertaken because the diagnostic possibility it represents, although extremely remote, is a serious one—like tuberculosis—that can be easily ruled out or represents a time-dependent threat like cancer. In the case of any apparently catastrophic illness, illogical or improbable tests may be done because the benign nature of the alternative offers an absurd hope of explaining the signs and symptoms in a happier way. This is not simply "defensive medicine" motivated by fear of a lawsuit but the accurate perception that the guidelines for diagnostic testing delineated by clinical epidemiologists are based on probability. Like the odd locution, "He deserves a CT scan," anecdotes are implicit reminders that the physician's duty is to the individual patient. For the sake of that patient's care, they record and commemorate the exceptions to the rule.

Comparative anecdotes are the prerogative of the senior faculty. The same symptoms could well have led to a different disease or a delayed diagnosis, and elders will recall perplexing cases that presented much as did the one being discussed today. An overlooked detail, a symptom or a sign not usually regarded as diagnostically important once turned out to be the clue that enabled the teller (or the teller's eminent teacher) to distinguish among the possible diagnoses. At professor's rounds where she is by definition the only faculty member present, a young internist makes up her own stories, rather like a law professor varying the details of a case to test the applicability of the covering principle. Once the case that has been presented to her is reaching a satisfactory conclusion, she asks, "What if this same patient came in, but had been on steroids for the past two months?" Then, "What if she were twenty years younger?" And "What if she had a history of heart disease?" Her hypothetical anecdotes test and enlarge the residents' knowledge of the possibilities they may encounter.

Just as the same symptoms may point to different diseases, the same disease may have several possible therapies, and brief anecdotes are often used to illustrate the wisdom of choosing one in some circumstances, a second in others. An elderly patient with an abdominal aortic aneurysm may prompt anecdotes on both sides of the question of whether to operate. In general, the instances alleged will run counter to the prevailing wisdom. That is, if the discussion tends toward "medical management" (in this instance, a benign neglect in view of the customary slow progression of the condition at the patient's age and the risks of surgery), then anecdotes will be told of a patient in her eighties whose aneurysm grew apace or of another who survived surgery in his nineties. But if the discussion itself runs counter to the received opinion on the subject—that is, in this case, if there is a rush to surgery—published studies of the poor outcome, the prevailing wisdom, will be cited.

Many comparative anecdotes are stories of mistakes. They serve as warnings; they illustrate adages like "Always think TB." To their tellers and to medicine as a whole they offer comfort that even mistakes are not wasted if enough can be learned from them so that they never happen again. The anecdote is one of the few means of support and counsel available to physicians in their everyday circumstances. Despite the difficulties inherent in trying to achieve accurate diagnoses and effective treatment, most specialties, as David Hilfiker has pointed out, have no regular procedure for confronting failure.[10] Only in the twentieth century has medical care been marked by notable success and only in the last fifty years has cure become routine. Rich with ritual at every other point, medicine is still developing a way of meeting what used to be its daily burden of ill success. Surgery has led the way. Perhaps because of their more active, more material task and its immediately visible results, and certainly now because hospitals require it, surgeons everywhere meet once each week in morbidity and mortality conferences to discuss a case that has not gone well for one of them.

Like all other conferences in medicine, these are teaching conferences. In tertiary-care hospitals, the presence of residents and students formalizes its character, but even in their absence surgeons go on learning. The conferences are also professionalizing rituals that bond practitioners and initiate the young, asserting without words that all are engaged in a common endeavor. One surgeon's mistake may save another from some future mischance, and the careful dispassionate investigation of what may have gone wrong is essential for everyone present. Charles L. Bosk has written about the moral education implicit in a surgical residency and the importance of the morbidity and mortality conference in modeling the assumption of responsibility.[11] In additional to its investigative and confessional character, the conference is also in some sense cathartic. The presentation of a case that embodies human error or mischance memorializes that case, makes it an object lesson, an evitational example. Through the very process of objectifying it, the presentation raises the mistake to the status of an intellectual construct. Both the process of examination and objectification and the comparative anecdotes the process evokes offer the surgeon—and surgery at large—the possibility of comfort.

In one such conference surgeons discussed the death of a patient during surgery, nowadays a rare but never impossible outcome. The case had been a complicated one with several close but well handled judgment calls and two or three pieces of bad luck: blood that threatened to clot, blood vessels that were crumbly and hard to suture, prolonged need for the machine that bypasses the heart and recirculates blood. After a time, the patient's blood stopped coagulating and she bled out uncontrollably. The pieces of the story were clearly understood both scientifically and surgically, but to these surgeons they were all ordinary difficulties. None of them would have been catastrophic alone, and everyone could cite instances (and a few did) when the circumstances had promised worse and the patient had survived. Physiology was scrutinized; an anecdote about heart surgery having produced the same result in the old days when ice was used to stop the heart was introduced as a possible analog. But the problem solving was finally inconclusive. No one had demonstrated the wisdom of doing anything other than what had been done. The attending surgeon, a man not quite forty who had answered questions for over an hour, at times taking the lead in the physiological brainstorming, brought the conference to a close.

"If any of you think of something," he said, "let me know. Because we haven't put our finger on anything—."

One of the elders commented with a world-weary resignation, "Well, we've seen it before—."

The answer was a firm, almost defiant, "Maybe. But I don't want to see it again."

The elder replied, "But you will. You will."

No one moved for a moment. Then the conference was over.

In its various shapes and sizes, then, the anecdote occupies a great deal of the physician's professional interaction, even—perhaps especially—in an academic medical center. Despite the opprobrium associated with subjective narration and the justified cautions about its use, these informal stories are central to medicine as an intellectual discipline which has as its task the understanding of and response to human variety. Along with their use for instruction and social bonding, anecdotes constitute an important means of recognizing and accommodating anomalies in medical practice. They foster a continuing and necessary awareness of the variant that does not fit the expectations of the observer, the odd detail that tests the general rule. They are reminders of medicine's ineradicable uncertainty.

The danger as always is anecdotalism, the inherent deception of drawing a broad generalization from very few cases. A pejorative cloud hangs over the anecdote in medicine. Exceptions are allowed: there seems to be little danger in the illustrative use of a similar case during the discussion of a differential diagnosis or in the citation of a notable exception as a cautionary example that marks the limits of a topic under discussion. And, it is generally recognized, when cases are too few or too rare to constitute a series, all reports necessarily must be anecdotal. In psychiatry what counts as research includes case reports, carefully documented accounts of single patients. Even in internal medicine, academic aspirants among residents traditionally have been encouraged to publish their observations of unusual findings in case reports or in letters. Anecdotes and the case reports that are their printed manifestation are in this way recognized as the beginning of scientific knowledge. The danger is that single observations will be taken no farther. They can come to substitute for peer-reviewed research of one's own; in the worst case, they replace knowledge of others' work. Two instances of a malady in a physician's practice can license the use of the phrase "in my experience," and three instances may move the subspecialist toward the locution, "in my series," whether or not the cases have been written up as a study.

Thus the anecdote's pejorative cloud is as functional as the anecdote itself, keeping storytelling within useful limits. It has led, however, to a professional blind spot: the anecdote is regarded only as an idle pastime, an unwarranted and dangerous assertion of personality in a scientific field, not truly a part of medicine and its discourse. On the contrary, carefully hedged about with ritual, dampened by the opprobrium of the profession, the impulse to embody and transmit information about anomalies in the form of stories is a fundamental, intellectually healthy one. Despite its abuse, the anecdote serves the skepticism that is essential to scientific medicine. It is of a piece with the nature of medicine, which requires the physician to recognize and treat in a particular patient the signs of a generalized disease abstraction. The use of anecdotes is consistent with the professional unwillingness to generalize—not only about medical matters but also about ethical ones. Whether it is a matter of judging another physician's treatment of a case or of moving from a course of action perceived as right in one instance to a generalized ethical prescription for all cases of the same kind, physicians remain just as wary of abstract ethical principles as of invariant pathological generalizations that will cover every instance of a disease. Anecdotes are a constant reminder that, in the uncertain domain of medicine, there will always be an exception that calls for investigation.

Anecdotes represent and preserve the recognition of this intractable particularity of the individual in medicine. They are a reminder of the fundamental nature of the object of medicine's study: the workings of an abstraction called disease in the individual human being. As the irreducible knot at the center of medicine as a discipline of human knowledge—the problem of a scientific discipline applied to particular cases—anecdotes are an emblem of the human science of medicine.

FIVE

WRITING UP THE CASE:

CHARTS AND CASE REPORTS

"There is nothing like first-hand evidence."
(*Sherlock Holmes to Dr. Watson*, A Study in Scarlet)

THE NARRATIVE unfolding of a single medical case may take several written forms. Every patient is the object of a highly abbreviated and written-to-the-moment entry in an office or hospital chart. Its goal is a clear representation of the patient's malady, the physician's treatment, and the patient's response. From the potentially bewildering details a pattern is discerned, a diagnosis ventured and confirmed. Unusual cases from which other physicians can learn may also be written up in a published case report, in an edited transcript of a clinical-pathological conference about the case, or in a brief letter to a medical journal. These written cases, like oral ones, are highly conventional in form and style, and like them they vary in occasion and size, audience, and provenance. Their characteristics are a matter of long professional habit, regardless of their authors' motivation or self-conscious awareness of form. They represent the patient's condition in all its particularity, recounting the physician's discovery of a pattern in its diverse detail or enabling a consultant or a subsequent investigator to fit the puzzling case to a clinical rule. They attempt to capture the phenomenal nature of illness, the passage of time, the observer's rational process, and the likelihood that this particular concatenation of events will be replicated in a statistically significant number of other patients.

A written case narrative may be short or long: hasty half-sentences in the patient's chart, a succinct letter reporting an unexpected clinical phenomenon, or a lengthy account scrutinizing the details of one particular patient's illness and treatment. At one end of the scale, the chart chronicles the day-to-day course of an all-too-familiar disease, an account that no one but the patient's caretakers will read. At the other extreme, the full and formal written case contributes a description of a rare or new condition to the body of clinical knowledge. In between—as a conference handout, a syndrome letter, or a published clinical-pathological conference—the written case reminds students and practitioners of all they have not seen, all they may know only as textbook possibilities. In each of these forms, the account is shaped by medicine's scientific concept of biochemical and physiological cause and by the physician's necessary focus on one patient's malady. Whatever its size, it is linear in its causality and diagnostic in its quest. Concerned with a disease in its human manifestation rather than with a person who is ill, the written case is intended to be read by others engaged in the care of patients, never by the patient whom it describes.

The Chart

The kernel of medical narrative is the patient's chart. It is the record of each patient's medical course, observed in one or more office visits or, in the hospital, from entry to discharge. Included in either place is the patient's report of the physical experience of illness from its onset until reaching medical attention. Graphs of vital signs, registers of drugs ordered and discontinued, itemized lists of problems, and printouts of test results make up part of its bulk. As the barest and most conventional of narratives, the chart's serialized entries are inscribed on a printed form by one or more hands in abbreviations that constitute a clinical code. Stapled to a folder in the office, the chart is a more or less idiosyncratic chronicle by a single physician. But added to a hospital binder, the collected pages of a chart document in successive scenes each of the patient's encounters with physicians, nurses, therapists, social workers, medical students.[1] Every entry is signed by its author, and thus it is a personal, eyewitness communication of what the chart writer has seen and heard.

The "write-up" in the chart records and thereby establishes the patient's medical history as he or she has reported it, the findings of the physical examination, test results, a list of problems in rank order, and entries for therapy started and discontinued, consultations requested and carried out. Daily progress notes may be keyed to the problem list and "SOAPed," that is, organized into Subjective, Objective, Assessment, Plan.[2] In an office the chart is a collection of private notes. In a hospital, it has at least a small audience of those who are its several authors. Its readers take part in the care of the patient and are known to one another but do not rely on oral communication. To guard against misunderstanding and, to a lesser extent, take advantage of the multiplicity of perspectives, physicians, nurses, therapists, and social workers write down their observations and their diagnostic and therapeutic activity in full detail. Before each new encounter these same caretakers consult the chart as it has thus far been written, interpreting the illness as they construct the plot of the case, determining its facts as they organize its story.

The parts taken by this chorus of hospital chart writers are varied. Physicians record the patient's history and physical examination, diagnose the ailments, order (and discontinue) tests and therapy. In the teaching hospital, medical students practice the physician's write-up, and, still relying on ordinary personal skills, they often supply a rich description of the personal situation in which the patient's illness occurred. Their entries must be signed by an attending physician who has read and concurred with the write-up. Often these are the fullest and most painstaking notes: the student's knowledge, skill, and perception are under evaluation, and these are measured by what is agreed to be the patient's condition. Interns, by contrast, are more nearly on their own as chart writers although in some states their orders for medication must be signed by a resident or attending physician. Second-year residents, the captains of the hospital "teams," are masters of the brief summary, as are the attending physicians and professors who supervise their work. Consultants typically appear as one-time narrators, perhaps at some length and certainly with authority, informing the "team" of the fine points that fall within the purview of their specialty and their recommendations for the case. All along, from entry to discharge, sometimes in segregated spaces, nurses chart the patient's physical and psychological response to treatment—vital signs, pain or discomfort, distress at being ill—and their own therapeutic measures and efforts at patient education. Therapists assess the patient's abilities and describe the response to their work. Chaplains, where they have charting privileges, note the patient's spiritual condition and, often, a request to forgo heroic treatment. In cases of chronic illness, social workers write about the patient's family and plans for community support. Each of the writers, it is presumed, reads the admission record and the most recent entries of the progress notes. But, in fact, the hierarchy of disciplines obtains in the chart as elsewhere in medicine. Chart writers are most likely to read notes written by members of their own discipline and those of the admitting and the most recent physician writers. Not surprisingly, concise notes are more highly valued than long ones. For emphasis writers resort to capital letters or underlining.

The hospital chart as a whole is an assemblage of these individual professional witnessings. Its scenes are observational samples recorded at regular intervals. Once past the first full entries describing the patient's condition at the beginning of medical care, the notes are slices of time: physicians' progress notes, nursing notes written at specified intervals. In this way, the chart is like a laboratory's bench notebook, by several hands, which tracks the progress of a scientific experiment—or several interactive experiments at once—day by day, interval by interval. Time's therapeutic use is widely recognized even in an age of technological sophistication: physicians speak with gentle irony of applying a "tincture of time." Its diagnostic use lies in the chart's record of the progress of the patient—or of the patient's disease.

With the passage of time, the chart takes on physical presence and a representational life of its own. As the repository of what has been seen and done in regard to an individual patient, it is the germ not only of the case presentation, the narrative coin of the medical realm, but also of any further written report of the case. As the historical record of the patient's improvement or decline, it is the basis for future evaluation and decisions about treatment. In the office, it is a loose chronicle of the patient's life events. In the hospital, it is the continuing daily—often hourly—record of the measurable details of the patient's physical condition, serving as communication among the caretakers and promising continuity despite staff rotations. Although in recent years the entry is often dictated aloud into a machine and then typed by a nonmedical worker, the chart remains a written medium, organized for rapid absorption, created to be read silently rather than to be read aloud.

What can be learned from a chart? If the reader is able to read and recognize it, it is a kind of hologram of a life story. Gerald Weissmann, in his essay, "The Chart of the Novel," speaks of its gripping opening lines and compares them to the opening lines of a novel. The chart is fully plotted, he claims, "an amalgam between the observational norms of the nineteenth-century novelists and the causal descriptions of the physiologist."[3] But not everyone is capable of reading a chart or of recognizing its representational power. It is not, after all, a novel. Not only is it not entirely in prose and not at all fiction, it seems scarcely to be a proper narrative. The patient's condition is represented by laboratory reports and visual signs such as electrocardiograms; graphs and flow sheets describe the course of various symptoms over time. The phrases that purport to describe the patient's condition are often not made up of words at all but are lumped letters that in turn substitute for arcane medical terms. If the patient seeks help for breathlessness after a having had a bypass, for example, the chart writer will note, "CC: SOB — SP / CABG": the chief complaint is shortness of breath, status post coronary artery bypass graft. Furthermore, the story's chronology, beyond its artful beginning *in medias res*, is so simplistic as to seem entirely unplotted. Details of character and motivation are suppressed in favor of objective information about physical findings—abnormalities and signifying normalities. Rita Charon's description of the process of learning to present a case is equally applicable to learning to write them up: "The genre, in the end, is the distillation of many medical lessons, and by teaching our students how to tell this type of story, we teach them deep lessons about the realms of living that are included and excluded from patient care."[4] Learning "to chart" is precisely the process of learning to eliminate individual detail, the life story.

If the chart is not quite a narrative of an illness (which would require much more about the sufferer's subjective experience and the significance the malady bears for the patient's ongoing life story), it is nevertheless a narrative of medical attention given to a malady. The document that results is at a minimum the chronicle of an individual's physical condition while under medical care,[5] the bare plot of which is governed by the determination of a diagnosis and the selection of a treatment. Such chronicity suggests that the chart could equally well be said to resemble an early epistolary novel like Samuel Richardson's *Clarissa*, or a self-consciously fragmented twentieth-century work like John Barth's *Letters*, or Helen Hanff's *84 Charing Cross Road*.[6] The write-up in the chart is, as its name suggests, written to the moment. Date and time are given for each entry, for the chart note represents a development in the progress of the disease and the workings of the therapy. At the beginning, diagnostic meaning is embedded in a plot that has not yet been constructed. Often determined inferentially through the slow accretion of facts, the diagnosis is glimpsed briefly in the write-up, speculated upon, encapsulated in the time of its telling. Progress notes will be brief, but each new chart writer begins by returning (at least cursorily) to the conventional opening of case narration to summarize the state of present knowledge: "This is the first Memorial Hospital admission for this 61-year-old black man, who presented to the emergency room July 12 complaining of severe chest pain . . .."

Despite the graphs and flow sheets and notations of test results—figural representations of the patient that plot the course of the malady under scrutiny—the chart narrative is obsessively narrated. Nothing vital to the physical condition of the patient is taken for granted. It is as if the details of illness have been set down—over and over again—not by an anonymous committee but by a collection of individuals, each a signatory, each commissioned to establish the facts. Each reiteration of the facts of the case testifies to the observer's thoroughness and his or her familiarity with the patient's condition. Over time, it is as close as mortals are likely to get to agreement on matters of perception and judgment.

Some repetition is due to the value of chart writing in clinical teaching. The precise replication of detail is a test of a student's skill in conducting an interview and a physical examination and of a resident's diagnosis and therapy. If the case presentation is the learner's oral report, the chart note is an essay examination. The entries of students and beginning interns are read and compared with the views of their teachers, the senior residents and attending physicians. Thus charts in a teaching hospital sometimes include marginal comments from a professor or a chief resident, such as "problem list unclear," "good history," "where are test results?" Like a student's or resident's act of memorizing the details of the case for oral presentation, this repetition is a pledge of the writer's own thoroughgoing attention to the case at hand. The medical story is told and retold from beginning up to the present moment as certification that the writer has considered and understood the whole.

Because the facts of the case are recounted as each successive caretaker begins to chart the patient's course, the story is elaborated over time, amplified with test results, interpreted by consultants, summarized by new voices. With its repetition and its multiple voices, the chart most resembles the musical score for a cantata. Individual voices are sometimes heard: Suzanne Poirier and Daniel Brauner have described the variations in the focus of concern among several physicians caring for a woman in a persistent vegetative state. They trace the important part placed by the entries of her fourth attending physician in turning attention away from her infections and back to her inevitable decline.[7] Various choral roles can also be distinguished: nurses, medical students, attendings, consultants all have different concerns that guide their observation of the patient, and these are reflected not only in the details they record but also in the tone and frequency (to say nothing of the authority) of their entries.

Every chart is a reiterative, cumulative manuscript: a veritable chorus of varied, but usually consensual, observation. Like the Midrash, the medieval collection of interpretive tales gathered around the sacred text of the Torah, each chart entry is intended to shed light on the central text, amplifying and elaborating it with a temporal extension of its truth. Yet, like the Midrash, each of these new accounts bears the potential for creating new puzzles of its own, and subsequent readers must make sense of these secondary texts as well. Tests may produce unexpectedly odd results, and with the investigation of those results, new entries may record a state of interpretive confusion, a "cascade of uncertainty."[8]

Against the ground of repetitive narration with its minimal, predictable variation, genuine discoveries now and then stand out. Occasionally a reteller will discover something new or reinterpret a fact previously noted and see in it new meaning. If the student who makes a physical finding that does not fit the categories learned thus far—the chest sound that is not an ordinary pleural rub—resists premature interpretation, a note in the chart can prompt a more senior physician to listen to the patient's chest and make the diagnosis. Or a consultant will observe that a runner's symptoms, while consistent with the head injury that is her chief complaint, are also those of hyperthermia, which actually caused her post-race fall.

On those occasions when the charted versions of the patient's story differ, whose view prevails? We hear of "chart wars," but the openness of charts to review by hospital utilization committees, professional-standards organizations, insurance companies, and governmental agencies has greatly minimized recorded conflict.[9] The medical hierarchy governs the choice among opinions. Where there are two conflicting, mutually exclusive accounts of one phenomenon, consulting specialists outweigh attending physicians, who prevail over the views of residents, who within their ranks have a strictly observed ladder of work and responsibility. There is room for disagreement in the chart, but traditionally there has not been much of it. What there is is subtle, almost silent. Differences about therapy, if serious, are addressed quickly, orally, and, in a discipline where change and uncertainty are expected, corrections are made and recorded without comment. Fear of lawsuits has reduced further the likelihood of recorded disagreement. Because courts regard charts as durable records of illness and medical care when time and self-interest may have warped the participants' accounts of the circumstances, professors in every health-care discipline now urge consultation and documentation as adequate safeguards against the charge of malpractice. As a result, physicians and nurses are now aware—as twenty years ago they might not have been—of the chart as a construction, a factitious (although not fictional) production of narrative art.

It is an art not normally accessible to most of us. The chart's mixed media—graphs, test reports, lists, and narrative entries in a strange language and in several unreadable hands—and the combination of brevity, repetition, and its narrative focus on physical phenomena render it formidably uncommunicative. "This isn't me," patients looking through their own chart are likely to respond. Like the representation of music on paper, the chart's code may be read and studied silently, as the record of its composition. Its written manifestation is also the basis of more public, "translated" performances. The case may be chosen for oral presentation at rounds, where its narrative structure is disguised only by the ritual sameness of the occasion; now and then, it will be submitted for publication in a medical journal, where with abbreviations filled out and X rays and graphs subordinated to the narrative text, the chart's story is conventionally readable. But the chart itself, like a musical score or a foreign language, must be read by someone who knows both the code and the cultural expectations that inhere in the situation it delineates. The reader must know the conventions of both medical representation and medical performance. Unreadable by the rest of us, even unrecognizable as something that might be read, the chart seems the property of the physician or the hospital. Courts of law have found that the actual paper or microfilm can be owned. But the information itself must be shared. The story, including its medical rewriting in light of details the patient sought the physician's help in uncovering, ultimately and legally belong to the patient.

The tone of these still relatively private notes in the patient's chart, like the tone of the performative summary in the case presentation, is cool and objective. The narrator of the write-up is effaced as befits the diagnostician's descriptive, analytical role. Only the signature, presumably, distinguishes one observer's account from that of another person in the same health-care discipline, and in that signature the rank—first the "MS 4" or "CC IV" (for a student who is a clinical clerk in the fourth year of medical school) and later the "M.D."—is of more importance than the name to which it is attached. Personal involvement is banished. The existence of the narrator is implicit, and the medical face is calm, ready to hear and record any human detail without revulsion or despair. Although the chart itself presses toward the future, toward diagnosis, treatment, resolution, as it is ideally written it is entirely nonjudgmental. In his essay, Weissmann asks us to consider an (imaginary?) opening line from a 1953 St. Vincent's Hospital chart: "This is the second SVH admission of a 39-year-old, obese Welsh male poet, admitted in acute coma after vomiting blood."[10] Who are we, the cool tone of the chart asks, to weep for Dylan Thomas at this moment when he needs so much else? Here in the hospital chart, as before death, we are all body, all equal.

The chart never quite adds up to a satisfying narrative. A lifetime medical reader like Weissmann may find poignant meaning in its opening lines (especially if the life story of the patient is also known) or gripping drama in the all-but-covert struggle between two diagnostic hypotheses or two choices of proper therapy. For the rest of us, it remains a story of medical care, told as it happens. It is apparently unplotted, and "what happens" occurs almost entirely to the body of its protagonist. The meaning of the events for the person who is ill (or for the rest of us) will not be found in the chart. Even the hospital chart of a dying poet will contain no general observations about human character, the struggles of creativity, or the costs of fame, not even about such a nearly medical matter as alcoholism. It narrates the bare physical facts; it depicts, enumerates, describes. Even the quest for a diagnosis, the circling between hypothesis and evidence, can be discerned only by an experienced reader. Causality is broken down into contributing factors, as if to fragment the narrative power that typically exerts itself on the oral and singly narrated case presentation. In recent years, the traditional tentative diagnosis, the "initial impression," frequently has been dropped from the admitting note, thus delaying a statement of diagnosis until the tests are in. Phenomena are merely listed as a list of "presenting problems" until the diagnosis is "nailed down." This deprives the chart narrative of some of its suspense, simplifying and perfecting the finished plot at the expense of recorded twists and turns.

The tone of the chart's narrative, along with its brevity and avoidance of all but physical detail, makes clear that despite its fundamental narration, the medical chart is not meant to be a novel, even a very modern *nouvelle vague* novel. In most other respects, the qualities of the chart write-up are qualities shared by medical narrative as a whole: its economy and immediacy, the effacement of the narrator with the consequent cool objectivity of tone, its claim to scientific status and its use of a special language. As in the case presentation, these characteristics are the consequence of medicine's attempt to control the subjectivity of the observer as well as to cope with the second-hand nature of reported facts. Chart writers strive to keep as clean a narrative slate as possible, admitting only those details determined in advance by their profession to be relevant to such cases as the one before them. Multiple narrators writing about differing concerns and the frequent reiteration of basic details are strategies by which the chart resists the narrative pull of an extramedical, human-interest sort. Chart writers hope instead to construct the sparest possible plot still capable of knitting up the details of the case and rendering it treatable. As the word suggests, the chart is a minimalist account. With its lists and graphs and flow sheets, it is the near-zero condition of medical narrative.

Even more than oral case presentation, where a slight inflection or modulation of the voice may convey recognition of much that is not put into words, the chart refuses awareness of the pain of human existence. Its minimalism is a goal of medical storytelling and an emblem of the efficiency that is an ideal of scientific medicine. The chart of a patient who suffers from a well understood and mild or easily remedied condition approaches untellability. What generalizations might be drawn from the patient's illness have been made and made again. It is, in Rorty's phrase, "normal discourse." Nothing more, it is believed, remains to be learned from this case or others like it. The disease mechanism is either well understood or not currently the subject of experimental study; the clinical course is predictable and the therapy uncontroversial. Diseases and injuries for which medicine has a cure fall cheerfully into this category, but so do such maladies as persistent vegetative states, some chronic illnesses, and dying as the "end stage" of a chronic disease. As medical narrative these conditions will remain chartbound, a story of one particular patient's illness that is so excessively exemplary as to be communicated with a label or a nod. Without the complications that generate commentary, further texts, the chart itself will be thin. Narrative requires difference, atypicality, and (like happy families) broken arms, appendicitis, or dying patients are all alike.

The criterion of narratability, then, even in the chart, is the unexpected, the medically interesting, the unexplained change. A well understood disease or an often seen or easily remedied one, even if it is life threatening and contagious, will not be written about except in the chart that confirms its routine ordinariness. It will not be published; it may not be retold at all. Certainly it will not be presented at grand rounds or professor's rounds. Unless it fits a pedagogical need to survey the major common maladies, it may not be presented even at sign-in rounds. Nor, except to the student or resident who encounters the malady for the first time, will it be sufficiently interesting to be the theme of an informal anecdote. The unsurprising case sinks from narrative sight.

But even the chart of an "uninteresting" case is narrative. Medical interpretation of bodily phenomena—the diagnosis and treatment of disease—remains a time-governed construction which must address the question of (at least) medical meaning before it closes. The requirement that the chart both account for the passage of time and come to some conclusion, however tentative, about the nature of the malady and the patient's future means necessarily that the chart is plotted. Given the potential variability of medical data and the uncertainty of medical knowledge, such narration is an attempt to deal with the transient and the phenomenal, to impose a pattern upon the myriad details of illness—and, on rare occasions, discover and establish a new or variant pattern. L. L. Weed's revolutionary problem-oriented medical record, which has gone a great way toward integrating chart writing into the modern clinician's investigative stance, brought a pared, thematic order to a wordy, encoded, multiauthored chronicle.[11] But even with its graphs and figures, the post-Weedian chart is far more than a chronicle. Its "data" are embedded in a narrative medium that retains the power of representing complexly the human situation of the illness. Narrative is required for an account of change that includes causes and contributing factors. For the malady that is easily recognized and understood, minimal narrative with an implicit and linear concept of cause is entirely adequate, especially when there is also an efficacious remedy. But where these conditions are not met, the chart blossoms into fuller narrative.

In the twentieth century, attention to a particular disease wanes with the discovery of a promising therapy and waxes as a therapeutic breakthrough proves, however efficacious, not to be a "magic bullet" that will remedy all human illness even of that one kind. Whether driven by its scientific aspirations or by its ideal of ameliorating human suffering, medicine somehow never rests with the merely technical but takes on further puzzles of causality and motivation. These lead inevitably to narrative. Peter Brooks suggests that in its extension, narrative possesses "a logic which makes sense of succession and time, and which insists that mediation of the problem posed at the outset takes time: that the meaning dealt with in narrative and thus perhaps narrative's raison d'être, is of and in time."[12] Clinical science, which has triumphantly rendered so many maladies "uninteresting," works to abolish narrative. But whether physician, patient, or virus, the living being seeks the new: the news, the novel, the narratable.

The Case Report

Drawing on the chart for its substance, the case report organizes and renarrates the story of the patient's illness and medical care. Its purpose is to report a new and newsworthy clinical point for publication in a medical journal. Despite its strong ties to history, to public discourse about social policy, and to narrative, the case report claims to be first of all a variant of the scientific report. It is the attempt by a scientifically educated, clinically experienced writer to convey a precise and generalizable account of one patient's illness. From the Hippocratic writings through the early years of the twentieth century, the case report made up the major part of clinical writing. Early medical education and practice depended on the narrative of the single case, and the advances in the identification and understanding of disease begun in the seventeenth century were founded on the case reports of Thomas Sydenham and his followers. The early twentieth-century *Surgical Clinics of Dr. John B. Murphy* was a serial collection of cases intended to standardize and advance modern surgical practice. Even in the era of the double-blind clinical trial, the present-day *Clinics*, descendants of that educational enterprise, continue to publish case reports that expand the vicarious experience of practitioners in every specialty.

Yet precisely because it is singular, the case report with its implicit claim to generalizability is regarded with scientific skepticism. In the late twentieth century, as medical education and clinical practice have become increasingly standardized, the case report has been confined to accounts of the new and rare. It is a report from the field (or, in medicine's more vivid war metaphor, the "trenches") not from the laboratory, and it is neither a prospective study nor subject to any but "historical controls."[13] The case report customarily concerns a newly discovered clinical phenomenon or a new interpretation of a phenomenon previously believed to be adequately explained. Thus early cases of toxic shock syndrome and AIDS were reported singly and then in studies with very small numbers, with variants often appearing as single case reports.

The themes of the case report are drawn only from those patients whose medical course is unusual and thereby narratable. The report describes and establishes a signal case, one that very probably began its long journey to professional respectability as an anecdote. Edward J. Huth, who soon after assuming editorship of *Annals of Internal Medicine* in 1971 folded its section of "case studies" into "brief communications," applies strict scientific limits to their publication: "Three kinds of case reports *still occasionally* merit publication: the unique, or nearly unique, case that may represent a previously undescribed syndrome or disease; the case with an unexpected association of two or more diseases or disease manifestations that may represent an unsuspected causal relation; the case with an unexpected evolution suggesting a therapeutic effect or an adverse drug effect."[14]

As a scientific account of a single instance of human illness, the case report reflects the mixed methodology of medical knowledge and accommodates as best it can this epistemological tension. Customarily understood to be reportage, a piece of a scientific puzzle, it nevertheless is a matter of storytelling accomplished more or less well and judged according to the conventions of medical narration. Because it is both an analytical report and a narrative history, the contemporary constraints placed on its publication are much like those placed on anecdotes. As a variety of the personal essay, the case report struggles with the problems of subjectivity and contingency, and these problems have earned it the suspicion of clinical scientists that is evident in Huth's description. At the same time, however, medicine's working assumption that the clinical phenomena can be explained in linear fashion, with chains of discrete cause and effect, is challenged by the impossibility of human beings explaining other human beings satisfactorily in a purely objective way.

In the case report the construction of the narrative that is fundamental to medical research and education takes its most compact, refined, and reworked form. As the written version of a case presentation that might be made at a departmental grand rounds well after the resolution of the clinical problem, it nevertheless differs from the the clinical-pathological conference. Unlike the "case records" of the Massachusetts General Hospital, the case report does not take the quasi-dramatic form of a transcribed grand rounds narration. Instead it is a personal historical essay that tells the story of the authors' investigation and treatment of an unusual or unexpected malady within an expository frame that argues the singularity of its presentation and its importance to the practice of medicine. It absorbs into its timebound telling all the numbers produced by sophisticated tests and represented by graphs and figures, and then uses that narration to illustrate its thesis. As the inescapably personal observation of a contingent event, it hedges its assertions with strategies that proclaim its authors' modesty and their scrupulous adherence to the assumptions and methodology, however tenuous, of retrospective clinical investigation.

One of these strategies is the use of a title that identifies the phenomenon to be described, specifies its noteworthiness, and renders it indexable: "Aortic Regurgitation First Appearing 12 Years After Successful Septal Myectomy for Hypertrophic Obstructive Cardiomyopathy."[15] Such a label distances the case report from the less formal oral case presentation and allies it with the conventions of the scientific paper. Its authorship tends to be multiple and includes the several physicians who in various ways were responsible for the patient's care. Then (also like the scientific paper but imitated these days in scholarly essays generally) the case report is summarized by an abstract printed in bold type following the title. There is thus no suspense in a case report. Were a report of one of Sherlock Holmes's cases to be given such a title and an abstract, we would have little interest in reading farther—except perhaps to study the circumstances and admire (or criticize) the method. "Enraged Swindler's Hieroglyphics Appear Years After Woman's Successful Escape from His Abuse," it might read, and then would follow something like:

> Mr. Hilton Cubitt sought professional advice concerning signs appearing on the outbuildings of his estate at Riding Thorpe Manor, Norfolk. Although there was no history of enmity in the neighborhood, the squire's beautiful American wife was reported to be greatly disturbed by the event. Upon analysis the hieroglyphics were determined to be threatening messages to Mrs. Cubitt, of whose previous history the squire was discovered to know little. The squire, not yet informed of the hieroglyphics' translation, returned home with instructions to forward further messages to London. Two weeks later he reported the following signs:

$$\text{ẊẊẋẏẊẋ-ẋ ẏẋ-ẋẋẏ}$$
$$\text{ẋẋẋẊẊẋẊẏẋẏẋẋ}$$

> The team arrived too late to prevent the squire's demise. The experience suggests that recipients of coded messages should be kept under close surveillance, especially when recently emigrated Americans are involved.[16]

Skimming readers need go no further—unless these particular circumstances seem relevant to them or they are curious about the method or, in this case, the error in judgment.

For readers wanting to know more, there are two to four pages to read. The authors stake the claim for both the readability of the case and the significance of the phenomenon by framing their narrative of the patient's illness and medical care within an essaylike exposition of the case. This essay-frame opens with a two- or three-paragraph introductory section that uses the stylistic conventions of the historical essay, highlighting the importance of the witnessed event and persuading the attention of an audience of solitary readers. Here we are told about the malady as it has been described in textbooks and recently published studies, and we learn the history of its therapy and the etiology as it is thus far known. This description of the state of the field before the discovery of the case that is about to be presented sets the stage for the subsequent exposition of the malady's unexpectedness and its importance for the future care of similar patients.

The case report proper then follows. This is the narrative of the case, often printed in smaller type than the essay-frame and is labeled "CASE REPORT." Although it has been preceded by an ample title, an abstract, and a paragraph of introductory exposition, the case narrative occupies the center of the case report as a whole. It is intended to be the physician's straightforward, objective account of a patient's disease and treatment, a scientific description of clinical reality. Included are charts, graphs, reproductions of X rays and test results, photographs—all the documents and aids to memory that appear on slides at grand rounds. The account proceeds in strict chronological order without hypotheses or scientific explanations. These are the facts of clinical science, and the same strict convention governs their reporting here as in the oral case presentation. It is as if there is something sacred about the individual case. The account of the patient's presentation, diagnosis, and care represents the lived experience of the patient-physician interaction that is basic to medical practice. Patterns may be drawn from it, of course, and that is why it is narrated and studied, but the details of one case are never perfectly replicated in the details of another. Thus the report of a case is never altered in the slightest. Not only may today's peculiarity become tomorrow's clue, but—more surprising—today's assumption may someday turn out to be precisely the matter most in need of investigation. The *New England Journal of Medicine*, responding to the use in its pages of "exemplary" (but, the writer protested, not quite "composite") cases, declared: "Alteration of minor personal details in a case report is an acceptable practice when it is necessary to protect the anonymity of the patient, but it should be acknowledged. A case report is an important primary datum, which may be used by readers for other investigational purposes. The facts should never be altered, even in slight detail, without full disclosure and explanation."[17]

The case report concludes with a return to the essay (again in full-sized type) that frames the patient's history. This is a discussion section in which the significance of the discovery and its contribution to clinical science are described. Mystery has been avoided throughout. It is as if

Sherlock Holmes's criticism of Watson's "backward" narrative structure were to triumph: as if the "adventure" began with an account of the crime, the criminal, and the motive and then proceeded to the story of their discovery—along with the reasons for eliminating other suspects, other possible motives. The narrator of the case report, as one might suspect, adopts a detached tone that bans emotion and pares the problem down to its clinical essentials. Without a third-party observer like Dr. Watson to narrate the case report and serve as a commentator on the reader's "peripheral" interests, we are left to imagine (if we care to) or to ignore the frustration, excitement, and satisfaction that must attend the solution of a puzzling, life-impairing problem.

As in a scientific report, "the facts" in the case are presented as formally and as objectively as possible. Yet what are these facts? Even where they are clear and reliable, they are webbed in a fashion more familiar to social than to physical scientists. The case report begins with a statement of the problem and a history of the question, yet for it to achieve the explanatory elegance of the scientific report is as impossible as to replicate that report's methodological rigor. Medical problems by definition are located in variable, experimentally uncontrollable human beings, and they express themselves at different rates through time. To account adequately for the phenomena they treat, medical reports must relate particular cases in all their detail and chronicle their alteration. To compound the problem of contingency, there is the equally troublesome matter of subjectivity: these accounts of instructive instances of illness must be the work of observing, recording, narrating—but not unidentified or uncommenting—physicians.

The physician authors are not wholly absent from the case report. It is true that much of it is written in scientific style: impersonal constructions in which conditions are the actors and human beings are acted upon. "Substantial aortic regurgitation developed in a patient with hypertrophic (obstructive) cardiomyopathy . . . who underwent septal myectomy." Not only is the patient in this sentence the site of the events, but clinical signs seem to exist and events occur independently of a medical actor or observer. Behind the impersonal, of course, stubbornly lurk accountable but at least theoretically contingent individual authors. For "Investigation revealed . . ." we are always to read, "Our investigation revealed (and, although we could be mistaken, we are fairly certain your investigation also would have revealed . . . especially since more than one of us observed it)."

As a sign of the ineradicably personal nature of the case report and an acknowledgment of its provisional status as clinical knowledge, the framing essay contains clear representations of the physician-observers who are now the narrators. Every physician is expected to stand authoritatively behind a chosen course of action. So absolute is this expectation by both patient and physician that it cannot be intensified even in a situation like those in case reports, one that is clinically unforeseen and perhaps unique. This responsibility is implicit in the physical presence of the narrator whenever a case is presented orally. As a written version intended to be read in the teller's absence, the case report must be more explicit. As a consequence, the framing essay and the commentary that closes it include, among the predominant impersonal subject-verb pairs, a few representations of the patient as actor and several strategically placed first-person pronouns—particularly the plural "we." The exposition that introduces the case includes, "We present the case history of a patient in whom . . ." and "We suggest that aortic regurgitation also may prove to be . . .." These first-person subject pronouns are used just as they would be in a personal essay written by an eyewitness to a historical event. Their use signals the authors' acceptance of the responsibility for the observation of the condition, its interpretation, and the treatment that follows, and it acknowledges the provisional nature of such as-yet-replicated knowledge. And while "I" and "Drs. Sanders, Levine, and Yancy" are never used, the use of "we" (not coincidentally) claims a shared but personal credit for the discovery.

The commentary that closes the framing essay and concludes the case report may also include one or two instances of the narrators speaking in the first person. Surrounded with impersonal descriptions of pathophysiological mechanisms, these instances are invariably statements of opinion, a personal summary of the significance of the case: "We believe this latter mechanism to be less likely, but it certainly cannot be ruled out." Here, as in the opening, expository half of the frame, the plural form both modestly invokes a team effort and anticipates the time when the phenomenon presented will be accepted by the clinical community as part of the common fund of knowledge. Although in any given report a narrator may be describing a nonce event—a possibility that according to the conventions of medical reportage is ritually acknowledged—the first-person plural proclaims an intersubjective understanding of the phenomenon that "we" believe will ultimately be shared by all of "us," scientific medicine in general.

By contrast, the central account of the facts of the case labeled "CASE REPORT," like the oral case presentation it formalizes, is told by an almost wholly effaced narrator. It is as if the narrative of the patient's illness and medical care were telling itself. In an oral presentation the resident stands before an audience, presenting self and skill and perception to be judged along with the facts of the case. In the case report, the authors are even less immediately present: although we know someone has observed, shaped, and written up this instance of illness, we must refer to the top of the first page where the authors are listed to know anything at all about them. In both narrations, the effacement of the narrator is a sign of a commitment to the rational scrutiny of detail. The bloodless conventions of the case, oral or written, declare the teller to be reporting facts and events in the standard, most nearly scientific way. If this is rather one-sidedly the teller's story, it nevertheless aims to be as closely as possible the story that, placed in the same situation, another, hypothetically inter-changeable physician would tell. The goal is an intersubjectivity that approximates scientific objectivity and the clarity of thought and commu-nication essential to good patient care. By means of such a minimally narrated case history, facts are to be established so that the causes of the malady may be identified and then blocked or modified therapeutically. Its publication in a peer-reviewed journal bids others to do likewise.

The story of illness told in the section labeled "case report" is necessar-ily more sustained and straightforwardly plotted and far less repetitious than the narrative found in the patient's chart, the account upon which it ultimately is based. Because the report is written long after the case is "solved," it lacks the immediacy of the chart's reiterated, dispersed, and not-yet-digested detail, and thus it is more easily recognizable as a narra-tive genre. Its smaller type encourages skimming, and this narrative body of the case report (reporting upon the body in the case) follows the con-ventions of oral case presentation:

CASE REPORT

A 51 year old white man had a heart murmur which was first discovered during routine examination at age 18. He was asymptomatic until age 30, in 1958, when he had two episodes of syncope while running. Over the next six years, lightheadedness, dyspnea on exertion and fatigue, orthopnea, parox-ysmal nocturnal dyspnea, angina, hemoptysis and episodic acute pulmonary edema developed. He was therefore sent in 1964 to Strong Memorial Hospi-tal, where the diagnosis of hypertrophic cardiomyopathy was established. Catheterization data are presented in Table I. Because of the severity of his symptoms, he was referred to the National Institutes of Health where a suc-cessful myotomy and myectomy were performed in October 1964.

Although a systolic murmur could still be heard postoperatively, there was no evidence of aortic regurgitation. After convalescence, the patient be-came functional Class I and returned to work. He received digitalis because of postoperative development of frequent premature atrial contractions.

During routine follow-up study at NIH in 1965 there was a provocable left ventricular gradient (Table I), but no diastolic murmur . . . [a summary follows].

When atrial fibrillation recurred in 1976, and was associated with return of significant effort and nocturnal dyspnea and angina, despite the admin-

istration of digitalis and diuretics, he returned to Strong Memorial Hospital
for cardioversion. For the first time, a grade I/VI diastolic murmur at the left
sternal border, indicating aortic regurgitation, was heard . . . [details of the
physical examination and treatment follow].

  When we saw the patient in August 1979 . . ..[18]

Although the author-narrators use "we" on three occasions in the expository frame of the case report, its rather startling introductory use in
the paragraph just quoted is the only use of the first-person in the case
report proper. Here it marks the reporting physicians' entry in the case. It
represents their assumption of responsibility from this point on (but no
earlier) for observation, testing, diagnosis, referral, and recommendations for therapy. In theatrical terms, the status quo ante is distinguished
from the present action by the introduction into the action of the characters who are the narrators. As the principal observers in the case, they are
the epistemological center of the report: at once the investigators and the
recorders, they are both Holmes and Watson, and, as the creators of the
narrative document, they are also Arthur Conan Doyle. Far from being a
mark of self-revelation, the first-person pronoun sets aside the epistemological questions in favor of the newly discovered fact.

  On the evidence of the case report, clinical medicine seems to have no
division of labor among observing, narrating, and writing. The case report's omnibus style obscures the distinctions in the work of caring for
the patient. Multiple authors are the rule in case reports, yet by convention they speak as one, observing the patient, presenting the case, and
writing it up in one voice. In fact, the custom of multiple authorship reflects the hierarchical nature of the clinical work in academic medicine,
and in "real life" the work of observing, narrating, and writing is divided
up among them. A junior author is quite likely to make the discovery; a
more senior author to interpret it and encourage its publication. The politics of priority in the list of authors—setting aside the politics of mere
inclusion—is complex. Generous elders frequently list themselves last;
indeed, to give up priority can constitute one of the signs of professional
maturity.[19] In some subspecialties, however, just as in some scientific
laboratories, the clinical chief, no matter how remotely related to the
research, is always listed and often listed first.

  Even in those case reports where there is only a single author, no distinction is made among these functions in the case report, except the inevitable and implicit one of time. With one author or six, there is a composite (and for the most part undifferentiated) author-narrator-observer.
Unless one of them has been solely responsible for a major part of the
study, the case report also depicts them acting as one: examining the patient, discovering the anomaly, treating the patient, referring him to re-

search subspecialists, caring for him after his surgery, and researching the question of the uniqueness of the case. We are accustomed to Arthur Conan Doyle speaking in Watson's voice, but the case report is written as if a committee of Conan Doyle, Holmes, and Watson pretended that none of them had ever known any more than any other and that the history of their communication among themselves was lost or nonexistent. This convention goes a great way toward controlling the human drama of discovery, and meditation on the interplay of character and chance is effectively eliminated. Here, as elsewhere, medical narrative obscures its epistemology in favor of a claim to objective realism.

The authors speak together with a foregone unanimity about what they have separately observed. Their use of the first person plural pronoun is thus a narrative convention, a convenient fiction. Yet to some degree it is a justifiable one. This unanimity serves to affirm the soundness of their observation and interpretation and to deny the contingency of the phenomenon and the subjectivity of their own perceptions. Their inclusion, near the end of the report, of a small series of similar patients "they" are following at one hospital bolsters their claim to reliability, as does the corroborating report from the National Institutes of Health. Ten years later they are dispersed in separate places—as indeed they may have been by the time they collaborated on writing up the case. But the pronoun reminds us that at the time for this patient they were a team, working as a unit with the observation of one, the supervision of another, and the breadth of knowledge of the third.

The effect of this compositely observed and narrated and written narrative is very different from the effect of the chart. Readers of the case report are barred from the immediacy of the experience of illness, diagnosis, and therapy. The narrators of the chart write as if they had just turned from the patient at the time of writing—and ideally, when charting is up-to-the minute, this narrative stance represents the reality. The reader, correspondingly, is led to feel "there," often caught in the suspense of the unfolding events. By contrast, the narrator of the case report has no such obligation to offer a moment-by-moment account of the facts. Writing long after the case has been solved, the case reporter is expected to digest that unwieldy and circumstantial matter and summarize it neatly for the reader's assimilation and use. Like a rather stiff autobiographer writing about childhood in later life, the author of the case report may give both a vivid picture of what is now believed to be the actuality and a perspective on its meaning that may not have been available at the time. But these concerns bar a representation of what it was like at the time. As readers of the chart, we can never be sure what will happen next; as readers of a case report, we are called upon to be less active and imaginative as the significance of the illness is discovered for us. Time has passed not only between the writing of the case report and our reading but between the unfolding of the course of events and the writing. In consequence, its tone is more reflective and conclusive. The chart is intended to collect the clues—and at regular scientific intervals. The case report is meant to establish a claim to have understood what it has all been about.

Case Narrative and Medical Causality

Because narrative bears the potential for expanding the web of causality to encompass multiple and interconnected circumstances that might (or might not) contribute to an event or fact, medicine resists its unscientific, contextual undertow. Thus written medical narrative (like oral case presentation) is narrowly conceived and standardized by strict conventions of tone, plot, and allowable detail, and it reflects medicine's simple, action-oriented positivism: disease lies out there in nature for medicine to analyze and explain. Not only is disease reified, but its causes are seen as linear and materialist: bacteria and viruses cause diseases much as accidents cause injuries. This pared-down enchainment of cause and effect, stimulus and response, is a mode of explanation that has been stunningly successful in medical research. Its parsimony is clinically efficient and, in a realm of uncertainty, its restriction of complexity has its own solid comfort. It is reflected in death certificates with their three blank spaces for the immediate, secondary, and tertiary causes of a patient's death. The request elicits a series of enchained events rather than multiple, simultaneous, interactive causes. The immediate cause of death is almost always the failure of heart or lungs, the secondary cause perhaps a myocardial infarction or pneumonia. Only the tertiary cause resembles the original diagnosis. What causes lie behind that diagnosis? They are not specified or speculated upon. Not only could early AIDS deaths be tactfully concealed in this way or a boastful oncologist claim, "None of my patients die of cancer"; but contributory factors such as violence, alcoholism, bereavement, poverty, iatrogenic complications, and inadequate health care are effectively erased from the etiology of illness.

The unifying, simplifying, reductionist force of biomedical explanation exists in tension with the need in clinical medicine for narrative's circumstantiality and explication of context. The case report, striving to achieve a scientific generality, nevertheless employs a retrospective historical frame and a narrational center in order to fit the singular instance to a larger scheme of scientific explanation. Physical facts are of supreme importance, but they must be narrated. To relate them to an audience is to relate one fact to another, hypothesizing and exploring the causes that link them. The act of relating a narrative makes an implicit claim about causal relations in time. Yet case histories are written and presented as if the connection of effect to cause were the narrative force that, by organizing and motivating both writer and the written, told the story. The facts, medical narrative asserts, speak for themselves.

Such representational, "transparent" reportage works best for maladies whose efficient cause is or soon will be well understood. Especially in those accounts that are routinely much the same for every patient—of myocardial infarction, for instance—facts do seem to speak for themselves. Data such as crushing chest pain, shortness of breath, and specified electrocardiograph readings can be linked with identifiable causes in every patient who presents them for diagnosis. So long as the report is trusted, the working assumption is that this case history needs no teller or that it achieves a scientific objectivity. This assumption is itself based on a grant of guarded professional faith: for, as we have seen, a physician's long apprenticeship is also an education in skepticism and assertion with regard to knowledge and authority. Every physician learns as a student and resident that each case narrative is backed by—and is itself a report on—the perception and reliability of its teller. When the reader or listener disagrees with the case report, the narrator is no longer a mere transparent medium for the "facts." Attacks on medical information quickly become attacks *ad hominem* that impugn the narrator's skill, reliability, experience, or rationality. Still, when there is no reason to doubt the facts, if the biological etiology is known and an effective therapy is available, the path from sign to diagnosis and treatment is wonderfully, almost storylessly direct.

Because medicine's notion of causality works to streamline its account of disease, in the second half of the twentieth century all narrative in medicine, whether written or oral, has been devalued, and its role and importance in the representation of causal complexity has been denigrated or ignored. For maladies that are "solved"—such as myocardial infarction or tuberculosis or appendicitis—the narrative is abridged. It is written only in textbooks, seldom told. Such abridgments rely on well-established knowledge of the mechanism of the disease, making assumptions about the relevance of that knowledge to a particular case. The manifestations of a patient's malady are readily explained by pathophysiology. Because its cause or causes are known, from the scientific point of view there is no "story" there: the symptoms are the disease.

Not all maladies are so well disposed of. Many maladies are not—or not yet—explained so simply and thoroughly as to make intervention feasible and effective. Even those "storyless" ordinary diseases, the kind that residents never label "interesting," can be opened up to narrative by investigative curiosity that goes beyond the familiar diagnostic and therapeutic givens. Good clinical teachers know that the new and anomalous are not the only medical sources of narratability, yet scientific explanation of the satisfying sort that eliminates the need for narrative must cover only enough of the etiology and mechanism of the disease to establish an effective cure or prevention. For good reason, then, scientific medicine since the late nineteenth century has focused on clinical phenomena, the appearance of disease in the individual case.

The investigation of new diseases and variants of old ones still engages and profits from medicine's strict enchainment of effect and cause and from the traditional narrative that organizes and presents the facts in this pattern. But such a narrow concept of causality leaves questions unanswered, particularly those about an individual patient's particular experience of disease. Why aplastic anemia in this particular patient? And why has it occurred now rather than last year or next? In addition, the prevention of disease and the care of patients who are chronically ill or dying requires a widened concept of causality and a richer narrative. If we ask how tuberculosis in an individual came about, the presence of the tubercule bacillus will not suffice. The patient lived in a small apartment with her family, cooked for them; their PPD tests for exposure to tuberculosis are positive, yet they do not have the disease. How has this happened? To ask this question—or the even larger one about our political failure to eradicate TB—is to make the trite story of a remediable infection narratable once more. A narrative of disease that addresses such details acts to complicate the representation—and thus the idea—of causality in medicine.

The medical narrative also must be widened when its province is extended from the diagnosis and treatment of disease to the remediation of illness. Dewitt Stettin's account of the medical attention given his macular degeneration occupies four brief sentences in his *New England Journal of Medicine* article.[20] A noted academic physician, he had consulted expert ophthalmologists in several medical centers renowned for their research. He was assured that nothing could be done to stop the progression of the condition or restore his eyesight; and, once diagnosed, his became a clinical story so short and "unremarkable" as scarcely to exist. If the practice of medicine were only a matter of addressing his disease rather than his condition, his ophthalmologists would have been correct. There was a great deal, however, that could be done for his blindness: optical magnifiers, the Talking Books Program of the Library of Congress, recorded journals, special radio stations, a talking clock, the Kurzweil reader. His account is an appalling compendium of all his physicians did not offer him.

The hope of achieving a minimal, streamlined scientific account in every instance of disease has created a sort of epistemological scotoma in medicine. It is a blind spot that obscures the usefulness of narrative in medical education, research, and the care of patients. For the present, it seems, narratives must be told and tolerated about the not-yet-under-

stood; often they are written up for publication. Yet as a method of grap-
pling with the new and inexplicable or as a way of framing the therapeutic needs of patients, narrative is largely unrecognized. Instead, medicine
awaits the day when the anomalous character of each malady will disap-
pear, and with it the need for all narration.

It is not surprising, then, that narrative as such has had little place in
the medical curriculum. Rules for writing up the case and for making
subsequent progress notes in the patient's chart are sometimes taught,
and beginners often practice oral case presentations, but in many institutions these skills are simply acquired without guidance or comment. Scientific education is the principal purpose of the organized medical curriculum, and only science and scientifically based clinical knowledge are
consciously taught. As a consequence medicine is not fully aware of its
own methodology or the degree to which it screens profound uncertainty.
The profession's lack of curiosity about one of its fundamental methods
of clinical investigation as well as a principal therapeutic resource has
deprived narrative of intellectual standing and any but a pejorative recognition in the profession.

In the scientific era the single case often has been poorly and prematurely assimilated to the general principles that govern clinical medicine,
and its narration has been something of a covert act. Not that the narratives themselves are concealed. Like Poe's purloined letter, they have
been hidden in plain sight all along, the basic coin of medical discourse.
There is no other method for transmitting reliably full and accurate information about the operation of disease in a human being. On those few
occasions when it comes to attention as a method of medical knowledge,
narrative, especially when used unself-consciously, risks provoking mild
derision. For the most part it is taken for granted, relied upon, forgotten.
Lodged in the center of academic medicine, narrative coexists more or less
easily with scientific knowledge in specialty groups whose members share
roughly the same biomedical knowledge and the same kinds of clinical
experience. Sometimes narrative will be scorned: by newcomers with
more knowledge or by the young, who have just read the latest clinical
studies. Because narrative is humanity's traditional—or, one might feel,
its "natural"—means of accounting for what cannot be measured or
counted, it apparently need not violate medicine's scientific focus on the
objective, replicable observation of more or less natural phenomena. For
most physicians, narrative is there, perhaps, but soon will be replaced by
science. It is to be ignored, forgotten, displaced, in favor of the quanti-
fiable and replicable.

There is, as we have seen, some justification for narrative's lack of
honor in medicine. Although narrative generally, like the anecdote in particular, is on the forefront of scientific understanding, identifying and de-

scribing cases that need fuller, scientific investigation, narrative evidence can mislead the unwary. Moreover, there is good historical reason for physicians' assumption that—like the complicated therapeutic measures Lewis Thomas has designated "half-way technology"—narrative is simply a stopgap measure, one that the discipline will ultimately "outgrow." For the moment it is enough that a new condition or a new response to treatment exists; scientific inquiry based on the biochemical knowledge of disease and an adequate number of subjects must then be brought to bear. In this view, narrative is a way station on the road to full scientific knowledge of disease. "Descriptive" studies, no matter how impervious to experimentation their material is, are regarded as "preliminary"; case reports seem to beg for the validation of a full series.

The case report, like the rest of medical narrative, is best understood as a practical response to medicine's radical uncertainty rather than as an outmoded, antiscientific tradition that biomedical advances will soon banish. For the act of premature banishment only obscures, without diminishing, causal complexity. Biomedicine moves closer to becoming a pure science in its laboratories, but at the bedside, rightly carried out, it remains a patient-centered interpretive practice. Given the requirements of a science whose laboratory is the living person, case narrative, despite its faults, is admirably suited to the task of reporting on its investigation. In some puzzling instances (whether temporarily or for all time) narration is the best account that can be given. Subsequent cases may cast light on them and, with luck and careful attention to recording the evidence, the narrative report will offer useful corroboration of future hypotheses. In other instances, the construction of case narrative is essential to good medical care. Not only is the first obligation of physicians to care for their patients, but increasingly illness and recovery are understood to have strong emotional and situational components. Clinical medicine, concerned with the care of sick people, requires of its practitioners both a scientific knowledge of disease and treatment and a particular understanding of the patient's illness. Sick people suffer from diseases about which much is now known and more will certainly be learned. The effective grasp of a patient's particular manifestation of a malady often depends not only on a careful written account of its physiological progression but on a recognition of its roots and its meaning in the life story of the patient. Narrative is essential to both these tasks.

SIX

AN N OF 1:

CLINICAL-PATHOLOGICAL CONFERENCES AND

SYNDROME LETTERS

"What a rag-bag of singular happenings!
But surely the most valuable hunting-ground
that ever was given to a student of the unusual!"
(*Sherlock Holmes, of the* Daily Gazette,
"The Adventure of the Red Circle")

CHIEF AMONG the medical narratives that, like Poe's purloined letter, have been hidden in plain sight are the clinical-pathological conferences and the syndrome letters published by the *New England Journal of Medicine*. Since the 1960s case reports have been dropped as "old fashioned" and unscientific from a number of medical journals. But in that repository of the best of American scientific medicine can be found regular accounts of singular happenings, studies with a numerator of one. In a journal otherwise governed by scientific criteria, such narratives are marked as idiosyncratic and unscientific by their very form. The clinical-pathological conferences are printed as verbatim transcriptions of academic occasions of the same name, and the syndrome letters, although they are now indexed by the National Library of Medicine, remain in form and content (and often in tone) personal communications. The clinical phenomena presented are singular, or idiographic, and although they may be useful for testing and refining the general laws of clinical medicine, they are meant to be taken as cautionary and not (as a case report might be) as nomothetic, or lawlike, themselves.

The Clinical-Pathological Conference

The clinical-pathological conference (CPC) is a quasi-dramatic reportorial form that attempts to capture the process of diagnostic reasoning. It holds up for praise and emulation the successful exercise of clinical ratiocination in a single, puzzling case. Although the custom of presenting troublesome cases to colleagues and experts dates back at least to Pierre Louis, the CPC as it was instituted by Richard Cabot in 1910 has become the pattern for medicine's traditional expository narrative. Published weekly in the *New England Journal of Medicine* as "Case Records of the Massachusetts General [or sometimes the Beth Israel] Hospital," the CPC is an edited, idealized transcript of medical grand rounds. Not only do its characters speak straightforwardly, the case presented is straightforward too. The focus is on the pathophysiological. However obscure the etiology, the disease itself is uncomplicated by other conditions. No personal problems mar the exercise or any distracting chronic problems exacerbated by this most recent admission. The pattern that governs this weekly drama is the quintessential medical plot. The diagnosis is the conclusion toward which that pattern leads, for the conclusion of this narrative, like that of other medical narratives, is governed by a "presenting problem" that makes its events narratable and, in fact, generates its plot. Here that presenting problem is (with conscious and informative patients) the medical version of the patient's chief complaint, and it is formulated by the physician as the narratable moment, the motive that begins the medical account. The physician then seeks a narrowly construed proximate cause in order to remedy those symptoms. Diagnosis with its concomitant therapy will be the conclusion. Only if the treatment is itself problematic does the medical story continue.

On the page the CPC looks like the script of a static, very wordy play: at the left margin speakers are identified by name as the source of the commentary that follows. But closer inspection reveals its narrative beginning, a long opening section without an identified narrator. Headed with a case number and labeled "Presentation of Case," this is a fully detailed, abbreviationless case presentation by an unspecified, scientifically omniscient voice. It is as if the record itself were speaking, although, knowing the custom of grand rounds, we may assume that a nameless, theoretically interchangeable resident who has taken part in the patient's care and has access to all the test data, is the narrative conduit of the case. After this introduction, the CPC takes the form of a drama. Its substance and rhetorical style are presumed to be the substance and the style of the speakers' remarks on that public occasion.

Two additional labeled sections make up most of the CPC: the "Differential Diagnosis" and the "Pathological Discussion." The first is a commentary on the various diagnoses that might obtain in this case (with mini-lectures on each) by a consultant unfamiliar with the patient. This expert is identified, as in a play script—"Dr. Schwantner:"—at the beginning, and the expert's commentary is in a style that can only be described as heavily edited verbatim of his or her remarks. The custom is to end with the several diagnostic conclusions: one that represents the consensus of those who cared for the patient, a second by the expert, and occasionally a third by residents or students. The pathologist customarily has the last word. The dramatic tension—always satisfactorily resolved—lies in whether these conclusions will agree.

Despite its apparent lack of action, then, the dramatic form of the CPC is not misplaced. The narrative of the case presentation gives the status quo ante, setting the stage; the action begins when the expert consultant begins to solve the diagnostic puzzle by plotting the best course of investigation and treatment. These steps are measured against what the staff at Massachusetts General chose to do in the actual case, and they in turn are an assessment of that action. The climax of the drama is that moment, after all the facts have been presented and the possibilities analyzed, when the physicians, home team and visitor, must lay down their diagnostic hands. The consensual "Clinical Diagnosis" is given in a phrase or two as a separate section, followed by the expert's opinion—"Dr. Schwantner's Diagnosis:"—which also stands alone, exposed to scrutiny. Then, after the discussion of the pathology contributed by local experts, the CPC concludes with the consensual "Anatomical Diagnosis," again a separate section of one or two lines.

If there is no autopsy report—that is, if the patient is still alive—a note in brackets or a sentence labeled "Addendum" may appear at the end, like a narrative voice-over, summarizing for the reader the patient's subsequent clinical course. It adds information that the auditors on the actual occasion may not have had. This relative subordination of the patient's fate reflects the focus of the CPC: unless the therapy offers some subsequent difficulty, the case is over when the diagnosis is agreed upon. The clinical-pathological conference, a common practice now throughout academic medicine and published for more than seventy-five years in every issue of its major journal, is an exercise in the emplotment of the medical narrative. It celebrates and promotes virtues essential to good clinical medicine:[1] careful attention to history and physical examination, a fund of clinical experience and scientific knowledge, strong reasoning ability, and the capacity for putting all the information together and reaching a decision that will be judged, often sternly, by subsequent events. Above all, the clinical-pathological conference reinforces the fundamental importance to the patient and to medicine itself of a correct diagnosis.

Therapy is mentioned, of course, but it retains the minor place it held in the early days of the CPC, when the pathologist was arbiter of the intellectual work of doctoring and "management" was intellectually unproblematic, a matter for nurses and family. The CPC comes as close to a report in the physical sciences as a clinical narrative can. How patients go on living, how they are helped toward rehabilitation or death, has never been a matter of concern in this genre. That is not what this exercise is about. Within its dramatic form, the CPC strives to be an accurate representation of the thinking necessary to reach an accurate diagnosis. There it stops.

We learn nothing directly of the scientific significance of the phenomenon that has occupied these speakers in the clinical-pathological conference. There is no overt expression of a "take home lesson," ordinarily so valued as the intellectual "bottom line" in medical conferences. By contrast, readers of case reports are supplied a preliminary idea of the condition's etiology and prevalence. It claims attention in its opening paragraphs for its rarity, and its authors balance their hypothesis about the "mechanism" at work, with the customary scholarly hedge that the phenomenon warrants further study. Implicit in the CPC is something like the experienced clinician's assertion, "We see this," an assertion that this singular happening is part of a common, if vicarious, experience. Yet the CPC's silence as to the significance and generalizability of the case under discussion is not simply a matter of relying on the obvious fact that the editors would not be publishing this conference in the *New England Journal* if readers were not to learn and alter their practice in its light. It is also the result of the CPC's dramatic form. There is no place in this genre for a "moral" to be drawn. Like the note on the patient's subsequent course, this addendum would require an omniscient voice-over, and rather than providing an understated close, such an additional conclusion would run the risk of dispersing the drama of diagnosis in bathos and cliché. The CPC remains instead a dramatic representation that replicates and reports a diagnostic investigation. Removed from the illness, removed even from the care of the patient, the action of this paradigmatic medical drama remains cool and intellectual. It is the stuff of which medical narratives are made: the rational progress toward the diagnosis of a disease in a single, distinctive case.

Letters to the Editor

If the CPC is medicine's most nearly scientific narrative, letters to the editor are surely the least so. Although case reports are in decline, letters concerning a single case continue to be published widely and regularly. Reporting on an unexpected diagnostic or therapeutic phenomenon, these personal communications come straight from the clinic, anecdotes that are scientific only in having been carefully observed and being now in search of corroboration. As accounts of a clinician's discoveries, as oddities that may advance scientific knowledge or improve the care of patients, they serve as reminders that medicine is not a finished science. There is work still to be done.

The occasional comic syndrome letters, for all their humor, take part in this. These are the "other" letters, bold, tongue-in-scientific-cheek reports of a hitherto unappreciated, but not-to-be-neglected clinical syndrome: french vanilla frostbite, space invaders wrist, credit-carditis. These letters are a minor art form, a funny, often ironic, and occasionally self-referential genre of medical storytelling. "French Vanilla Frostbite," for example, reports on inadvertent research conducted at a neighborhood ice cream emporium on a single occasion by the infant daughter of two physicians.[2] "The Tight-Girdle Syndrome" reports an unusually comprehensive series, as one might expect from its author, Paul Dudley White: he describes three cases, each an interesting, reportable variation of the malady.[3] Like scientific articles, syndrome letters provoke replies and inspire collaborative investigation. We owe our present-day knowledge of ski-boot syncope, for example, to the multiletter interdisciplinary discussion inaugurated in the early 1970s by Robert J. Joynt, neurologist, dean, and "skier without parallel."[4]

Like the straightforward letters they parody, comic syndrome letters are written anecdotes, abbreviated narratives of an isolated instance of illness. Their concern with a single, subjectively observed, perhaps unreplicable case is unscientific on its face. Even more surprising, the serious tone they adopt in their description of an absurd or trivial disorder parodies the investigative spirit that informs the *Journal*'s featured articles, the source of its scientific preeminence. What are these comic letters doing in this place? Because the *New England Journal of Medicine* functions as arbiter of the acceptable (rather like the commissioner of baseball in that other realm of skill and chance), we must assume that narrative reports with an N of 1, comic as well as straight, are in the best interests of scientific medicine. How is this possible?

The existence of the comic letters, particularly juxtaposed with their more serious models, nicely addresses the principal problem of medicine's knowledge. Syndrome letters are a means of conveying information about isolated clinical events, and thus they broaden the practitioner's vicarious experience of rare occupational injuries, environmental maladies, and the unexpected complications of therapy. Like anecdotes, they have a vexed status. What is the relation of this exception to the rule from which it departs? To what degree can it be relied upon? With what confidence can it ever be ignored?

Regular *Journal* readers can expect to find such a bagatelle every few weeks, a bit of (usually) diagnostic wit among other, more serious syndrome letters. The serious variety predominate, and in fact, the comic variants could not exist without a well established, recognizable, standard form for reporting the nonce case. The value that these singular, odd bits of clinical experience often have for medical practice is also essential to the humor. Even the funniest letters are also serious medical reports (or, more rarely, social commentary) that supplement the physician's textbook knowledge. Although they are comic, they share the standard syndrome letter's goal: to advance clinical knowledge in the interests of good, thorough patient care.

The Straightforward Syndrome Letter

While the two forms of the syndrome letter are readily distinguished, their boundaries are not absolute. At one end of their range, the comic syndrome letters have strong affinities with other epistolary divertissements published by the *New England Journal*,[5] letters about the physiology of ordinary life[6] or the diagnosis of ailments in literature[7]—matters about which medicine is called to do absolutely nothing. At the other end of their range, the comic syndrome letters merge almost imperceptibly with the straightforward letters they imitate. Those quite serious letters report the preliminary results of research or warn of the limits of particular therapeutic choices. The fun of the comic letters is rooted in their likeness to their straightforward models, a similarity of form and phrase which an exaggeratedly solemn scientific tone emphasizes. Inevitably, then, both straightforward letters and their mock variants fall into the same identifiable subgenres: they concern new diseases, iatrogenic complications including side effects of new or trusted drugs, pathognomonic signs, and, in great abundance, the "social diseases" constituted by occupational, environmental, and sports syndromes.

Some of the straightforward letters concern the discovery of genuinely new phenomena: a hitherto undescribed hernia of the fascia of Scarpa[8] or a case of toxic-shock syndrome occurring not just in a man (uncommon in itself), but in a man with an infection not ordinarily attributed to *staphylococcus aureus*.[9] Other letters, like "Elevated Serum Interleukin-2 Levels in Chronic Progressive Multiple Sclerosis,"[10] concern discoveries that offer clues to the mechanism of disease, or, like "Two Cases of Herpes Simplex Virus Encephalitis in the Same Family,"[11] describe epidemiological oddities that suggest genetic or environmental factors in disease.

More common are letters about iatrogenic maladies. These may be new complications of old procedures: "Periumbilical Hemorrhage Complicating Percutaneous Liver Biopsy"[12] or "Ipsilateral Horner's Syndrome as a Rare Complication of Tube Thoracostomy."[13] More urgently reported are side effects of new drugs or of old drugs put to new uses: rifampin may turn contact lenses orange;[14] atropine in eyedrops may be toxic in the elderly.[15] In 1979 a newly introduced synthetic catecholamine, dobutamine, was reported to cause necrosis at the site of its intravenous infusion.[16] Recently, aplastic anemia was attributed to tocainide, a drug prescribed for ventricular arhythmias.[17] New and desirable drug uses are also the subject of letters: the reported use of a scopolamine patch to limit excess salivation in wind instrument players—a serious letter about normal, if troublesome physiology—straddles the line between the serious and the mock forms.[18]

Diagnostic clues are the subject of a number of straightforward letters. Physicians who discover new pathognomonic signs—or the neglect of old ones—rush to spread the word of their usefulness. The crossed-straight-leg-raising test as a means of diagnosing a herniated disk in patients with lower back pain is reported to be far more sensitive than a lumbar myelo-gram.[19] A neck click—not among the heart sounds physicians have learned to listen for—may indicate an otherwise undetected case of mitral valve prolapse.[20]

The Comic Syndrome Letter

Recognizable to a rapidly scanning eye only by their promisingly clever titles, the comic letters share the formal properties of the far more fre-quently published straightforward letters. This essential ground of com-parison is promptly undercut by the lavish use of as many of the conven-tions and phrases of scientific reportage as can be crammed into one or two short paragraphs—and all for a topic distinguished either by the ab-surdity of its etiology or by its triviality.

"Frigid Headache" illustrates the genre. Not at first glance a letter about the perils of the palate, its title lures us to read about one of the frustrations of uncontrolled appetite:

> In the light of the recent surge of interest in neurologic esoterica, evi-denced by the report of Grocery Bag Neuropathy, we are compelled to re-port a therapeutic breakthrough in a heretofore unnamed, poorly under-stood, yet common neurologic affliction—namely headache, predominantly frontal in distribution, precipitated by excessively rapid ingestion of "slush" or similar products cooled to nearly 0°.
>
> In a well controlled study of uncontrolled consumption by two senior medical students over a three-month period, the pathophysiology was clari-fied to our satisfaction. The probable trigger zone of cryogenic cephalagia involves the palatal thermoreceptors, and through vascular response via palatocortical pathways, yields frontal pain. The symptoms were apprecia-bly ameliorated by lingual-recoil therapy, whereby the tip of the tongue is curled back and pressed against the soft palate. This act presumably warms the palate.[21]

The authors, medical apprentices at the time, convey scientifically appropriate attitudes not only in the display of their recently acquired vocabulary but in the order and content of the report: the history of the question, careful observation of the malady and its etiology, meticulous description of investigation undertaken, a pathophysiological hypothesis, and, at last, the "therapeutic breakthrough," "lingual-recoil therapy." Its very overdoneness is a characteristic satiric strategy intended to give away their intention. What is the target of this fun? The victims with their "uncontrolled consumption"? The recently acquired scientific vocabulary and the physician's capacity, all too often utilized, to translate the commonplace into the esoteric? The status of scientific facts in medicine? The *New England Journal of Medicine* itself? The answer is, to varying degrees, all of the above.

The immediate satiric target of every comic syndrome letter is the straightforward letters published regularly in each issue and, beyond them, the status of knowledge in medicine. Syndrome letters reveal the profession's dedication to the minute particular, and thus to the hitherto unknown "fact." Medicine must explain such facts and, given a rare stroke of luck, the comic letter writer actually may explain something about disease. But the syndrome letter reminds us that knowledge in medicine is, fundamentally and finally, incomplete and uncertain.

Subgenres

Comic letters are published in every one of the straightforward categories. Newly discovered phenomena are often heralded. The genetic transmission of the hitherto unappreciated photic sneeze reflex (existing in one-quarter to one-third of those surveyed at Johns Hopkins Medical Institutions but known to a mere 8% of the neurologists responding) has been established by the birth of the index patient's daughter, herself a sunlight-sneezer at four weeks.[22] The authors, father and daughter, call for further research.

There are comic versions of the "side effects" letters, but for sound reasons the sufferers are never patients but the therapists themselves. "Hot-Watch Syndrome," for example, despite the promise of its title (an allergic reaction to goods sold in shadowed alleys?) describes the danger of overlooking radioactive contaminants on the stem of an experimenter's watch.[23] Gaussian carditis is a clinical parody of this variant. An iatrogenic complication of MRI-scanning, this malady renders useless the credit cards of nearby physicians and technicians.[24] This unexpected hazard of medical therapy, we should note, is unrelated to—and therefore ungeneralizable from—the earlier credit-carditis, a neuropathy of the hip due to a card-stuffed wallet.[25]

Newly discovered pathognomonic signs also inspire comic letters. "The Succussion Splash as an Infant 'Burp' Sign,"[26] and its successor, "Tympany in Traube's Space as an Infant 'Burp' Sign,"[27] are contributions by medical parents to the literature of middle-of-the-night diagnostics. Debate over the proper interpretation of the "Cloret sign" arose in 1978 when two investigators reported that, in the case of a depressed 74-year-old with a history of psychiatric illness and the complaint, "My smile is not right," an asymmetrical green stain in the corner of her mouth pointed toward a neurological rather than a mental deficit.[28] A respondent reminded us, however, that this new phenomenon should not be confused with "the more prevalent 'Cloret sign'—the 'green tongue' of occult alcohol abuse" and "wonder[ed] why the 74-year-old depressed woman . . . was using 'Clorets.'"[29] Yet a third letter pointed out that green urine, while "not pathognomonic of Cloret abuse . . . may be useful in identifying patients clever enough to disguise their tongues after taking Clorets to hide the telltale alcohol breath."[30]

Occupational, environmental, and sports syndromes are the subject of at least half the mock syndrome letters, and their many variants suggest the rich possibilities of combining the serious and the entertaining in this form. Occupational disorders traditionally have been well reported. New maladies occur as new tasks or new machines are introduced, and, given the assiduity of medical science, few escape report. Occupationally related bursitis of the knee received thorough attention, including its etiology and epidemiology and a promise of further study, in "Carpet-Layer's Knee," a 1982 letter from the National Institute for Occupational Safety and Health.[31] Priests were omitted from the table of occupations afflicted, and this oversight was corrected in "'Genu Genuflectorum,'" published the following year.[32] International debate ensued: the Latinate coinage was criticized in the British Medical Journal[33] but was subsequently defended as designating a noninflammatory condition distinct from the well established Anglo-Saxon clergyman's knee.[34]

Although none of the conditions reported in these letters approaches the morbidity and mortality of earlier work-related diseases such as miner's lung, the injuries are painful, often disabling, now and then life threatening. Two types of pipetter's thumb, a scientific work-related disorder, have been reported,[35,36] and pricer palsy appeared soon after bar-code scanners were introduced into grocery check-out stations.[37] Buffer's belly, a more serious condition, was reported in a floor refinisher whose ruptured sigmoid colon presented deceptively as an intra-abdominal infection.[38]

Letters about occupational conditions are parodied by correspondents who pretend the activities of daily life are occupations in the customary sense. "Lawn Mower's Arm," for example, continues the roll call of sprains. ("The therapy recommended . . . is avoidance of medical consultation and continued exercise of the affected limb."[39]) Neuropathies abound: the aforementioned credit-carditis (which would top the list in a Syndrome Citation Index), its corollary back-pocket sciatica,[40] grocery-bag neuropathy,[41] handlebar palsy,[42] back-pack meralgia,[43] and the endemic paresthesia of ponderous-purse disease.[44] There are seasonal epidemics: the autumnal pumpkin carver's palm,[45] the winter (male) jogger's dreaded penile frostbite,[46] and springtime's frisbee finger,[47] an extended discussion of which ended with the following editorial note: "Frisbee finger, Ingelfinger regretfully acknowledges, has not been adequately covered in the pages of the *Journal*."[48]

Sports injuries are an unfailing source of syndrome letters. As subject to fad and fashion as maladies due to high heels and long scarves,[49] those related to running, skiing, and cycling have been thoroughly reported in the last twenty years. No one doubts the usefulness of any of these reports, although many of them—like attacks by birds as a side effect of running[50]—boast a touch of the absurd. A few, like "Jogging and Suppression of Ovulation,"[51] have actually warranted the further research for which letter writers customarily call. Others, like the reports of cycling injuries, have a long but not very conclusive tradition. Reports warning of the dangers to health—appendicitis, cyclist's neurosis, kyphosis bicyclistarum—created by that newfangled contraption, the bicycle, appeared in the the *Journal*'s predecessor, the *Boston Medical and Surgical Journal,* and elsewhere in the mid-1890s.[52]

Dancing, too, inspires syndrome letters. The foot and leg injuries of professional dancers are well established maladies in orthopedic textbooks. Syndrome letters necessarily concern the most recent popular dances, like Saturday night palsy,[53] a neuropathy of disco fervor, and break-dancer's neck (in all its variety).[54] The potential inclusion of a finger injury, the unintentionally punning disco felon,[55] has been the subject of a corrective letter.[56]

Food and the perils of its preparation and consumption provide richly suggestive subjects for syndrome letters both straight and comic. As with drugs, new substances may cause difficulty: diarrhea caused by the newly introduced sorbitol was reported in "Side Effects from Dietetic Candy" in 1966.[57] Old foods may also be newly abused. Popsicle panniculitis was well known from a case report with accompanying photograph in 1970.[58] French vanilla frostbite merely established a new agent for this phenomenon. Similarly, the gloriously Latinate Hydrox fecalis has extended our knowledge of excretory coloration beyond its previously established frontier.[59] In this instance as in many others, physicians have used themselves as experimental subjects, following in that tradition of self-experimentation celebrated most recently in a historical account by Lawrence Altman.[60] Nothing, both sorts of syndrome letters tell us, must hinder the progress of medical science.

Occasionally the absurd circumstance in which a malady has been acquired seems to license a letter's comedy, but even then it is less the patient's condition itself than the style of the report that is amusing. The patterned cleverness of the names given to these injuries is part of a comic pretense that we live still in the days when the giants of diagnosis and treatment bestowed eponyms like Adam naming the animals. Where the maladies are not life threatening, their victims may have the satisfaction of knowing their suffering is so recognizable as to have a name. For physicians, identifying a troublesome syndrome and placing it in the clinical taxonomy is a source of pleasure; their tongue-in-cheek tone is a nod to the weightier matters that occupy medicine and the other pages of the *New England Journal.*

The letters at which we laugh most freely are those that report the minor or fast-healing consequences of pastimes and fads that are in themselves social epidemics, like "Space-Invaders Wrist"[61] or "Urban-Cowboy Rhabdomyolysis."[62] Some injuries are more serious than others, and thus produce more serious letters: those in 1971 describing an epidemic of fondue-pot injuries are an example.[63] But even the least serious syndrome would not be funny were it not reported in the language and style of careful observation and objective reportage that characterize the science of clinical medicine. When the physician's prescriptive advice can include the entirely preventive "No more video games" or "Stay off the mechanical bull for a while," the malady is rendered harmless and the letter is even funnier.

The Epistemology of Medicine

The humor of the comic syndrome letters has serious roots in the epistemology of medicine. An aura of scientific discovery surrounds clinical medicine, and not only because the laboratories are nearby. The diagnostic refinements and therapeutic wonders of the twentieth century support the illusion that in time, perhaps soon, diagnosis, prognosis, and treatment will be matters of certainty for every malady in every patient. Students and residents are taught to work rationally—and to regard such methods as the differential diagnosis and clinical epidemiology as scientific. Practitioners recognize medicine's uncertainty, yet few are aware that clinical reasoning about medical diagnosis and therapy most resembles the procedures of the human sciences. There, in disciplines such as history and anthropology—as in clinical medicine—hypotheses grow out of observation and return to the "facts" for their corroboration rather than being rigorously separated.[64]

It is not surprising, then, that the ethos of medicine both scorns the anecdotal and provides for the careful reporting of single instances. No doubt many of these cases represent interesting but insignificant details: orphan facts. But others will turn out to be supremely useful and, as with anecdotes generally, it is not always possible to tell in advance which are which. Certainly the letter by Steven A. Samuel in the spring of 1981, "Apparent Anaphylactic Reaction to Zomepirac (Zomax),"[65] alerted the medical community to an unanticipated life-threatening side effect in a new nonsteroidal anti-inflammatory agent hailed as a "wonder drug." Scientific studies supporting his observation could not have been published so soon. This is merely the most striking of recent examples. Despite the Food and Drug Administration's testing program, medicine remains dependent upon physicians' reports in such instances, and due in part to the scientific attitude inculcated by medical education, it is an effective system. Physicians are educated to attend to the minute detail and to fit it to a pattern. When a detail is truly anomalous, the physician's duty is to report it—and a medical journal's is to publish it.

Science and the Single Case

Far from challenging this delicate accommodation to uncertainty, comic syndrome letters exist for many of the same quite serious reasons. With some justification they pretend to be exactly the same sorts of letters as the sober scientific ones, and the line, as we have seen, is often blurred. Patients do suffer from the syndromes these letters describe so amusingly, and there is the same alert sounded in regard to the sequelae of mechanical-bull riding as for the side effects of a new drug. Pain, wasted time, and the unnecessary expense of elaborate testing and treatment can be avoided if the practitioner is equipped with the new information—to say nothing of being spared the embarrassment of missing something obvious.

The comic syndrome letters embody the problem of the proper relation between medical generalizations and the particular case. At the same time that they participate in clinical research, they also mark the limitations of that effort. Although concerned with the hazards of modern life—the perils of fashion and fad, the consequences of our leisure obsessions and sensuous excess, the penalties of our attempts to stay young and to defeat death—their satiric targets include the tradition of clinical observation.

The letters remind us that, although physicians must not stop trying, not everything can be learned in advance of the clinical encounter. Even as they recommend the consideration of such maladies as *Jaws* neurosis[66] and pigmenturia from "Loving Care" hair dye[67] in differential diagnoses, the comic letters' mock heroic version of scientific reportage also warns physicians not to take too seriously such "science" as a single instance represents. Their parody of clinical science—with its Latinate vocabulary, "objective," factual reporting style, and, above all, its attitude of careful observation—mocks the anxious desire to contribute to the body of medical knowledge and the dream that such a body can be objectively possessed.

The *New England Journal of Medicine* has recognized medicine's ambivalence about the single case in two ways: directly in a 1985 editorial defense of publishing straightforward scientific letters without peer review and indirectly by its continuing publication (and thus its tacit encouragement) of the mock syndrome letter. The editorial defense was provoked by a letter calling for the peer review of letters on the very grounds that the *Journal* in other instances has been at such pains to protect and defend: its prestige and authority as a purveyor of exact and reliable medical knowledge.[68] Granting that the issue is worrisome, Arnold S. Relman nevertheless replied, "Clinical science, after all, does not consist exclusively of randomized controlled trials or fully documented laboratory studies. Not all useful new data come in full sized manuscripts." He noted that letters provide physicians and investigators with timely though inconclusive information. Recognizing the "tentative and incomplete nature of the[ir] evidence," he concluded, "we . . . hope that readers will read them with the interest—and the circumspection—they deserve."[69]

As a reminder (consciously undertaken or not) of the circumspection required in reading about any single case, the *Journal* publishes comic syndrome letters right alongside the straightforward ones. They are emblems of medicine's frustrated reliance upon the anecdotal. Potentially valuable, always to be explained, the anomalous "fact" is never to be trusted. In rounds and conferences the anecdotal is hedged about with precautionary statements—but never omitted long. So, too, in the *New England Journal of Medicine*. By the fact of their publication, comic syndrome letters proclaim the importance of detail, and at the same time signal silently that too much attention to the single case leads to aberrant absurdity.

But how much attention to detail is too much? How can the individual clinician achieve a balance between attention to detail and scientific generalizability? A pair of letters published in 1970 plays upon the tension between the importance of a single case "discovery" and the need for sound clinical investigation of the phenomena. In "Grand Rounds Whiplash" Stephen G. Pauker reports his own signal case of that well known, but hitherto unreported occupational hazard of medical residency. Given a chronic lack of sleep, he suggests, perhaps residents should be issued prophylactic Thomas collars.[70] But this conclusion is not backed up with a prospective epidemiological study nor, we discover, have the causes been entirely understood. In a letter replying to Pauker, H. C. Gilman faults the etiology he has proposed for grand rounds whiplash and charges him with failing to take a careful and complete history. It seems that not long before the onset of symptoms Pauker had occupied a seat in Gilman's aircraft: "Since we all try to learn from all things in medicine," Gilman writes, "the lesson must be that all 'acrophobic fellows' should not fly with me before going on Grand Rounds. This might be much less expensive than the suggested prophylactic Thomas collars."[71] It is an ironic imitation of medicine's characteristic suspicion of the nonce case; the subject may be comic but the criticism is traditional and sound.

The *Journal* has also published a cautionary letter suggesting that syndrome-letter reading itself may be hazardous to the physician's health. David Bateman's masterly "Syndrome-Reader's Scowl"[72] describes the case of a colleague who seemed at first only ordinarily depressed. Consultation with a specialist, however, reveals serious trouble: "'Note the pained curl of the brow, the wandering, fearful eyes, the cowering posture.'"

> "C'mon, Brandon," I said to my friend. "you just need to have a little fun. How about some exercise?"
> "Not on your life," shouted Brandon. "I might get tennis elbow, runner's knee, or frisbee finger."

The narrator proposes a movie instead—but no, Brandon fears popcorn eater's grimace, a malady that involves "intense, repetitive movements of the tongue and facial muscles in response to a morsel of popcorn lodged near the tonsils." Opera? "Never. If I enjoy it I'll get applauder's palms." Psychotherapy offers no hope: there's the dreaded shrink-seer's sputter, "an uncontrollable compulsion to speak openly about one's feelings." Brandon drops from sight. "There were rumors that he had fled to the Bowery, where he has allowed a bad case of tippler's elbow to progress to doorway-sleeper's hip."

The warning is clear: too much letter reading will weaken you. Learn too many facts and you'll fall their victim, drown in their uselessness, apply them where they are not needed. By taking the single case as the rule of the whole, the physician's judgment becomes skewed. By focusing on the details and not the pattern, the physician will be unable to act. But what is the cure for this parlous condition? Shall we ban syndrome letters? The end of Bateman's letter suggests not. The narrator is left sitting inert,

> the pile of unopened journals on my desk, tapping my fingers, fearful of the next revelation. Finally I can bear the pain no longer. I return to the specialist. He looks at my hands.
>
> "Procrastinator's fingertips," he says sternly. "Be very careful."

Bateman's metasyndrome letter captures the conflict exactly. Physicians must balance the facts, especially those newly discovered, with the need to take action that will benefit the patient. They must continue to learn, keeping up with new developments, recent research, even nonce cases. But they need equally to preserve an ability to act, even though scientific advances mean that today's action might have been contraindicated a decade ago and will be outdated a decade hence. Syndrome letters, like the anecdotes they record, reinforce this openness to change—but they risk, as Bateman's letter suggests, an attendant incapacitation. The physician, however learned and aware, must continue to act.

The *New England Journal of Medicine* syndrome letters, straightforward and comic, are a sign of the value of the single case study. Published without peer review, they assert the importance of the scientific attitude in medical practice: in the everyday care of patients, careful observation and an open mind will save lives, relieve suffering, restore well-being, prevent injury, save resources. Although the heroic age of medical discovery has passed, the attentive, thorough physician may still refine the stock of medical knowledge. The malady may be transient or there may never be enough cases for a genuine study; but once it is reported, other physicians will take note and refine their practice. Despite the serious limitations of their use, then, syndrome letters, like anecdotes generally, serve as a reminder of the irreducibly experimental character of medical knowledge. "Not everything is in the textbook," they trumpet. "Use your wits. Learn from everything."

The truth of science is presumed to be guaranteed by a system of knowledge and not by an individual, yet the syndrome letter asserts the same subjectivity that is implicit in the case presentation and chart write-up.[73] Like much of clinical discourse generally, the letters base their claim to our attention on the reliability of their authors' observation of a single case. We must trust that the speaker is skilled and educated as well as honest. Both medical education and the genres of clinical narrative can be viewed as ways of controlling the variables of medicine's necessary subjective observation of singular events. Syndrome letters are a part of this. Comic or straight, they participate in the medical naturalist's catalogue of the new and the odd, while the comic letter has the added task of reminding its readers that such minuscule, case-by-case colonization of the medical unknown is even more uncertain and fraught with intellectual danger than more scientific studies. Read against medicine's principles of scientific inquiry and a tradition, far longer than the *Journal*'s, of reporting the single case, the comic syndrome letter is mock heroic in tone. It carefully balances an awareness of the patient's suffering against the certain knowledge that few of the world's suffering will have been at Gilley's three nights in a row riding the mechanical bull.

A physician's judgment is constantly educated, honed, and refined by clinical narrative. Because clinical judgment is always subject to revision, every practitioner, no matter how ordinary the practice, is educated and admonished to be "scientific," open to new phenomena and willing to work to make sense of what he or she observes. In the best interests of medicine, then—both to encourage careful observation and open-minded inquiry and to warn of the limitations of the nonce case—the *New England Journal of Medicine* publishes studies with an *N* of 1.

SEVEN

PATIENTS, PHYSICIANS, AND RED PARAKEETS:

NARRATIVE INCOMMENSURABILITY

"You know my methods in such cases, Watson;
I put myself in the man's place, and, having first gauged
his intelligence, I try to imagine how I should myself
have proceeded under the same circumstances."
(Sherlock Holmes, "The Musgrave Ritual")

THE PATIENT's account of illness and the medical version of that account are fundamentally, irreducibly different narratives, and this difference is essential to the work of medical care. Sick people who seek a physician's advice and help are in quest of exactly this difference, for physicians are believed not only to know more about the body but also to see its disorders clearly and without shame. Yet because it is scarcely acknowledged by either patient or physician, the difference between their accounts of the patient's malady can warp understanding between them.[1] Expectations of care that ignore the difference between physician's and patient's stories contribute to the widespread dissatisfaction with contemporary medicine. If the incommensurability of the two narratives cannot be altered or avoided—or if in fact it is essential to medicine's therapeutic benefits—then some recognition of its existence and effect may prevent or reduce the misunderstanding and harm that are among its side effects. As a philosophical problem or even a political one, such coexistent and competing narratives have been well described in anthropology.

Incommensurability

The Bororos of South America are reported to assert that they are (or at death will become) the red parakeets that are so plentiful in their part of the world. Since the late nineteenth century, anthropologists have asked either directly or by implication how we, who have very different ideas about death and the provenance of parakeets, can understand this claim. As an emblem of the problem, these parakeets have been a recurring motif in the debate about rationality conducted by social scientists in recent years. Jonathan Z. Smith, who has suggested that if a totemic animal were assigned to anthropologists and historians of religion it would be the Bororos' parakeet, poses the problem succinctly. If we understand the Bororos to mean what they say about being or becoming red parakeets, either their statements make no sense to us and we decide they are "pre-logical" or irrational, or, despite the meaninglessness or absurdity of their statements to us, we conclude that they serve well enough for the Bororos.[2] In either case we have not understood the Bororos or their beliefs about who they are. The problem of how we are to make sense of their claim to parrothood is an epitome of the incommensurability of our discourse and theirs. Neither can be entirely understood in—or translated into—the terms of the other.

Physicians, too, have some claim to the emblem of the red parakeet, for their way of making sense of the patient's story has much in common with the anthropologists' investigation of the Bororos' account of their postsecular destiny.[3] The narrative in each case belongs to a human being who is an object of scientific study and to that person's world of lived experience and belief. Indeed, as a part of that study, the narrative is itself the object of investigation and interpretation. The physician's task, like the anthropologist's, is to make sense of the story in the generally accepted terms and concepts of the scientifically oriented world. Both the story and its teller must be explained and placed in a rational order of knowledge. Yet the two narratives, the physician's account and the patient's story out of which it was made, continue to exist in the world side by side. Although the patient's story is contained in and explicated by the physician's, it has not been replaced by it. Nor are the two narratives simple "translations" of one another. They are incommensurable; neither can be comprehended in (or satisfactorily reduced to) the other's terms.

The medical interpretation of the patient's story bears great power for healing. As the location of the malady in the social universe, a diagnosis relieves suffering in itself as well as in the guidance it provides for therapeutic action. Like all power, it must be exercised with care. Just as the anthropologist's account of the Bororos' parakeets is constructed for other anthropologists, the medical narrative is the interpretation of a subjective account intended for a professional audience. The physician's task, like the anthropologist's, properly concludes with the return of this newly constructed account to those who were its objects for comment, clarification, and reconciliation of all that does not seem to fit.[4] Here the difference between the subjective, experiential story and the outsider's objective, scientific interpretation is most evident. Patient and physician, Bororo and anthropologist are barred from a perfect understanding of one another: their assumptions are different, their worldviews structurally alien. No matter how close their relationship, each member of the dyad is bound to a viewpoint that leads each to be only partly understood by the other. The impossibility of explaining the experience and consciousness of another human being is exactly what is at issue. No doubt this is why the task of returning the medically interpreted account to those who are its objects is sometimes postponed—or neglected altogether. In anthropology this amounts to intellectual colonialism. In medicine, it is a therapeutic failure. Just as therapeutic potential is wasted when the medical interpretation of the patient's story is incomplete, inattentive, or dismissive, so when that story is not returned to the patient, the physician-patient encounter is incompletely healing. Like the anthropologist's account of a bit of another culture, the medical narrative not only offers its maker and its professional audience an insight into the life of another human being's experience, but also runs the risk of losing touch with the meaning of its original narrative, even occasionally of missing it entirely.

There are times, of course, when communication between patient and physician appears to be quite simple. If physician and patient are known to one another and the malady is neither life threatening nor unfamiliar, the two narratives seem rather easily translatable each into the other. Mr. Jefferson makes an appointment with his physician to report, "My ulcer's acting up again." After ruling out new complications, the physician may point out the added stress of the patient's holding a second job, and then prescribe again the medicine that worked last time. Studies have demonstrated the poor correlation between gastric pain and the presence of an ulcer,[5] yet these two people, physician and patient, can be said to understand one another. Under the conditions of normal discourse—each knowing something of the context of the other's statements—their narratives are already half translated one into the other. The patient has described himself in part in medical terms; the physician has interpreted the trouble and responded (also in part) in experiential terms familiar to the patient. Pressed further, the two would surely reveal quite different understandings of stomach pain: not only their words but their emplotment of the event would differ. For the purpose of the medical encounter, however, each has made an effort to accommodate the other's reality.

This is not the only kind of interaction between physician and patient. Setting aside those overtly troublesome occasions when physicians use opaque language, attempts at understanding may be blocked by different assumptions and concerns.[6] The illness may be complex, life threatening, or puzzling to either patient or physician. Or, in the apparently simple case of recurrent stomach pain, the physician may choose to apply the knowledge that something more than (or perhaps entirely different from) an ulcer could be the source of the patient's distress. In these instances of abnormal discourse, the patient's narrative, like the Bororos' account of red parakeets, poses for the physician the same problems of understanding and translation and the same potential for reductionism, condescension, and contempt.

As patients we often tolerate this incommensurability because it accompanies the promise of health. We consult experts precisely because they are knowledgeable and experienced. But the experience of physicians as patients suggests that incommensurability is not entirely a matter of a knowledge differential. Even with full grasp of the medical facts, the gulf yawns wide between the question that obsessed Tolstoy's Ivan Ilych, "Is it very serious?" and the one that absorbed his physician, "whether it was a matter of the vermiform appendix or a floating kidney."[7] In one of his last essays in the *New England Journal of Medicine,* Franz Ingelfinger tells of the sound advice he received after numerous consultations with colleagues about his illness. He had cancer in the very part of the body that was his specialty, and consultation with his physicians had left him confused and in fundamental ways uncared for. The sound advice? "Get a doctor."[8] He badly needed someone to take on the responsibility of reconstructing and representing the subjective account of his suffering in the medical world and then reconciling that medical version with his experience of illness. "Arrogance" is the quality Dr. Ingelfinger said his consultants had lacked, and we can imagine that sorting through the therapeutic possibilities for so eminent a physician took something like that. What was lacking in fact was the attentive care physicians provide ordinary patients every day, but Ingelfinger's label reminds us of what is always required of someone who reorganizes and retells the experience of another, questioning, reinterpreting, and sometimes ignoring reality as that person has reported it.

Incommensurability and the Closure of the Medical Plot

Accounts of an illness by even the most uncommunicative patient and physician have much in common. They are evoked by the same phenomenon, the patient's distress; they seem to ask the same question—What is wrong here?—and they seek the same ends of relief and remedy. One might expect the two stories to reach a common ending in cure or death. But this is not the case. The hospital medicine learned by almost every medical student and resident in the United States seems to an outsider painfully deficient in closure. What happened to Ms. Ferrier? If she is still in the hospital, the resident in charge of her care will know the answer in minute detail. But there is no assurance that the other residents, who heard Dr. Sanders present the case last Tuesday, will remember her at all.

Even Dr. Sanders, although she will almost certainly recall her admission, may not know her condition now if she is no longer responsible for her care.

For those who do not take care of the patient, the case is over—and has been since the medical presentation of her case concluded with the diagnosis and treatment. The case presentation, like the initial write-up in the chart, customarily ends with the choice of therapy and a plan for care, or with the decision to call in a surgeon or a subspecialist for consultation. But these are part of the denouement and they flow from the resolution of the crisis of the medical plot, the quest for a diagnosis. The determination of the diagnosis and the consequent choice of treatment bring the medical plot to a close. We do not sit on in the theater after a film is over, expecting to have "happily ever after" played out on the blank screen nor (very often) hold a finished novel on our laps thinking it might be possible to wring something more from its endpapers. If Ms. Ferrier's case should be presented subsequently at professor's rounds, a departmental conference, or at grand rounds, the narrative related at that time will differ surprisingly little from Dr. Sanders's first presentation at morning report so long as the intervening days or weeks, which may have brought about her recovery or her death, have been predictable, "uneventful" by the criteria of medical narrative. A sentence or two regarding her course of treatment and its outcome will be added to confirm the diagnosis and illustrate the interest and the difficulty of the case. But they are nevertheless a coda: in medicine narrative closure is achieved by the diagnostic resolution of crisis.[9] Subsequent events, whether her response to treatment or an autopsy report, merely confirm the diagnosis, playing it out in time.

In the patient's story, closure is governed by a different plot, one which has a structure almost as invariant as the medical one. The restoration of health or its inalterable loss will close the story, just as loss of health, real or foreshadowed, was its genesis. Ms. Ferrier's account of her illness and the accounts of her family and friends, however much they may vary among themselves in emphasis and detail, will all begin with her falling ill, and they will all end with the resolution of the illness in her recovery (or, in the case of chronic illness, with the course of treatment she has embarked on) and the place of this episode of illness in her life. Diagnosis and choice of treatment are important turning points in this plot, but they are not its closure.[10] For most physicians, however, the details of the patient's story that are not perceived as medically problematic are not medically narratable. This irrelevance includes much of the subjective experience of illness: suffering, uncertainty, helplessness, fear of death, anxiety over loss of control. These are matters about which medicine in general and physicians in particular customarily have little to say. Indeed, without corroborating signs, a patient's subjective experience of illness does not raise for most physicians a narrative-provoking question. (Or a liaison psychiatrist may be called in to construct another sort of story to provide its explanation.) Physicians are prompted to tell stories as they sort their clinical experience; their criterion is not the degree of their patients' observed or reported pain and fear but the opportunity to cure or ameliorate a disease. For them the meaning to be sought in the events of Ms. Ferrier's illness has to do with the speed and accuracy with which the source of her trouble can be identified and the reliability with which she can be treated. Physicians do not assemble to discuss the patient's story. Their plots are medical plots, their endings medical endings. Closure fixes meaning, and the meanings of medical plots concern diagnosis and choice of treatment.

The Patient's Story

The patient's story, far from being dismissed or destroyed in a healing encounter, is itself subjected to medical treatment. Like the Bororos' account of the parakeets, it tells something vital about its teller, and those who would understand that narrator must understand the story and its place in the narrator's world. In psychiatry this concept of the symptomatic story is foundational, but in an era of chronic, environmentally induced, and psychosomatic illness the insight is equally applicable, if somewhat more metaphorically, to the rest of medicine. Whatever else may take place, the opportunity for a sort of narrative therapy is an integral part of every medical encounter. The physician always begins by hearing the ill person's story. Even in an emergency room or in the treatment of comatose patients, a version of the patient's story is sought from friends or family or the medical attendants who have brought him for help. "Was he wearing a seat belt?" The question is a fork in the road to diagnosis; the answer will guide the search for injuries along one logical path rather than another.

Accepting the patient's story as itself a text produced by the illness, physicians ask questions of both story and body, then set about constructing the medical account, a metastory about disease or injury. Their minds are stocked with biomedical knowledge, medical assumptions about causation, and the practical wisdom that comes from more or less extensive experience treating maladies of this and other sorts. From this stock they shape the patient's story into a diagnostic plot open to therapeutic alteration. Michael Balint, the psychiatrist who aimed at the integration of psychological awareness in British general practice, saw this process as interactive, unconsciously negotiated,[11] as do more recent medical theorists who have been influenced by social anthropology. The construction of a metastory about the patient's story interprets the events of illness, testing them against the taxonomy of diagnostic plots and settling on one that is sufficiently likely to warrant therapeutic intervention. This is the fundamental act of patient care. The medical account retains its connection to the patient's story even when augmented or substantially changed by the physical findings and the answers to the physician's questions. The patient's story—her expectation of "appendicitis" rather than the less corrigible cancer that is diagnosed—must still be attended to.

Freud described his work as the repair of the patient's story,[12] and the idea of the treatment of the story is not quite so farfetched nor so exclusively psychiatric as it may seem. It took place literally in the seventeenth century. Stanley Joel Reiser has described how English physicians diagnosed and prescribed by mail, offering their opinions and recommendations to the afflicted who wrote describing their illnesses.[13] Far more willing than modern newspaper doctors to diagnose and prescribe for maladies described by their correspondents, these physicians kept up a thriving consultative practice. Their patients, in a more nearly literal sense than modern patients, were texts written entirely by themselves for the physician's interpretation.

Modern medicine is strikingly different. No one today would diagnose from the patient's story alone—much less by mail or (despite their appearance and popularity) in a syndicated column. No matter how often teachers of interviewing skills tell of maladies diagnosed solely from the patient's history, no one thinks of eliminating the physical examination. Careful examination of the body by the physician is the act that grounds the patient-physician encounter. Tests and instruments, which have become increasingly routine since the nineteenth-century introduction of pathological anatomy and physiology into medicine, extend that examination. Sir William Osler reflected the late nineteenth-century clinicians' consensus that an improved biomedical science could never substitute for firsthand knowledge of the patient when he wrote: "To study the phenomena of disease without books is to sail an uncharted sea, while to study books without patients is not to go to sea at all."[14] It is not simply that observation and knowledge are both essential to scientific medicine, but that observation of the phenomena is the source of medical knowledge—both the general kind that appears in textbooks and the particular information about the patient who is ill.

Even with superb diagnostic technology, the patient's history continues to exert a powerful influence, and narrative remains central to knowledge in medicine because the patient is its focus. Book knowledge and clinical observation isolated from one another will not suffice. Narrative is required to apply one to the other. Residents occasionally joke that ambulances in the not-too-distant future will be backed up to the doors of various hospital scanners—CT, MRI, PET—and in one swift motion unsounded, unstoried patients will be admitted, examined, and diagnosed. That day will not arrive. Textbooks and handbooks, which residents sometimes call "storybooks" as a sign of their distance from real life, are actually storyless in our sense. Their paradigmatic descriptions of illness lack the sense of a lived body, an experienced malady. Narrative, which organizes and stores knowledge of the individual case, is required to interpret the paradigmatic case, and this the patient must supply. Likewise, the scanned but silent, untouched body yields facts that without a narrative can be incoherent or difficult to make sense of. Narrative constructed out of the patient's account of illness, then tested against the ill body and augmented with answers to the physician's inquiry, makes sense of the facts as it discovers them and serves, too, as a context for treatment. Although ordinary physicians are unlikely to discover a new phenomenon or to work out a new etiology or therapy, they are confronted dozens of times every day with the medical scientist's situation in little: What accounts for the malady experienced by this patient? Careful observation guided by the patient's story of the illness and the process of "matching" the plot of the constructed medical metastory to biomedical principles must supply the answer. Physicians still rely on their eyes and ears and hands, and stories are still elicited and retold as part of the process of careful observation and analysis. The patient presents a malady in both body and story, hoping for a rewriting of the narrative of illness in and through the medical narrative, an interpretation that will lead to an understanding of the symptoms and thereby to their relief and cure.

In this process, the incommensurability of the patient's story does not authorize either its erasure or its replacement by the medical account. As the originating narrative, the foundation of clinical knowledge for each particular case, the patient's story remains the source of much of the medical narrative and the first and final focus of its inquiry. Not only does it persist in the consciousness of the patient, where it remains accessible to the physician who asks again, "What brought you here?" but it survives in the physician's case, embedded in the chart and subsumed in every presentation, maintaining its difference even there from that transformed and transforming medical narrative. As the "chief complaint" and the "patient history," the narrative of the patient's subjective experience supplies the data for the clinical investigation, serves as a guide for tests that will confirm a diagnosis, and remains a touchstone for the medical care that follows.

The medical narratives that physicians traditionally employ in their efforts to understand and represent the unfolding experience of human beings who are ill are not simply the patient's story retold by a different narrator. Whether presented orally to colleagues, cited anecdotally in discussion, written up for publication, or simply recorded in the chart, the medical narrative appropriates and reorganizes the patient's story as a part of a diagnostic plot. Like an anthropologist's report of the Bororos' stories about parakeets, these clinical accounts of the patient's illness are interpretive reconstructions of the data the investigator has gathered. In each case, the subjective experience or belief of the object of investigation becomes the investigator's material, providing information that guides subsequent questions and observations. The words of patients, like the words of native informants, are scrutinized for clues that will reveal more about the experience they represent; in each case, the professional investigator replaces the experiential account with an "objective," explanatory report that has scientific status. The parakeets are visible in the branches of the trees, and the anthropologists see them there, but theirs is not the Bororos' reality. Is their scientific account faithful to their informant's subjective experience? Can subjective truth be explained with justice both to scientific knowledge and to the experience of the teller? Can that subjective experience be made sense of in a way that not only adds to the investigators' store of knowledge but also is recognizable and perhaps useful to the informant?

These questions are vital to the medical recognition of the patient's story and thus to the success of the physician-patient relationship. In the process of its medical retelling, the patient's account of illness becomes to some degree irrelevant; indeed, the physician's narrative (to say nothing of the physician) is capable of proceeding without further reference to the patient's experience. Once it has yielded its information, the patient's version of the events of illness, as well as the life out of which it is told, is often ignored. Like the Old Testament in the reign of the New, the patient's story has been superseded—not by being forgotten or denied or controverted but by being interpreted.[15] Its details now support a new set of meanings. Once told, the patient's experience seems to make sense in the medical realm only by being related and understood in medical terms.

Healing Narrative

The medical retelling of the patient's story, like other powerful aspects of medical care, has potential for healing and for harm. It is at the center of medicine's power to affect the lives of patients. Sick people seek medical attention expecting to present their wound or pain to the physician's knowing scrutiny and to tell the story of their malady to a willing, interested listener. They come to have this change in their ordinary state of being interpreted and recognized, to have their fears allayed or confirmed, their malady cured or its consequences minimized. Physicians hear the

story, ask questions, and examine the patient's body, translating and reconstructing the story into a medical version that approximates one of the
model narratives in the taxonomy of disease. This hypothesized version is
tested against (and refined by) the signs and test results and the statistical
likelihood of its occurrence in this present patient, someone with this life
history. When a fit is achieved and the diagnosis leads (by the same investigative oscillation between theory and detail) to the choice of a therapy,
the physician in turn retells the story of the malady to the patient, interpreting the symptoms that led to the consultation and the signs that have
been discovered there. This retelling replaces the patient's account with
the medical version, entering the ongoing life story of the ill person, sometimes leaving scarcely a mark, sometimes altering it with earthquake
force. The medical interpretation returned to the patient may be a welcome reassurance or the diagnosis of a serious illness. It may institute a
new life stage—chronic illness, incapacity, parenthood—or a new regimen: exercise or pills or unaccustomed abstention. The story and the
therapy that follow from the medical interpretation may restore the patient's previous state of health, or may require patience and courage.
Then it is, once more, the patient's story.

Three things are essential if this narrative interaction is to contribute to
the healing of the patient. The first, prior to their encounter, is the physician's understanding that a patient's account of a malady is and will remain distinct from the medical version that patient and physician are
meeting to construct. The second and the third are integral parts of the
patient-physician interaction: in the beginning the case must be constructed in a careful interview and physical exam; at the close, the story in
its medical version must be restored to the patient.

The Reification of the Patient

The patient's story is not only the raw material for medical interpretation
but a thing in itself. It is the presentation of the patient's illness experience
(and often an epitome of a life) and not merely the precursor of the medical "truth." The physician's recognition of this is narrative's first contribution to medicine's healing task. Medicine's appropriation of that story
is unavoidable, but, given that the patient has come voluntarily seeking
help, it need not be a *mis*appropriation. Nor is the accompanying objectification of the patient necessarily harmful. Impersonality is a virtue of
medicine that these days, given the perceived diminution of medical caring, fails to receive its due. Intrinsic to the permission we grant physicians
to touch our bodies, impersonality is not only a part of the scientific
stance, it is also understood as an open and charitable, even an egalitar-

ian disinterestedness. Patients are guaranteed acceptance and care no matter who they are or what their lives have been, no matter how tired the physician may be or how horrible the malady. Impersonality is not inattention.[16] Walt Whitman's wound dresser in *Drum-Taps*, his collection of poems about nursing the Civil War wounded (1865), embodies this disinterested care:

> I dress the perforated shoulder, the foot with the bullet-wound,
> Cleanse the one with a gnawing and putrid gangrene, so sickening,
>   so offensive,
> While the attendant stands behind aside me holding the tray and pail.
>
> I am faithful, I do not give out,
> The fractur'd thigh, the knee, the wound in the abdomen,
> These and more I dress with impassive hand, (yet deep in my breast
>   a fire, a burning flame.)[17]

Whitman's wounded soldiers rely on him for that impassive attention no matter who they are; he is there despite the sickening sights and smells. That he identifies them by their conditions is a metonymy—the use of a part for the whole—that at once forces him to face the horror of their bodily condition and protects him from the painful details of their individual lives, which he is helpless to alter.

As a part of the care provided by a physician, a respectful, impersonal attention is important to the therapeutic relationship. It can imply a recognition that the sufferer is more or other than patienthood presents to view. The person who is ill seeks help, in part, for the sake of the physician's discriminating but nonjudgmental interpretation. Like those who bring their mysteries to Sherlock Holmes, patients seek above almost all else, sometimes even beyond cure, an explanation of what is happening to them. "Is it a matter of life and death with me?" Ivan Ilych asks his physician; and the physician cruelly ignores him, not simply by translating his question to the medical question of whether the trouble is the appendix or a floating kidney but also by stopping there, leaving Ivan Ilych in doubt about the meaning of those alternatives. The patient in North American culture wants above all to know, because to know is to retain some control and to preserve a sense of an undamaged self. Suffering is independent of pain, beginning or ending even when pain is unchanged. The abstraction of our selves in the medical narrative parallels and accompanies our willingness to uncover our bodies and our lives to medical scrutiny. We undergo this impersonalization trusting in the privileged nature of the patient-physician relationship—what is discovered will be held in confidence—and in the common humanity of the physician who, we presume, will recognize in us a fellow creature asking on this occasion for help.

As the example of Tolstoy's physician suggests, incommensurability is a part of the functional ontology that guides clinical action. Physicians work as if diseases were real entities that have invaded the body of the sick person and can be both known and counteracted. Although this concept is rightly, easily criticized both philosophically[18] and microbiologically,[19] it is part of an attitude toward what ails us that can be quite appealing in someone we trust to be active on our behalf. The ontological view sets aside a more sophisticated scientific awareness of the reaction of the body at the cellular level to bacteria and viruses, for a positivist, all-but-binary view of disease: you have it or you don't, and if you do, we'll try to get rid of it. With its emphasis on recognizable entities—"clinical pictures"—this clinical ontology facilitates the acquisition and retention of knowledge in practice, enabling the physician to think about and treat illness in another human being. It also encourages the objectification of the patient's illness, and this potentially alienating side effect of medical care is bound up with the therapeutic effect of the medical reinterpretation. As readers of Alexandr Solzhenitsyn's *Cancer Ward* are reminded, the objectification of the patient is a modern memento mori—not only the consequence of a bureaucratic society but also a token of our common humanity in a secular world where such tokens are often in short supply.

The incommensurability of the experience of illness and the medical accounts of it may be an ineradicable part of Western medicine. As both an outgrowth of the clinical ontology that facilitates the daily work of medicine and the inevitable consequence of the medicine's appropriation of the patient's story, it is almost certainly unavoidable. Yet without the physician's awareness of all that is (or is not) taking place at the level of narrative, this incommensurability has a deleterious side effect: physicians and other health-care workers begin to speak and think of patients as if they had become their diagnoses. The patient comes to be seen only as the locus of medical activity. Thus, Ivan Ilych is to his physician and then to himself and to others the troublesome floating kidney (or perhaps the appendix) that is believed to be making him so irritable and unpleasant. Reified in this way, people who are chronically ill or dying have only an abstract medical existence, for, in this view, when "nothing more can be done" for a disease, the physician's work is over.

A careful distinction must be made between this reification and the impersonalization that someone ill undergoes in the medical interpretation of illness. The act of becoming a "patient" is itself a first step in assuming a nonpersonal, medicalized identity. The translation of the patient's story into the medical discourse involves the substitution of the case for the person: the patient is impersonalized, represented in the medical arena by an objectifying medical narrative. This generalizing view of the individual aids diagnosis and may even offer the patient some comfort. The person who has presented with an illness and become a patient takes on a metonymic existence: she becomes a case, the narrative of her malady. In the ordinary discourse of medicine, as we have seen, Ms. Ferrier becomes the narrative of her medical care that is written and read in the chart and in a teaching hospital presented by a resident and mulled by senior physicians. Ms. Ferrier's medical currency is as "a case," and her medical existence is as a story, told and retold, her signs and symptoms analyzed and examined, her "numbers" recorded, her response to treatment documented. The case narrative that represents the patient to the medical world comes in that world to *be* the patient. This substitution is a useful, understandable bit of mental shorthand—not unknown outside medicine. Certainly it reflects the fact that the medical story, her case, stands for her, actually stands in for her; as we have seen, she herself need not be present to be presented. Yet it is not necessary or understandable that she by extension becomes the disease itself, "the bowel cancer in 714."

Reification may be an outgrowth of the impersonalization effected by the physical examination and construction of the medical narrative, but it goes farther by substituting the disease rather than the case for the patient: "I've admitted an aortic aneurysm," "Did the broken leg go home?" No doubt, like the impersonalization of chart writing and case presentation, this clinical habit is the outgrowth of regarding diseases as if they were things in themselves. Clinical ontology encourages speaking (and then thinking) about maladies as if they were entities identical with the bacteria or viruses that are their most immediate and necessary (but not sufficient) cause. This practical clinical assumption literalizes a metaphor that takes the contributing factor for its effect, and it may be inevitable, at least in our culture, where diseases are forces to be countered, invaders to be repelled. But the further step, the reification of the patient, is an unnecessary and depersonalizing side effect of medical care.

Patients seek medical care both for the explanation of a malady and for its relief, and they accept, even welcome, their translation into medical stories about their conditions. Reification, however, is an altogether different matter. In the collapsed metonymy of person and disease—"We sent the MI to the unit"--the medical story is reduced to its diagnostic label, the myocardial infarction. Reified, the person who is ill is no longer a medical story—for instance, a case of bowel cancer (substitution enough)—but its epitome: the diagnosis, an objectified disease. For its usefulness, we tolerate and even seek out medicine's re-presentation of the patient and its attendant substitution in medical discourse of case for person. Reification, however, reduces the patient to a mere diagnosis or to a stage of dying. She is no longer equated with a medical narrative intended to represent for objective scrutiny the situation in all its complexity; the patient has now become the disease. Without a saving recognition of the reality and persistence of the patient's experience and its incommensurability with its medical interpretation, the diagnosis replaces the case history as a representation of the patient. The medical object, the disease, comes to stand for the patient. The patient in this view is nothing but the disease, and the disease is the enemy.

As an inextricable part of medicine's power to replot the patient's illness and reshape its ending, this tendency toward hypertrophy renders the medical narrative potentially harmful both to patients and to the physician's rational process. Reification goes beyond the defensible, useful "translation" of the patient into a case to the summary reduction of that case to a diagnostic label. The physician—or the philosophy of medicine—that fails to recognize the inalienability of the patient's story and the experience it represents will be unable to honor the separateness of the patient's experience from the medical story and will offer little resistance other than mere etiquette to reification. When the two stories are thus collapsed, a reductionist view of the patient's story, and thus of the patient, is the consequence. The recent autobiographies of illness are eloquent about the damage this causes to the spirits of people who are seriously ill. Indeed, many authors have been inspired to write about their illness by a defiance aimed equally at the unkindness of fate and their medical reification.

Along with its benefits, then, the medical practice of reconstructing and thereby interpreting the patient's experience carries the risk of overreaching its goal of diagnostic generalizability and rendering the patient a mere thing. An apparently easy but harmful progression leads from the distancing inherent in the narrative encapsulation of patients' stories to the further step of turning patients into disease objects. The subjective experience of illness must be transformed into a recognizable category of disease; this is an abstraction essential to the physician's construction of the case. Yet this transformed narrative need not come to be regarded as a medical entity altogether detached from the patient's experience. Ms. Ferrier's account of her experience is always available to the medical investigator, who has only to ask her once more about the events that brought her to seek help or to look at the record of those events in her chart. But she is seldom asked, and the original history of the present illness is customarily consulted only if there remains an unsolved diagnostic or therapeutic problem.

Academic subspecialists engaged in clinical research might argue that reification, like impersonalization, is the unavoidable and therefore justifiable by-product of their scientific concern. As experts who treat only the difficult or critical cases in their field, their principal work is to consult and advise other physicians, to collect data, to conduct clinical research in order to improve the understanding of the mechanism of disease. Their focus is not the person who has the malady. Would we, they characteristically ask, prefer to have our hands held sympathetically at the cost of a lower level of scientific knowledge? The parallel clinical argument is that in the modern hospital, particularly an academic one, time is precious and the patient's suffering calls for immediate action. In these circumstances, reification is a shortcut, no more harmful to patients, they claim, than the representation they undergo in the construction of the medical narrative and the presentation of the case. What is important is the treatment administered and the cure to which it may lead. Physicians, this line of reasoning goes, must focus on the purely biomedical, even at the cost of turning people into scientific objects, because that is where significant effects on outcome can be made.[20] After all, what can be done about a patient's life story? Even if one grants that these matters affect the patient-physician interaction or the illness itself, medicine is not obligated to attend to patients' irremediable material or social circumstances, their childhood and education, their beliefs, hopes and fears, loves and hates, ambitions and defeats. Such circumstances, of necessity, take second place to saving the life that supports them.

Appealingly practical though these justifications are, they are not the principal motive for medicine's reification of the patient. Nor is reification found only in academic medical centers. The emotional protection reification offers all physicians is a far more powerful reason for its existence than either scientific focus or high-pressure clinical pragmatism. The person who becomes a case of bowel cancer is a problem in therapeutics to be addressed, but a person who has become the bowel cancer itself is a fait accompli. Bowel cancer is a congeries of qualities and events with a known course requiring physical attention but no investment of self. Is she dying? Is she anxious or confused? Afraid? All that might represent her memory or hope is blocked out as irrelevant. As in Walt Whitman's "The Wound Dresser," reification focuses the attention on the domain where care may have some physical effect. Biomedical science has little to offer the emotions and experiences that are our common human denominators. It might be sufficient if physicians were to recognize this limitation and, particularly, restrain the application of technological wonders in the care of the dying. But their avoidance of pain also has its price both for them and for the quality of medical care. Dialogue between patient and physician at that point is blocked. The tendency to see the patient as an object with only a medical existence and only a diagnostic meaning is solipsistic and controlling. It fosters avoidance or automatic, unfeeling care, and, by precluding careful observation, it makes possible, even probable, inadequate treatment and misunderstanding of further symptoms. The patient in effect is deserted. The living spirit is ignored in its reduction to a morbid body. Not only do physicians lose their patients, first to inattention and then to death, they are deprived of restorative contact that can validate their life work and the possibility of further learning.[21] Given medicine's authority to define reality in our medicalized society, reification encourages patients themselves and their friends and families to understand the chronically ill and the dying in this way. To themselves and to others, patients reified by medicine become a disease acting itself out in a treasonous body. This is an unnecessary, cruel consequence of the incommensurability of discourse that otherwise, when recognized and controlled, is an efficacious part of scientific medicine.

Physicians who fail to understand the incommensurability of their account of a patient's illness with the patient's experience exacerbate the frequent ill effects of medical therapy. Very likely they believe that, given some additions and clarification, the patient's story is identical with the medical account, or even that the two are different but the medical account is the more real and better able to explain the subjective experience. The latter view is encouraged by patients themselves, who after all hope to be understood and set right by their physicians. In either case physicians are prevented from acknowledging and attending to the very different reality of the patient. The differences between the two narratives—particularly in plot and closure—are not only elements of incommensurability but obstacles in themselves to the physician's necessary return of the narrative to the patient. A belief that the medical narrative consists simply of facts that the patient must accept contributes to a lack of understanding by both parties of what medicine is and does. When the medical narrative obliterates the patient's story, physicians confuse their own uncertainty and helplessness and their patients' deaths with failure; patients, when angered by inattention, are likely to confuse them with malpractice.

Rewriting the Patient's Story

The second contribution of narrative is in itself a healing act: the physician's careful construction of the medical case. The therapeutic relationship is grounded in the patient interview and the history the physician takes, and a narrative view of clinical medicine accords this activity the importance it deserves. A malady cannot be understood nor therapy effectively prescribed unless the patient's experience is captured accurately and translated into a recognizable medical version. The interview is the source of primary data essential for the work of diagnosis even in the era of computerized taxonomies and nuclear magnetic resonance images, and the act of "taking the history," passive and transparent though the phrase assumes it to be, is part of the construction of a distinct medical narrative. The work of medical reasoning and the process of including and excluding information takes place as physician and patient talk. One internist has said, "Surgeons have scalpels; the interview is our tool. We take a history in order to understand the patient and determine the needs of particular individuals."[22] The usefulness of the patient history is universally asserted, but—perhaps because it runs counter to the main thrust of modern medicine, to eliminate the subjective—medical education often neglects the considerable skill the interview requires. The goal of medical education is the uniform diagnosis of illness no matter who physician or patient may be. The medical facts are assumed to be "out there," and the patient history, given a cooperative patient, is assumed merely to record them. The case histories that result are often "thin description," the very opposite of Clifford Geertz's prescription for the successful understanding of another's experience, the "reconstruction of the imaginative universe in which human acts are signs."[23]

The medical rewriting of the patient's story that takes place in the interview is an integral part of diagnosis and treatment. Just as the patient's account guides the physician's observation and then serves as a measure of the case narrative, so its rewriting enables physicians to exercise the cognitive skills involved in clinical medicine and to care for the patient. The rewriting locates the malady in the spectrum of disease, works out for this situation the operation of biomedical causality, and, at the same time, preserves a sense of the complexity of circumstance in which the malady has occurred. By this means, medicine is capable of recognizing multiple causality even as it seeks the necessary and sufficient straw that broke this camel's back. Once the proximate cause is known, the physician can work to counteract it in an effort to restore the patient to health.[24]

Medicine has the power not only to rewrite the patient's story of illness but also to replot its course. The therapeutic prescription, which follows from the reorganizing, diagnostic plot, enables physicians often to change an appalling, life-threatening outcome. The natural history of a disease that has initiated a chapter in the patient's life story may be altered, even halted, by an accurate diagnosis and prompt treatment. Appropriated and transformed, the chapter, with luck and skill, can be returned to the patient with an uneventful (which is to say, a happy, nonnarratable) close. The patient seeks medical advice and care for just this reinterpretation of the symptoms. "Is my case very serious?" Ivan Ilych asks. The physician's contempt for the irrelevance of such personal concerns is part of the price Ivan Ilych pays for the consultation. He accepts it, as those who petition him as a judge accept his quite similar behavior toward them, but it is wounding nonetheless. Even in the case of chronic or fatal illness, when the ending is not to be a happy one and other clinical stories between now and then will inevitably be generated, the medical account of the malady is returned to the patient. "Ms. Ferrier, this is what we've found," the physician says. "Here is what we can do. These are your choices and this is my recommendation."

Recent attempts to improve medical care, concerned with more than advancing technology or problems of access, have encouraged dialogue between physician and patient. They follow a tradition that dates from the late 1920s when Francis W. Peabody gave his talk on "The Care of the Patient." Ill himself and troubled by what he saw as an unassimilable amount of scientific information while so many of a physician's patients had nothing organically wrong, he set out his fundamental axiom of clinical practice: "The secret of the care of the patient," he wrote, "is in caring for the patient."[25] Not long after, L. J. Henderson, the physiologist who worked out that bane of medical studies, the Henderson-Hasselbach equation, argued for considering the patient and the physician "scientifically" as a unified system. Influenced by his participation in the social scientists' Pareto Circle at Harvard, Henderson wrote: "In an interview listen, first, for what the patient wants to tell, secondly, for implications of what he does not want to tell, thirdly, for implications of what he cannot tell. . . . I suggest that it is impossible to understand any man as a person without knowledge of his environment and especially of what he thinks and feels it is, which may be a very different thing."[26]

Recent studies of cultural and psychological barriers to communication between physician and patient have begun to augment that knowledge. Alan Harwood has described the Galenic concepts Puerto Ricans bring to the medical encounter,[27] Loudell Snow the beliefs of African Americans;[28] and Lyle Saunders the practices of Chicanos.[29] These and other studies have provided insights into patients' health beliefs and customs and, at least by implication, suggestions that can enrich the construction of the medical story. The physician's awareness of cultural assumptions is necessary in the care of patients from "majority" groups as well, even those with whom the physician shares ethnicity, class, and age. Muriel Gullick has written about the medical beliefs of the American middle class,[30] and Eric J. Cassell has based a philosophy of clinical care on the cognitive regression even the mature, well educated person undergoes when seriously ill.[31] These last two studies suggest that even if cultural factors are recognized and controlled, incommensurability will remain the fundamental reality of patient-physician communication. In the absence of obvious cultural barriers, the gulf between patient and physician still exists. Physicians and patients, by virtue of their roles in the illness encounter, are always engaged in the narrative construction of different realities, telling different stories about what is nominally the same malady. This is the irreducible substrate of communication in medicine.

Does this mean that patient and physician can never understand one another? Surely this predicament need not be worse for them than for other human beings. We are all always alone. Patients and physicians are only a frequently more anguished case of our common fate, the human condition caught at a critical moment. To capture the patient's experience, an attention that goes beyond the anthropological is needed. It is a storyteller's attention. Essential to healing, whatever the background of patient and physician—perhaps especially when they are remarkably similar—is the recognition that the two do not quite speak the same language. They will not tell the same story of the illness to which they turn their mutual attention. The physician especially must be aware that the patient's account of illness has its own ontological and epistemological status, apart from whatever medical translation it may undergo, and that insofar as it is practicable, this account must be recognized and represented in the case history and in the care of the patient.

A narrative view of medicine emphasizes the constructedness of the case history that is shaped in the medical interview. Such attention to the patient-physician interaction is part of an attitude toward the ill person that is healing in itself and has the homely virtue of connecting with the physician's own sense of a professional and a personal life. It grants that other human beings may be finally unknowable but it does not then turn to solipsism or narcissism. It asks, instead, to know the other person's story. The physician's focus on the healing relationship has as a secondary benefit the cultivation of a professional interest in daily practice. Alternately dulled by routine and assailed by death and the failure that death seems to imply, physicians easily become hardened to suffering, not the least their own. A narrative view of medicine—the recognition, first, that the patient is the source of narrative unsubsumed by the medical case and, second, that the case is a medical construct rather than a natural object—can help preserve physicians' understanding of medicine's healing activity and their appreciation of the intersection of their lives and the lives and deaths of their patients.

Re-storying the Patient

The third narrative act of healing is the physician's return of the story to the patient, an acknowledgment that no medical story—not even chronic illness or impending death—is a life story. Here, as the medical interpretation is related to the patient, the incommensurability of the two stories is most evident, and the physician's failure to recognize the differences between them can result in any number of small—but to the patient earth-shattering—miscommunications. Although the stories arise from the same physical phenomena, no neutral language can encompass them both. The differences in plot and closure affect so ordinary an exchange as the concluding interaction between patient and physician in a routine office visit. At this point physician and patient express some common understanding about what is wrong, the degree of its seriousness, and what each of them is to do next. The physician declares what in the medical view has caused the symptoms and seeks the patient's cooperation in continued care: a prescription, a change of habits, a return visit, referral to another health professional. Whatever else may transpire, the narrative of the malady is in effect handed back to the patient. She learns the medical interpretation of the illness and, often, is persuaded to alter her own evaluation: the little lump is serious and will require further testing, perhaps surgery; the debilitating malaise is a virus that will soon be better. The patient is sometimes asked to accept the unacceptable and all too often must accept it in terms that make no sense or whose sense is unintentionally deceptive.[32] Much of the tension in medicine concerns who is to tell the story of the patient's malady. The pain caused by a poorly returned narrative runs contrary to the profession's commitment to serve the ill. It is the source of much of the contemporary societal dissatisfaction with medicine.

As an investigation in which hypotheses are shaped by the fact, clinical diagnosis resembles in its method the work of anthropologists. In describing the latter, Barney G. Glaser and Anselm L. Strauss set out the principle that results must be returned to those who were its object.[33] This is not only a matter of ethics but of adequacy and reliability. Such sound reasons hold for medicine as well as other human sciences. In rare instances, the investigator may have gotten it wrong. The patient's experiential account tests the diagnosis and the plan of treatment, just as an anecdote tests clinical rules, and on rare but important occasions alters them. Strong therapeutic reasons also support the return of the story to the patient. He or she has sought help in the form of information, advice, and care from another human being; now the physician gives an account of all that has been learned and all that can be done to remedy the matter.

The narrative that is returned to the patient is the medical one, which has appropriated and replotted the patient's story in its own prescribed, conventional way. Like all medical narratives, its conclusion is consistent with that plot: the quest for the proximate cause of the patient's distress ends with a diagnosis and recommendations for treatment. The patient has the task of integrating this medical ending into that story of the experience of illness, and this task may be accomplished more or less skillfully—or not at all. In this closing exchange, the incommensurability of narratives surfaces again, and if the two are too widely disparate and the physician fails to recognize the distance between them, the interaction founders. The medicine will go untaken, the consultation unsought, the prescription unfilled. Little in medical training prepares the physician to see the patient's narrative as a separate reality and not merely the primitive version of a freshly established medical truth, yet this is precisely what must take place if two narratives are to be accommodated. For the physician not to recognize the existence of the two narratives and their incommensurability is to risk patients' leaving unconvinced and uncooperative, "noncompliant" or even more isolated and suffering than when they arrived.

Physicians have a strong and enduring stake in the incommensurability of the two stories because it protects them from the suffering experienced by patients. Not only is the medical version quickly constructed to take the place of the story of illness, but, beyond the initial chief complaint, patients' firsthand reports of the subjective experience of illness are not themselves a part of the medical record. In the medical version that suffering is the prescientific given, the very thing that is to be investigated. What the patient has experienced comes to be a minor part of the case as it is constructed by the physician.

In turn, patients are shielded by custom from medical stories. Long before the contemporary anxiety over malpractice suits, physicians concealed their medical records from patients as not suitable for their sensibilities. The medical version, in this view, is the real story, the truth from which ill people must be sheltered. Even today, when truth telling has become a professional standard and is an essential part of eliciting the patient's informed consent to treatment, the custom of closed records continues. Physicians prefer to return the story to the patient at a moment and in words of their own choosing. Social custom prescribes these opportunities: at the close of the office visit with the patient dressed again, and perhaps in the physician's office if the news is serious or, these days, if the malady is routine, more quickly at the end of the physical examination. The daily hospital visit by the attending physician is another such occasion and was long before rules about Medicare billing were invented. Indeed, in a teaching hospital, a summary of the medical story for the patient may be the major purpose of the attending physician's visits, for residents have assumed the actual care of the patient. Such control of the narrative is not simply arrogance, for the act of returning the story properly involves its reinterpretation in the terms of the patient's experience: "It looks as if the incision is having a hard time closing, but you'll still be out of here by Friday." Were patients to read their charts or listen to the presentation of their cases, not only might they find it difficult to recognize themselves among the physiological details, but even the medically knowledgeable would be likely to feel chilled by their caretakers' external, "clinical" view. The patient has become the object rather than the subject of a narrative of medical attention. The chart, the case presentation, and the published case report make no accommodation to the patient's experience and ignore its incommensurability with the medical version they present. In those forms the patient's account of the experience of illness is objectified, stripped of emotive power, all but unrecognizable. Custom protects patients from this cold, objective view of themselves.

Ultimately, however, the objective view must be returned to the patient and entered into the life narrative it came from: it does seem to be bowel cancer, but it's not hopeless. Although the physician-patient relationship depends upon the transformation of the patient's story into medical terms, its healing power does not reside in the medical story itself. The therapeutic use of that story is essential; for healing requires not just the power of specialized knowledge but the return of the medical interpretation to the world of action, both in the form of a therapeutic decision and in its careful retelling to the patient. The physiological intervention licensed by the interpretation is essential, but alone it is seldom enough. For life or death—for an uneventful, unnarratogenic close or the opening chapter of the last section of a life story—the rewritten, replotted account of illness must restored to the patient, re-storying the ill person. An attempt must be made to reconcile the clinical view with the patient's experience of illness and sense of life. However incommensurable the patient's and the physician's accounts, this return of the story to the patient is a powerful part of the therapeutic relationship, and the physician's recognition of their incommensurability goes a long way toward overcoming its potential side effects.

A concern with the patient's life story works against medicine's customary sense of narrative closure. Georg Lukács's comparison of the function of narrative plot and scientific theory, each guiding "the dialectical movement from concrete reality to abstract representation and back to conscious participation in reality's progressive tendencies,"[34] can apply as well to the whole of medical care as to the quest for a diagnosis. The "concrete reality," the phenomena to which the plot must faithfully return, is made up not only of the patient's body but the patient's story. In the diagnostic circle, it is not the disease but the patient's account of the experience of illness that generates the diagnostic quest and refines the differential diagnosis. The interpreted and replotted story must be returned to the person who is ill: diagnosis, prognosis, recommendations for treatment. There, tested against the subjective experience of the disease, theory enters the world of practice. Every office visit, every hospital stay requires this concluding conversation between physician and patient. It is to the patient's experience—and to the patient's understanding of that experience—that the diagnostic conclusions ultimately must be referred.

While the patient's story of illness is to the medical world a subjective version of a familiar story, to the patient it is a piece of a larger life story in which the medical interpretation of this illness must be reembedded. Good physicians acknowledge the truth that, despite the medical narrative's enormous importance, it is only one story, a part of the whole story, about the patient. It does not wholly account for or express the experience of illness embodied in the patient's account. The patient's life story may seem to be altered, perhaps shortened, by the imposition of the medical narrative, yet that more objective version does not replace who the patient is or the meaning of his or her life events. Especially in the event of a poor prognosis, a physician must acknowledge what in health can remain implicit: this bad news is not the whole story. A diagnosis is not the whole of a patient's life story, and, finally, it may have little bearing on that life's meaning.

The defamiliarization essential to the medical interpretation of the patient's subjective experience is an essential part of the knowledge and care the patient has sought. Yet once the diagnosis is made the problem of how to fit the medical interpretation to that private experience requires thought and therapeutic care. The physician's interpretation must be returned to the patient with some consciousness that, while it is not at all the patient's story it must somehow be fitted to that account of life experience. A fatal diagnosis only makes the matter more difficult. These days no one doubts the cruelty of Ivan Ilych's physician, who takes refuge in a diagnostic puzzle and refuses to return any story at all to his patient. It may be equally cruel to tell a truth that the patient is not ready to hear—"truth dumping," it has been called—or to tell it in such a language that it cannot be understood. Physicians who recognize the existence and strength of the patient's own life story and its incommensurability with the official medical account often wait for the patient's questions, rather like enlightened parents responding to a child's questions about sex, answering as they unfold. But how do physicians make themselves available for the questions that arise after the patient has gone home? And how do they make certain that they are open to such questions, particularly to the doubts and uncertainties of those who are old or shy or depressed or of a different class or ethnic group?

Some questions medicine is ill equipped to answer. Individual physicians may attempt them, but for medicine itself many of the patient's concerns are as familiar and as resistant to objective explanation as the Bororos' account of their souls' destiny to their anthropological visitors. Like that account, they embody for their tellers the meaning of the experience they relate. How illness is connected with life events and why the same disease follows a different course in different patients,[35] whether the patient bears responsibility for illness,[36] what effect fear or anger provoked by the illness may have,[37] what control (including taking prescribed medicine) the patient may exercise over the disease and its consequences[38]—on these and other themes important to patients' stories, medicine itself is largely silent.

In only the mildest of maladies do diagnosis and prescription provide closure for the patient's narrative. Luckily, for most of us, for most of our lives, these are just the encounters we have with physicians. A broken arm or a strep throat may not require the physician to attend to the experience of illness. But for all those diseases and conditions that a simple treatment does not cure, those that are serious, that linger or recur or worsen, something more than a narrowly medical interpretation is required for the patient's closure. Of the three questions Edmund D. Pellegrino and David C. Thomasma have described as essentially medical— What is the matter? What can be done? What should be done?[39]—the first two are not, first of all, questions about the life of the patient or the meaning of illness. They are questions that are answered in the medical narrative by the diagnosis of illness and the choice of an appropriate treatment. The third and equally important question—what should be done *for this patient*—must be answered in the context of the patient's life and values. Alasdair MacIntyre has argued that ethical considerations are bound up with the narrative character of human life.[40] In medicine, such consideration of the patient's life story may modify, may even determine, further testing and the choice of therapy. The narrative therapy that began when the physician elicited the patient's original account of the malady properly concludes with the physician's attention to how the patient will integrate the medical interpretation into his or her life story, what the diagnosis will mean to the person who is ill. Above all, it is necessary for the physician to acknowledge the patient's story of loss and change and its incommensurability with medicine's quite successful story of, for example, the rapid identification of a lymphoma or macular degeneration.

The return of the constructed narrative to the patient at once grants the persuasive power of the physician's role and marks its limits. Patients need more than the medical facts of their case; they need to be able to translate that knowledge into the terms of their lives. To help them achieve this is good medicine, of course. For a physician to attempt to reconcile the medical account with the personal meaning of the illness is an act of great persuasive power: advice will be more readily taken, consultations sought, medicines bought and used. As Leon Eisenberg has pointed out, even if all the recent theories about therapeutic efficacy of such attention are not proven, it is at a minimum a gesture of common decency.[41]

If narrative is healing, why have physicians so often been silent? Pedro Lain Entralgo has described the tradition of the physician's silence that extends from the death of Aristotle to, he believes, the inception of Christianity.[42] Jay Katz has argued strongly that its recent manifestations are a controlling exercise of power.[43] Modern medicine differs from ancient Hippocratic practice both in its capacity to cure and in its equally important commitment to care for those it cannot cure. It is not knowledge or therapeutic power that calls for narrative but our sense of all we do not yet know about human illness and our care of the chronically ill and dying. These last require the silence to be broken.

A wise clinician's advice to beginning physicians on communicating with their patients might bear a strong resemblance to the advice given the young narrator of Albert Murray's "Train Whistle Guitar." Little Mister and his best friend have jumped a freight, meaning to leave their small town in the Depression South to join up with their hero, Luzana Cholly, a traveling man, decorated in World War I, guitarist and gambler, teller of tales and doer of deeds. To their surprise, Luzana Cholly sets the boys firmly on a train headed back home with strong words about the benefits of schooling. His parting words address the problems of all those placed at risk by an incommensurability of discourse:

> And then he was talking about Negroes and white folks again, and he said the young generation of Negroes were supposed to be like Negroes and be like white folks too and still be Negroes. He sat looking out across the water then, and then we heard another freight coming and he got up and got ready and he said we could watch him but we'd better not try to follow him.[44]

Murray's hero gives us a model for the right relation between general biomedical rules and the particular circumstances of illness. It is an epitome of the physician's threefold task: to acknowledge the subjective experience, to reconstruct it as a medical version that can be matched to taxonomic abstractions and explicated with biomedical laws, and, returning that interpretation to the patient, still to understand and affirm the life narrative of which it is now a part.

EIGHT

A CASE FOR NARRATIVE

*"You have perhaps erred in attempting to put colour and life
into each of your statements, instead of confining yourself
to the task of placing upon record that severe reasoning
from cause to effect which is really the only
notable feature about the thing."
(Sherlock Holmes to Dr. Watson,
"The Adventure of the Copper Beeches")*

ARLY IN HIS ILLNESS, Tolstoy's Ivan Ilych recognizes in his physician the "new method" he has perfected for himself as an examining magistrate. In that office he "acquired a method of eliminating all considerations irrelevant to the legal aspect of the case, and reducing even the most complicated case to a form in which it would be presented on paper only in its externals, completely excluding his personal opinion of the matter, while above all observing every prescribed formality." Now, with his physician, there is

> the sounding and listening, and the questions which called for answers that
> were foregone conclusions and were evidently unnecessary, and the look of
> importance which implied that "if only you put yourself in our hands we will
> arrange everything—we know indubitably how it has to be done, always in
> the same way for everybody alike." It was all just as it was in the law courts.
> The doctor put on just the same air towards him as he himself put on to-
> wards an accused person.[1]

Although impartiality and restraint in the new bureaucratic administration of power are preferable to bribe-taking and favoritism, we are meant to see the deficits of the "new method" for Ivan Ilych—first as a person who practices it and then, once he is ill, as the victim of such cool professionalism in its medical form. Patients need more than diagnoses, and to supply their need physicians must have richer case narratives than the traditional medical case history.

Narrative shapes clinical judgment. In medical practice, the vast body of knowledge about human biology is applied to the patient analogically through narratives of the experience of comparable instances. The capacity to provide good medical care depends upon both the physician's stock of clinical stories and an understanding of how they are (or are not) relevant to this particular case. Maxims and rules are absorbed during clinical training, just as the principles of the biomedical sciences are memorized in the first two years of medical school. But despite the increased specificity of practice-based maxims, their applicability is still often uncertain. As in other case-based inquiry—law, moral theology, criminal detection—judgment in medicine is shaped (and the relativism of the individual interpretation of principle controlled) by comparing the narrated circumstances of the present case with others of more or less the same kind.

The prevalence of narrative in medicine suggests that this case-based, experiential way of knowing is well accepted in clinical practice, even if its implications are seldom acknowledged. Ethical decisions are made in much the same case-based way, and as a consequence, philosophers fresh from the classroom in the early days of the bioethics movement were frustrated at what seemed to be physicians' ignorance or unconsciousness of the overarching principles that guided their ethical decision making. They soon learned the strength of case-based deliberations. Not surprisingly, the recent defense of the philosophical position of casuistry has been undertaken by philosophers working in medicine and influenced by the methods used in the work of their clinical colleagues.[2] Medicine, as Leon Kass has observed, is a fertile ground for understanding "the moral relation between knowledge or expertise and the concerns of life."[3]

The construction of the case history is an integral part of medical thinking, essential to clinical education and to making decisions about the care of an individual patient. But good decisions about patient care beyond the diagnosis call for a richer narrative than the traditional medical case. In an era dominated by chronic disease, a physician's narrative stock should include not only clinical cases, which traditional medical education provides, but also a practical knowledge of human character and life patterns for both the well and the ill. In addition to an encyclopedic, Sherlock Holmesian knowledge of pathological cases, physicians need a literary sense of the lives in which illness and medical care take place. In the past twenty-five years medical thinkers have sought to broaden the practitioner's understanding of the individual case. Whether by increasing the number and kind of "facts" regarded as relevant to the grasp of a case, by organizing what is observed into a more coherent chronicle, or by attending to narrative shape and subtleties of representation, these critics have expanded and enriched the concept of the "case" itself. Taken together, they are working toward reshaping the medical narrative. Their arguments have met with only mixed success at a time when medical practice has been altered by technology and economic constraints. Yet these pressures only make more necessary a richer sense of patients and their life choices. Physicians feel strongly the danger of becoming mere technicians. Whether they treat patients in brief, almost anonymous encounters or take care of the chronically ill, intellectual and moral support for patient care can be found in the "color and life" of enriched case narrative. A larger sense of the patient's story enlivens the everyday practice of medicine and improves the quality of attention given to the person who is ill.

The Shield of Achilles

In the midst of the *Iliad* Homer interrupts the progress of the war to describe the making of a new shield for Achilles. It is a narrative digression that (among other things) is itself about narrative art. Because the besieged Trojans have driven the Greeks back to their ships, Achilles has allowed his friend Patroclus to go into battle disguised in the armor Achilles inherited from his father. Patroclus has been slain by Hector and his body and the armor have been taken captive. Grief-stricken and enraged, Achilles is ready at last to return to battle, and his mother, the nymph Thetis, persuades Hephaistos, "smith of the strong arms," to forge new armor for her son. At this turning point in the war Homer gives us a long digressive account of the wonders of the god's creation. The shield is marvelous. Homer describes it as "fivefold," five layers thick, but it is easy to imagine that the phrase might mean five layers folded like pages, for the whole world is represented there. First is the physical universe:

> earth, heaven, and sea,
> unwearied sun, moon waxing, all the stars
> that heaven bears for garland.
> (XVIII, 557–560, trans. Robert Fitzgerald)

Next are two cities, one at peace, celebrating weddings and adjudicating a blood quarrel; the other at war, besieged like Troy, refusing a treaty, attempting an ambush, breaking into open battle. As Homer describes them, these are not still scenes but moving pictures, full of action. They are eventful slices of narratable life. Only with difficulty can we anchor such descriptions to static representation on the surface of a shield, and as readers immersed in the narrative we do not try. It seems right that this visual representation convey action over time; it is, after all, a god's handiwork.

Cosmology and politics are not the shield's only themes nor, evidently, has Hephaistos begun to fill the available space. He adds a field being plowed, the gathering of a king's wheat, and the preparation by the people of a celebratory feast. Elsewhere, an irrigated vineyard is harvested by singing children; cattle in a pasture are surprised by a pair of lions; shepherds not far away tend their sheep in a quiet valley. Last, there is a dancing floor where young men and women link arms, moving effortlessly in a circle, and all around the shield's rim runs the circle of the mighty ocean stream.

Here in the midst of the *Iliad*'s account of bravery, death, and loss we find a full, richly detailed representation of human life, and, moreover, it is a part of what we might have expected to be a simple piece of military equipment. The digression's unexpected length and its intrusion on the principal action of the epic suggest the importance of the shield and its art. Despite Achilles's renown and his connection with the gods, the scenes represent small, ordinary events. They are the life out of which the story of the *Iliad* arises. Their representation of the whole of human experience places war and the epic poem itself in a larger context of human activity, and we are led to feel that this representation is a part of the protection offered to the hero returning to battle.

The shield is an epitome of narrative and its representation of human life. Works of art generally give us intellectual pleasure by representing to us the things that are not. These are not lies, of course, but fiction: true accounts of the way things would be, if only we had experienced them in just this way. In the ninth year of the Trojan War, Hephaistos paints enameled pictures of a besieged, chaotic city and a peaceful, orderly one. We recognize Troy in the one and are reminded, perhaps reassured, that, outside the *Iliad*, the other still exists. Beyond is the countryside at peace where life is marked by (and stories are part of) the regular events of the seasons—plowing, harvest, festival. There nature and art provide all that is narratable: lions rampage; one boy among the happy grape harvesters sings "a summer dirge"; two tumblers handspring across the circle of the "magical" dance.

The representative wholeness of Hephaistos's creation, which might be a metaphor for all art for all of us, seems to have a special relevance for physicians. Literature in particular constitutes a source of knowledge. For those to whom the experiences are familiar, narrative is confirming; for those reading about something new, the view of human possibility is enlarged. This is especially useful for physicians and for medical students. Their education often proceeds as if the practice of medicine were only a science and not also a social enterprise subject to cultural and emotional variants. Illness is assumed to be an inhuman evil, death is wrong, and medicine's task is simply described: to restore the sick to health, preventing or at least forestalling death. There are few sick people and no physicians at all in medical textbooks and none of the human experience that gives illness and the practice of medicine their meaning. "Cure sometimes, relieve often, comfort always." Only the old maxim, more often read than heard these days, exists as a reminder of medicine's role in the face of the entropic reality of human life.

Literature and Medicine

Where does medicine look for an understanding of its activities and its values? What is the source of its ideas about its place in the sum of human activity? In its confidence in its knowledge and the significance of that knowledge, the medical profession emulates early twentieth-century positivist physical scientists rather than the social scientists and the humanists whose work physicians' work more nearly resembles. The human sciences, by contrast, have begun to study themselves obsessively. Anthropology and sociology puzzle over how other human beings can be reliably understood, and historians are absorbed by the impossibility of separating the event from its telling. Social science generally has been gripped by debate over its suspension, like quantum mechanics, between the knower and what is known. Literary scholars approach their texts armed with theories of reading, writing, and knowing, and philosophers debate not only the foundations of knowledge but their very possibility. Medicine, however, has remained turned resolutely outward toward the "real world."

Medicine cannot of itself address questions of its meaning or the meaning of illness. This is not a part of its province as it is currently conceived, but is rather the province of religion, the humanities, and the values-oriented social sciences. Philosophers, historians, and sociologists have studied medicine as they have studied science, and these studies include valuable descriptions of what medicine is and does. Although many literary critics find inadequate the view that literature provides an unmediated record of social reality, it is nevertheless a vivid means of understanding the physician's often quite lonely job, the hard work of nursing the desperately ill, the patient's experience of illness, the process of dying. Fiction, poetry, and drama all offer medicine their visions of human experience. Within its representation of the full range of human possibility, we may see how doctoring, being sick, and learning to heal fit into the whole.

Literature and medicine are distinguished from most other studies of humankind by the particular account they give of individual experience. Just as literary criticism can be abstract, so can medical knowledge, especially in its textbook form; but as medicine, it has meaning only in its applicability to the individual case. The medical case history, like literary narrative, can be about only one set of circumstances at a time. Medicine has its origin—in several senses—in the patient's presentation to medical attention, and it has its end—also in more than one sense—in the treatment of that sick person. Like literature, the medical case history embodies the attention medicine accords the individual. The case history concerns instances that at once test our generalizations about human beings and embody the aggregate of human experience.

Reading about Patients

This particularization of widespread experience is easily seen in contemporary stories about illness. In recent years, the patient's story of "my operation" has gathered force in a flood of books and articles. There are a few traditional plays and stories in which illness plays an essential part—the Book of Job, Sophocles's *Philoctetes* come to mind. But only recently, as we have begun to live long enough to fall victim to chronic disease, have very many stories been written to examine illness as the individual experiences it. Thomas Mann's *The Magic Mountain* is in some ways the model of the genre, yet in that novel the hero is distanced from the narrator and both are distanced from the author; its story becomes a metaphor for a sick society. The contemporary narrative of illness in the United States is instead a midlife version of the growing-up novel. Hero-narrator and author are collapsed into one figure in an autobiographical (or autobiographically fictional) account of an individual's growth in circumstances not of his or her choosing.

The lack of choice compels our attention. As medicine has become central to our understanding of what it means to be human in an unreligious, technocratic time, a voracious public appetite has developed for medical narrative: fiction, autobiography, reportage, played out in drama. These stories are about the failure of control and the threat of extinction. They enable us to think about the value society places on a human life, about the meaning of pain, the definition of the person, the limits of even an American autonomy, and our attitudes toward authority, choice, chance, and the death of the individual. Much of our public discourse, even before the AIDS epidemic, concerned disease and medical care. Fleshed out with "human interest" detail, case narrative has become the stuff of the well publicized adventures of transplantation teams. It is a mainstay of television's daily dose of hospital crisis and intrigue. Pathographies of the seriously ill have become a subgenre of contemporary biography.[4] Issues of health-care policy are debated and necessarily have their legal manifestation not in the abstract realm of public policy but as individual cases. Names of individual people come to stand for issues— and now and then for their resolution: Dax Cowart, Karen Ann Quinlan, Baby Jane Doe, Elizabeth Bouvier, Rock Hudson, Baby M., Nancy

Cruzan. Medical cases are often the germ of fiction and, especially, drama. Brian Clark's *Whose Life Is It Anyway?*,[5] which stirred public discussion of unwanted life-sustaining medical treatment, was very probably inspired by the 1975 discussion of Cowart's case by Robert White and H. Tristram Engelhardt, Jr., in the *Hastings Center Report*.[6] In 1985 Larry Kramer's *The Normal Heart*[7] and William Hoffman's *As Is*[8] gave their newly alarmed off-Broadway audiences a glimpse of the human and political costs of ignoring AIDS. We look to such accounts of illness to tell us who we are as a society. Their crises concern the exercise of individual rights, the problem of balancing conflicting interests in decision making, and the allocation of resources that our political choices have made scarce. In their imaginative exploration of the ordinary person's opportunity for self-definition and even for heroism, they depict for us a boundary condition of our humanity.

These stories and plays and autobiographies are based on what are, at other times and places, with other narrators, plain, stripped-down medical case histories. They go beyond the conventions of medical storytelling to supply plots and themes missing from medical narrative. Indeed, pathographies, especially first-person narratives of fatal illness, seem to have been written by patients precisely to supply those things that the case history rigorously excludes. Many of them are quite forthright about this motive. They write not simply to supply that lack for us as readers (although, having few other ways to think about the unthinkable, we are morbidly curious about fatal diagnoses) but primarily to repair the loss to themselves. As Eric Cassell has pointed out, suffering is quite distinct from pain and even from dying, and, although the goal of medicine is the relief of suffering, many patients suffer not from their disease but from their medical treatment.[9] Pathographies address and sometimes seek to avenge the damage done by medical care to their bodies, care that took no care of them. They tackle complex questions of human suffering and response to illness, the difficulties and hopes of the doctor-patient relationship, the acceptance or rejection of medical therapy, and the meaning of illness in the life of the person who is ill. In so doing, they bring to bear on the medical "facts" of the case assumptions broader than rigorously scientific ones about causality and consequence in the course of human illness.

Physicians' familiarity with patients' stories may ultimately enrich their understanding of medical cases, but pathography cannot substitute for case narrative. However valuable pathography may be, its focus is on the patient rather than the disease. The case, by contrast, serves an essential diagnostic purpose, and for this purpose its narrowness makes sense. It orders the messy and confusing details of experience and filters out clinical "irrelevancies." It promotes medicine's focus on—indeed, its obsession with—the particular in the care of patients, for it serves as a constant reminder that not all cases of the same kind are actually the same. It clarifies medical intervention by preserving the physician's awareness of the problematic relation between general laws and a particular circumstance. It encourages a tolerance of uncertainty by providing the means of recording and memorializing exceptions to the rule. For all these reasons, case narrative is central to the epistemology as well as to the practice of medicine. It is a construct of that epistemology, necessary to rational investigation in a domain where subjective experience (and subjective accounts of that experience by another person) are the original and grounding data of clinical care. As patient history, narrative makes possible the communication of one human being's experience to another and underlines its status as mediated fact: it is often the best we have to go on. As the account of a patient's course of illness, the case narrative's representation of change through time is an essential tool of clinical reasoning, facilitating the comparison and contrast of developing patterns. Narrative accommodates the uncontrolled, uncontrollable variables of the individual circumstance, making possible a clinical flexibility that dare not ossify into inalterable rules. Scientifically it fosters a fidelity to the phenomena and a recognition that they are the final arbiters of the explanatory power of the principles themselves. Pedagogically, narrative encourages and improves clinical judgment by making possible a kind of practical, clinical knowledge that mediates biological principles and the facts of the particular clinical case.

Nevertheless, in any situation but acute emergency care—and sometimes even there—the traditional medical case is restrictive, limiting the practice of medicine and the care of patients to diagnosis and prescription. Just as that narrative hones clinical judgment, so fiction and pathography enlarge the physician's awareness of the human problems that are the context of disease and injury. Knowledge of cases sharpens the awareness of clinical possibilities; knowledge of life stories helps cultivate attention to patients, an interest in their oddities and their ordinariness— and a tolerance of both. Especially in primary-care practice, this interest and attention can be vital. John Berger in his portrait of a physician, *A Fortunate Man*, describes the daily rounds of a general practitioner in the north of England. By the standards of a resident in a North American tertiary-care hospital, the array of illness this village physician sees is grindingly "uninteresting."[10] Its only distinction from a general practice anywhere at all lies in the recent decline in the region's standard of living as industry has departed. What fascinates the physician (and thus the narrator and his readers) is the role he plays in his patients' lives: for them he is the "requested clerk of their records."[11] It is a historical, even a literary task. He is not simply a bystander in the unfolding story of their lives. He knows the hard truths. He understands something of what goes wrong in their lives. William Carlos Williams, fascinated by his own quite ordinary patients, admitted, "my 'medicine' was the thing which gained me entrance to these secret gardens of the self."[12] But fewer physicians these days have such a practice, and, although "continuity of care" has been a medical buzzword off and on for more than two decades, few schools set out to prepare their students to understand its pleasures.

Is reading autobiography and fiction necessary to the formation of this narrative sensibility? The wisdom and sensitivity of experienced physicians may have been gathered without benefit of literature through a lifetime of careful attention to patients. But what are young practitioners to do before they have acquired a store of cases on which to found a sustaining overview of life? And what are middle-aged physicians to do when the physical consequences of bad luck and folly and human evil lead them to harden themselves to the life stories of their patients? Physicians turn to professional journals for accounts of difficult or unusual cases and new developments that offer hope of altering the plots in old stories of disease. Likewise, in fiction, autobiography, and drama they can broaden their knowledge of human beings not only beyond the textbooks in human behavior but beyond the ethnic and chronological limits of their own experience. The physician who has read Tolstoy's *The Death of Ivan Ilych*, for instance, has imagined a patient's unwilling slide toward death. He or she is also able to entertain the possibility that the horrors of illness are not entirely physical; an apparently self-possessed, successful, now terminally ill patient may lack the support of family and friends, but in some sense may have before him the discovery of an authentic life. Years of practice may provide wisdom to equal this awareness, but, unrelieved and unassessed, those years may also callous the physician who has "seen it all."

To cultivate practical wisdom in the diagnosis and treatment of patients, physicians are taught to employ a narratively mediated casuistry. The residencies are long apprenticeships that at once foster the accumulation of a large number of cases and guide the new physician in their judicious use. Most physicians, especially those who enter primary-care practice, extend this case-based reasoning beyond diagnosis and treatment to judgment about the people who are ill and how best to provide effective care. To some degree, physicians are prepared for this by attention given during their education to "case management."[13] To increase this preparation, the Association of American Medical Colleges' 1984 report on the general professional education of the physician, *Physicians for the Twenty-First Century* (the GPEP Report) calls for, among other things, more experience in ambulatory care.[14] Such exposure gives students an opportunity to begin to acquire a fuller collection of cases, one that takes into account the vagaries—economic, social, psychological—of the human beings who are ill. For effective and satisfying practice, a collection of life histories is needed. Years of experience taking care of patients may foster the clinical wisdom necessary to handle difficult cases well, but meanwhile for physicians, as for all of us, the vicarious experience offered by narrative increases familiarity with the range of human character and the life outside office and hospital to which medicine aims to restore them.

In particular, literature is a source of knowledge about the operation of values through time. Just as medical narrative is the repository of much of the professional ethos learned by students and residents, so narrative generally—biography, fiction, history—shapes moral sensibility and models clinical distance. Several recent works by physicians make this point. Robert Coles's recent book, *The Call of Stories: Teaching and the Moral Imagination,* extends the argument of his 1979 *New England Journal of Medicine* essay, "Medical Ethics and Living a Life," to argue the centrality of narrative in moral education.[15] In the earlier essay, which addresses the moral life of physicians, he distinguishes ethical reflection from its more academic cousin, ethical analysis, and recommends reading novels about doctors (*Middlemarch, Arrowsmith, Wonderland*) for their account of the peril that lies in wait for the unsuspecting and, particularly, the idealistic practitioner. In *Stories of Sickness,* Howard Brody finds an even more practical role for literature in delineating the responses to illness that govern the lives of patients.[16] With an eye to developing an ethical analysis grounded in the story of the patient's life, he surveys (among other works) *Philoctetes, The Magic Mountain, The Metamorphosis,* and *Cancer Ward* to offer physicians what he sees as the best available knowledge of the experience of illness. Arthur Kleinman samples the life stories of actual patients in *The Illness Narratives,* a framed collection of mostly autobiographical accounts of the experience of chronic disease.[17] They are ordinary, sad, sometimes frustrating, often heroic, always revealing about the role of medicine and health-care practitioners in the lives of the ill. Kleinman argues persuasively that the patient's culture is one the physician must enter carefully, ethnographically, openly.

Narrative, in medicine and out, cultivates the power of observation. No one is able to observe carefully details that are not known to exist or have dropped from memory. Narrative's clinical usefulness is most obvious in constructing the history of the patient's present illness. Into what category does this illness fall, the physician asks, and does it differ in any way from the index case of its kind? What has the patient's life been? How has it contributed to this illness? How will it help or hinder recovery? The conviction that such information is important must be acquired.

It is not standard equipment that comes with a medical education. Medical students in the late-twentieth century find in Francis Peabody's 1927 essay, "The Care of the Patient," a still painfully accurate description of information overload and the neglect of the patient. But it is the actual experiences of illness in which they begin to take part that, for them, will illustrate the diagnostic and therapeutic importance of life histories and make Peabody's essay most persuasive. Familiarity with the life stories in fiction and drama fill out the range of human possibility. Many medical students, for example, have not known well a vigorous, healthy old person; outside their families few have known someone alert but steadily failing. Stereotypes abound, and narrative about the lives of the elderly— D. L. Coburn's "The Gin Game," Alice Adams's *Second Chances*—can subject them to scrutiny. William L. Morgan, Jr., has given the pages about Aunt Leonie from Proust's *Swann's Way* to his residents in internal medicine. Near ninety, she takes to her bed and from that vantage rules the family and the neighborhood. When she naps, "three streets away, a tradesman who had to hammer nails into a packing-case would send first to Françoise to make sure that my aunt was not resting."[18] "Is Aunt Leonie ill?" the residents were asked. "What should be the goals of her physician?"

A narrative view of medicine does not neglect the biomedical sciences. Instead, it adds to that scientific view a privileged humility in the care of the patient through its recognition that the larger biological story in which each human being participates moves, with or without medical attention, from birth to death. We may organize our life stories, plot them, change their course, shorten them—but their direction and the fact of their end are givens. For most of us these days disease is a small part of life—and as we move into our seventh decade, a not unexpected part. The perspective offered by this larger pattern of life-narrative can ease the expectation (held as often by physician as patient) that death can be defeated. By locating us all on the common narrative trajectory from birth to death, narrative restores the physician to the proper place in the patient's story. This larger view may offer help to the physician in thinking about and communicating prognostics: the meaning of the illness for the patient may be set by the medical meaning—the diagnosis and the customary course of treatment—but it is not confined to it. Likewise, even in chronic or fatal illnesses, the meaning of the illness is not the meaning of the patient's life. Thus hope need not always be construed as the hope of cure,[19] and therapy may be tailored to the patient's life stage and wishes.[20] Of little use is the enthusiastic athleticism that expects of every patient a no-holds-barred struggle against death or a run for the record books that is often more valuable to clinical pioneers than to their patients. Good physicians offer their patients all that is appropriate, urge them to make use of technological advances that are promising in their case, soothe fears, alleviate pain, persuade. But they do not lose sight of the lives out of which patients' choices come and into which medical therapy must intrude.

Narrative also offers physicians a way of confronting the pain of a patient's illness or loss. A physician who does not ask an elderly patient about her family because the answer may be, "There's no one; my husband died this last year," might justify the reluctance by saying that such a question will "make her sad." But such a physician has either a maimed sense of what causes sadness or a partial, perhaps rigid, sense of life patterns. The real threat is surely that the physician will feel the pain of her sadness. This is at once egocentric and much too self-deprecating: the question does not cause the sadness and may in fact do much to ease its pain. The bereaved are not all sad in the same way. Some are sad for reasons that can be addressed, some feel guilt and anger, which the physician as an arbiter of normality can render less painful. Many are stronger and healthier for having their sadness acknowledged. Physicians who read more than the bodies of their patients and are acquainted with more life stories than the ones in which they are asked to intervene are better prepared to see an individual's life as a moral trajectory and have a firmer grasp of the challenges we face at every stage of life.[21] They see more clearly the mix of pain, pleasure, and loss in most people's lives and know what, if anything, suffering may be good for. An understanding of the human condition gained from literary narrative may make it easier to meet patients' suffering with an educated innocence, an openness of observation that in itself can be some comfort to the patient. "It is difficult/ to get the news from poems," William Carlos Williams wrote, "yet men die miserably every day/ for lack/ of what is found there."[22]

By enabling us to envision the whole of life into which our lives somehow must fit, literature, like Achilles's shield, offers us a little shelter from inevitable pain. Although it was forged for his protection, neither the shield nor the representation of life's wholeness emblazoned on it can save the hero from the death he is bound for or restore his friend Patroclus to life. Achilles knows it: his mother has told him that he will not long survive Hector, and it is Hector he means to kill. The gods know it: Hephaistos acknowledges the hero's mortality even as he agrees to set to work on the shield. The shield has a problematic, even paradoxical usefulness. It alters Achilles's fate not one bit. He nevertheless cannot return to battle without it. It will cover him meanwhile, enabling him to fight again, protecting him while he goes on to meet his fate.

Like Achilles, we readers retain our vulnerability. There is no protection from death or from the loss of the people whom we love—even for those of us who become physicians. In a literal sense, the work of art, like

Achilles's shield, may be entirely useless. It serves no practical purpose in the world, but it is difficult, sometimes impossible, to return to battle without it. It sets its bearer's action in a context of meaning: violence and death are all around, but although inescapable, they are not all. The work of art shelters us meanwhile from injury and pain. Physicians, whose profession is not a protection from human suffering but a deliberate exposure to it, stand in need of that shield. Literature enables medical students and seasoned clinicians alike to face the onslaught of experience, bearing a knowledge of life that is both painfully particular and clear-sightedly whole. Reminded that the single individual has only a small part in the scheme of things, no matter how heroic, they may better equip themselves with a protecting, protected concern for those who seek their help. Literature's representation of life provides its readers a little space between themselves and the onslaught in which to see clearly both their own deeds and the lives of others.

Literature, History, and the Enrichment of the Medical Case

In recent years there have been a number of proposals for the improvement of the medical case history. Because the case is a representational narrative, a number of these proposals participate—wittingly or not—in the historiographic critique that history-writing as a whole has undergone.[23] Like historiographers of the same period, Alvan R. Feinstein addressed the futility of a quest for covering laws in his field. His 1967 *Clinical Judgment,* an epistemology of clinical data, introduced statistics into medical thinking about the individual case.[24] Applying the principles of epidemiology to the care of patients, he demonstrated that, with a given probability, particular patients can be fitted into the statistics for their condition. Without ever quite raising the question of medicine's status as a science, Feinstein's work nevertheless supplies his answer: not quite, not yet. His argument for "clinimetrics"—the "new science basic to medicine"[25]—appeals to mathematics as the foundation of scientific knowledge, but his work moves medicine toward a certainty that, while greatly improved, inevitably falls short of the predictive power of political science on election night. In 1968 Lawrence L. Weed argued that the case history as recorded in the chart was so haphazardly organized and impressionistic that it often failed to take account of physiological fact. His "problem oriented medical record," like the cliometrics movement in history writing generally, is intended to "elevate [the medical history] to the level of a scientific document."[26] Addressing the undoubted difficulty of assessing and treating multiple problems in a single case, Weed's work challenges the explanatory function of narrative. Flow charts and graphs and lists of observable phenomena replace subjective and narratively recorded impressions of change. Yet the methodologies that underlie these changes in the case history are readily recognizable, despite their scientific flavor, as those used by historians and social scientists.

In historical studies generally social history and the experience of the everyday have also gained advocates in the last twenty-five years, and medical history writing has been no different. Here and there in geriatrics and in family medicine the scope of the medical case has been widened to include the observable facts of ordinary lives. More careful attention is now given the habits and capabilities of patients and the circumstances in which disease and injuries occur. In academic hospitals psychiatric-liaison services are consulted in the care of "difficult" patients in non-psychiatric units; George L. Engel's "The Need for a New Biomedical Model" provides their bio-psycho-social manifesto.[27] Since the early 1980s, a working group in the Society for General Internal Medicine has been devoted to the study and teaching of the medical interview.[28] Holding the biomedical model so narrow as to be ultimately "unscientific," Engel has described this attention to the person who harbors the illness as the "science of the art of medicine." It also bears a strong resemblance to the historian's shift from an exclusive focus on kings and battles (or germs and surgery) to a broader sense of the arena in which historical events are shaped and played out.

Nor are the application of statistics and a wider attention to the phenomenal world all that has occurred in the epistemology of the social sciences. In the same period, history and anthropology (to name the most obvious fields) have been learning at a great rate from Continental philosophy and literary theory.[29] Provoked by new views of knowledge, these disciplines have undergone a theoretical upheaval, reassessing (among other matters) the role of narrative in the account of social reality. Can medicine do likewise? Certainly quasi-scientific improvements have not eliminated narrative from medicine; clinimetrics and cliometrics have been matched by renewed interest in the patient's experience. Like history itself, the medical case history must take account of epistemology and literary studies. What have literature and literary theory to offer?

First is the simple recognition of the existence of narrative in a scientific field. The patient's account of illness is not the only story in medicine. Literary criticism and literary theory take seriously the case history as narrative and narrative as a legitimate, thoroughly medical way of knowing. Early writing in the field of medical narrative had as its primary theme the flattening and, often, the loss of the patient's story.[30] This needed recognition badly, in literary terms, but further laments are far less effective than asking, Where does the patient's story go? What remains and how does it work? Is this the case narrative we want? These questions amount to a literary critique of medicine.

Second, literary theory enables us to recognize that, however scientific the innovations of clinical epidemiologists may be, they do not establish medicine as a "hard" science. Despite their use of mathematics and the objectification of knowledge in charts and statistical operations, the numbers are applied as they are in the social sciences, to bits of human behavior that must be counted rather than measured. Moreover, these phenomena, while generalizable, are not necessarily replicable. Clinical epidemiology has increased the precision of post hoc explanation and improved prediction and therapy, and these are invaluable contributions to the microepidemiology—and to the rationality—of clinical decision making. As a consequence, physicians are better able to apply the knowledge of human biology and the aggregate insights of epidemiology to the particular patient. But to do so they still need narrative. Thus, the aim of clinimetrics and the problem-oriented record remains the improvement of clinical narrative and the refinement of medical interpretation.

Third, literary criticism offers a means of analyzing medical narrative on its own terms. The case history is not the patient's story, nor is it meant to be. It subordinates the patient's experience to the medical reconstruction of events, rigorously ignoring the fear and bewilderment, the loss of control and the suffering that may attend the experience of illness. The patient is flattened, the narrator is almost effaced; the narrative as a whole is relentlessly passive. This is not cruelty, but what the patient has come for: an objective gaze that can establish with relative certainty what the matter is. The result is an objectifying report. But it is nevertheless a narrative, one meant to establish with relative certainty what the process—the cause and the cure—of those events may be. Rhetorically the genres of medical narrative proclaim the observer's careful attention and reliability: other observers with the same training, they assert, would observe and report just the same thing. Yet because we are accustomed to the self-presentation of the narrator that is characteristic of nonmedical narrative, we may miss in the case history a sense of that personal self. Instead, a professional self, standardized, with eccentricities erased, presents the case history and is presented by it. In mastering the case history (and thereby their profession) it is just this "objective" self that students learn to assume. An awareness of literary conventions suggests that whatever alterations are proposed, the case history cannot stray far from this narrative pattern.

Finally, in a search for a means of enriching the case history, literary criticism offers guidance in sorting through the narrative genres that have grown up around medicine, narratives that have suggested themselves as models for improving case history. Pathographies must be set aside. Although useful for the enrichment of medical sensibility, autobiography, drama, and fiction that have illness and patienthood as their theme are not practical for reshaping of the medical case precisely because they are patients' stories. Instead, we must look to versions of the physician's story. An enriched case history must retain the virtues of traditional medical form since, within its limits, the case is a clinically useful way of organizing knowledge. Along with its brevity and clarity, changes that hope to succeed must retain the case history's presentation of the physician as knower and narrator and, inevitably, a vivid jargon that normalizes the world of suffering and injustice. How to enrich the representation of the patient's experience within the constraints of the physician's narrative is the problem that remains both for medical narrative and for medical practice.[31]

Outside the confines of the case history, physicians write movingly about their care of patients. David Hilfiker,[32] Richard Peschell,[33] Julia Connelly,[34] and the recent "pathographers" of medical education[35] tell wonderful stories of the patients from whom they have learned vital lessons. Increasingly during the 1980s such accounts appeared in medical journals where they offer psychic refreshment and moral encouragement to members of a profession that has not traditionally fostered self-disclosure. Being a physician is hard work. These narratives about doctoring, especially in a time of change, are valuable for representing the subjective experience of physicians meeting difficult patients, puzzling or frightening patients, patients who may sue. Like the fiction of William Carlos Williams, Richard Selzer, and L. J. Schneiderman or the poetry of Williams and contemporaries John Stone, Dannie Abse, and Jack Coulihan, such reports "from the trenches" tell us something never included in the medical case history: the physician's thoughts and feelings about the medical encounter. Here the physician is free to speculate—still in the context of the care of a patient—about such matters as the creation of the therapeutic relationship and its effects, the interaction of mind and body, and the mutual influence of the illness and the character of the person who is ill.

But, like pathographies, these works are not case histories. Although their "facts" may be recorded in a medical chart and their form derive from the case presentation, works by physicians—essays, fiction, and poetry—characteristically define themselves against the case history. Fully as much as pathographies, they are the untold stories of medical care. In rounds such material is often communicated nonverbally: a physician's emotional response to a patient can be readily transmitted by inflection, gesture, or facial expression. Such subtlety is unscientific—not because it admits emotion, but because it affects listeners while depriving them of the data upon which the narrator's response is based. What has been the experience of the physician in caring for the patient? What has been the experience of the patient? No one doubts that, with the exception of some emergency and life-threatening situations, these questions are important to the quality of care provided the patient. Our thoroughgoing neglect of them as therapeutic data not only has been detrimental to the patient-physician relationship but has contributed to the invention of the patient-denigrating language of "crocks" and "gomers." Some inclusion or acknowledgment of the physician's subjectivity, however small, would add to the usefulness of the case history. Narratives by physicians about doctoring may persuade us that this would be an important inclusion. But in themselves they go well beyond the case history. Valuable as reflections on the work of patient care, they are not a part of it and thus cannot serve as direct models for an enriched case history.

More promising are the extended case studies of Sigmund Freud, A. R. Luria, and, recently, Oliver Sacks. As medical as they are literary, these cases set the standard for physicians' full empathic and analytical narratives of illness and treatment. They were conceived as antidotes and supplements to the standard case history so as to embody their authors' enrichment and extension of their medical fields. Freud's case studies, such as "Fragment of an Analysis of a Case of Hysteria" and "From the History of an Infantile Neurosis," laid the foundation for an understanding of the mind for the next three-quarters of a century. Indeed, we know the patients he describes so well that these works are called not by their titles or the maladies they describe but by the patients' names: Dora, the Wolf Man.[36] Freud himself recognized the amphibious nature of these studies. As he constructed the concepts of psychoanalysis, he demonstrated them with nonlinear case histories that, as he worried in the preface to "Fragment of an Analysis," might seem to be fiction rather than scientific contributions.

The need for narrative in the organization of clinical investigation has been embraced by Oliver Sacks. With the extended cases of A. R. Luria as his inspiration,[37] Sacks writes full, phenomenological narratives of people whom he sees as neurological patients, conveying to us what it is like both to live with their maladies and to interact with them. Jimmie, "the lost mariner" with severe Korsakov's syndrome, for example, has no short-term memory and no memory of the last twenty years; his need to reconstruct his world every few minutes leads Sacks to speculate on the nature of the self. The relation of disease and self is also raised by Witty Ticcy Ray, who has Tourette's syndrome; he leaves off his haldol medication on weekends to pursue his virtuosities as a rock drummer and ping-pong player.[38] Luria called such studies "romantic science" because, as attempts to capture the whole of the malady in the life of the person who is ill, they focus on the concrete individual experience—the excesses as well as the deficits—regarded as trivial by "classical science." Sacks describes his project as the restoration of a holistic neurology, the reunion of "a soulless neurology and a bodiless psychology."[39]

Here in neurology and psychiatry are full, well told narratives of an illness and its place and meaning in the patient's life, together with an account of the patient-physician interaction, and these case studies are still tied, however loosely, to the expectations of the strict medical genre. Their narrators are physicians and their quite nonfictional focus is the understanding of the sick person who is receiving medical care. Their goals are both therapeutic and cognitive: the amelioration of the patient's condition and the advancement of medical knowledge. Yet they are not themselves usable models for much of medical care. By animating both the patient and the physician-narrator and widening the focus of the storyteller's concern beyond the measurable pathophysiological details, the extended case study necessarily violates the conventions that shape and constrain the case history and control its troublesome, ineradicable subjectivity. Whether Freud's circular, exploratory narratives, Luria's "novels," or Sacks's briefer sketches—these case studies become something new and other. It is significant that these are psychoanalytic and neurological cases, accounts of patients whose maladies are not immediately life threatening nor easily cured. Their symptoms, more than those in more general medical cases at this stage of our knowledge, may be said to constitute the disease. These cases aim to be foundational in their disciplines, for in their different ways they are creating the diseases they describe. Freud explores the sources and meaning of "hysteria," describing the workings of the mind and establishing diagnostic criteria and a psychomechanical explanation for a range of hitherto uncharted emotional maladies. Luria and Sacks acquaint us with the oddities of neurological malfunction, domesticating maladies that are exacerbated by a general misunderstanding of their symptoms and the patient's behavior.

It is in finding larger themes than the diagnosis and treatment of a particular patient that these case studies set an impossible standard for the everyday, working narrative of patient care. Indeed, how many cases like Dora's or Witty Ticcy Ray's can be written? Not only is time too short in the day-to-day care of patients, but the story now has been told. These are the index cases, and, as with the classic accounts of a disease of the heart or kidneys, the phenomenon is now established. Only if there are new developments that call for new interpretations are these cases "reopened"[40] or additional cases written about the malady. Like fiction and autobiography about illness and doctoring, such foundational case studies broaden our understanding of patients and medical practice. Yet their comprehensive, exploratory, subjective method remains anathema to many physicians, for they represent the very tendencies that the strict conventions of the case history are meant to control.

The Subjectivity of Physician and Patient

Case narrative is tolerated grudgingly in medicine because it enables clinicians to describe the nonlinear, subjective, and uncertain aspects of their experimental field. But, as the profession's prohibition against anecdotes recognizes, narrative that bursts the generic constraints of the strict case history, especially narrative of any length and fullness or speculative force, inevitably pulls against medicine's commitment to the objective, scientific study of human illness. The medical case history is, after all, a history: a narrative that attempts both to control the subjectivity of the observer-narrator and to stabilize and evaluate the encapsulated narrative of the patient who is its object.

How, then, can case narrative be enriched without doing violence to its acknowledged value in the care of patients? It is necessary to enrich it and not to replace or overwhelm it (as the patient's story might) or to so enlarge it that it cannot be a useful part of everyday medicine. What is needed is a simple, compact means of moving away from the illusion it fosters of objectivist, scientific reportage and toward an acknowledgment that it is a human and humanly constructed account. Two things are essential: first, both tellers and listeners must recognize the narrator of the case history as contextually conditioned, and, second, the lived experience of the patient must be acknowledged.

Some progress toward the first of these, the recognition of the case as narrated by an individual with a history and a social context, has been made in psychiatry. Following Jacques Lacan, some theoreticians of psychiatry have adopted a narrative, "constructed" conception of both the patient's illness and the psychiatrist's therapeutic reworking of the patient's story. Roy Schafer has argued that psychological theory—especially the principles of Freudian psychomechanics—be set aside in favor of a careful description of the clinical work of psychoanalysis: its narrative construction of both a personal past and a "present subjective world."[41] Such a subjective construal of reality by psychotherapist and patient is central to the distinction Donald Spence draws in his book on therapeutic interaction, *Narrative Truth, Historical Truth*.[42] This "antitheoretical" theory of psychoanalytical knowledge has been put to work

on a practical level as well: James Hillman has described teaching narrative method to psychoanalysts as a way of improving their grasp of both
the analysand's life story and the unfolding of the therapeutic interaction
in which it is constructed.[43]

Many of these insights have been introduced into the specialty of family medicine, whose residency education customarily includes a rotation
in psychiatry. In an effort to ground their designation as "family" physicians in something firmer than the care of clusters of related patients,
family physicians are encouraged to construct genograms representing a
patient's family and to take a brief "life history." They may be members
of a Balint group, where they discuss their responses to patients, and
"counter-transference" is more likely than in other specialties to be a familiar term.[44] It is not uncommon to hear family medicine residents introduce a case at grand rounds with a brief account of their feelings about
the patient and the course of medical care: "I've gotten really involved
with this case," one may say, or "This patient has been difficult to take
care of." Given this narrative frame, the interaction of physician and
patient and "management" problems such as the care of the dying, conflict with family members, or the refusal of treatment are more likely to be
discussed.

The second requirement for an enriched, workable case history is that
it acknowledge the patient's reality. Renato Rosaldo has argued that
"depth" of understanding is not only a matter of "complexity," that favorite academic attribute, but also is associated with the more emotive
quality he calls "force."[45] It may be that physicians need not untangle the
strands of their patients' lives in order to understand them; some degree
of imaginative participation in their plight could be enough. Anatole
Broyard may be missing something like this when he says, "I would like
my doctor to spend five minutes meditating on my case."[46] Physicians
might replace the often overmedicalized and now often useless "chief
complaint" with a comparable "existential complaint." The answer to
"How are things with you, Ms. Ferrier?" could be recorded like the chief
complaint used to be, in the patient's sometimes quite revealing own
words. The objection has always been that there is no time, and certainly
this is often the case in tertiary-care hospitals, where work loads are
heavy and survival is often at stake. There, at the locus of late twentieth-
century medical education, only spare and purely diagnostic case histories need apply. Yet fuller narratives that may be unwieldy in the hospital
by their broad focus have an instructive place outside the hospital where,
after all, most medicine—even in rushed and harried subspecialties—is
practiced. Certainly in an era of chronic disease students and residents
need preparation for the care and understanding of sick people.

The search for a workable case narrative is likely to spread. Psychiatry and family medicine are "special" specialties focused on long-term care and therefore (logically if not quite necessarily) on the patient. Increasingly other specialties are turning their investigation to the nature of illness in the individual patient, particularly in general internal medicine and geriatrics and in behavioral and developmental pediatrics. One of their common concerns is the interview, the origin of the case history and the occasion of its construction. There the patient's story is told and the physician begins, first with questions and then with the physical examination, to plot the medical interpretation of the phenomena the patient has presented and reported. Incommensurable though these accounts may be, they are present there together and have a strong shaping effect on one another. Such matters as open-ended questions not answerable by yes or no, the relative and symbolic physical positioning of doctor and patient, and patterns of eye contact, verbal interruption, and breathing patterns contribute to the success or failure of the interview and are open to investigation and instruction.[47] Among the most valuable strategies for patient-centered interviewing are questions about motivation and meaning, questions customarily regarded as literary. George Engel's questions— "Who is there at home?" and "How is that for you?"—are excellent keys to a patient's life situation. These concerns enable the physician to construct a case history that acknowledges matters literature has traditionally taken for its themes: courage, loneliness, anger, alienation, fear of death. In his study of the physician-patient interaction, *Talking with Patients*, Eric J. Cassell adds three other matters of importance: "The patient's definition of the problem, the solution(s) which, from the patient's point of view, would be adequate, and the methods employed by the patient to cope with the illness."[48] William Donnelly's recent call to return the case history from Weedian chronicle to narrative proposes that residents add to their history of the present illness a sentence or two describing "the patient's understanding of the illness and how that illness [is] affecting the patient's life."[49]

Can such concerns be integrated into the case history and into the day-to-day practice of medicine? The goal is not fiction, but an attention to patients that is at once enriched and shielded by the physician's knowledge of life stories and their themes. Such attention will result in better, even more expeditious care, a patience with patients, and a pleasure, now often missing, in the practice of medicine. The patient-centered interview with its few well chosen questions about the patient's life circumstance and the meaning of the present illness is both more probingly diagnostic and more therapeutic than much of current "history-taking." Often it is just what is needed by a patient who was coping well enough with the same symptoms last week. Along with an appreciation of the role of narrative in medicine and the growing awareness of the case history as a narrative genre, the patient-centered interview resists the enchantment of technology and goes a long way toward remedying the neglect of the sick person that has marred late twentieth-century medical care.

Sherlock Holmes and Medical Narrative

For 150 years, as human beings have conquered infectious disease, the literary genre that has most resembled the case history has been the detective story. The archetypes of the genre, the Sherlock Holmes adventures, were written by a physician. The detective story is not a narrative of illness, but like the physician, the detective seeks to identify the nature of apparently random evil in the world in order to eliminate it. The semiotics of detection are precisely those of medicine. Except in emergencies, Sherlock Holmes receives those who need his help in his rooms. He hears their stories, observes them and the physical evidence they present carefully, even microscopically, and asks pertinent if sometimes unexpected questions. Then he sets about solving the mystery, identifying the criminal and replotting the unknown agent's mode of action. Dr. Watson, like an amiable, eager resident, keeps the records from which he organizes and presents the case. At first, like a student or an intern, he is confused and left woefully behind, but, like them, he attends to "the method" and improves with time. The stories he writes about Sherlock Holmes's adventures resemble the case presentation, narratives of investigation and interpretation. The narrator in each genre has the task of telling us both "who done it" and how the puzzle was solved. Holmes's ratiocination bears a strong resemblance to clinical reasoning. Each is a comparative process operating through time, and this dialectic of discovery and understanding is well suited to narrative representation. With their purposeful, chronological organization of particular events, both medical and detective narratives mediate the application of a body of professional generalities. The signs and clues of the individual case are seen to unfold according to pathophysiological or criminological principles. The signs match the descriptions of disease distilled in textbooks or the crimes catalogued in Holmes's vast memory of hundreds of cases, and they bear out the rules of thumb developed in the practice of the respective art. The plot that emerges from the investigation is the diagnosis: a narrative reconstruction and explication of a subjectively reported sequence of events whose signs have been scrutinized and interpreted by an expert. Both Holmes's reconstruction of the crime and the physician's of the disease are working stories, essential to the understanding of the case. Their investigative reconstruction not so much proves as narratively demonstrates what the matter has been.

But the detective story has its limitations, and these, too, are very like those of the case history. Indeed, the case history stands in much the same relation to the full and thematically rich narratives of illness as the detective story stands to the rest of fiction. Both narratives are capable of excellence in their kind, but they are finally inadequate as a steady narrative diet. No matter what is uncovered through Holmes's methods—his careful attention to the story told by the victim, his close scrutiny of physical signs, his brooding on the store of case narrative already known to him—in the strictly patterned detective story, much else is rigorously excluded.[50] Hints of complex characterization and emotion of any subtlety or depth make their way into the detective stories only because Watson (as Holmes often complains) succumbs to the seductions of storytelling, beginning in the middle and embellishing the cases with detail the master regards as extraneous. It is not narrative itself that Holmes is suspicious of, for he knows quite well that he works by constructing a story: "Our case becomes rounded off and difficulty after difficulty thins away in front of us," he tells Watson in *The Hound of the Baskervilles*. "I shall soon be in the position of being able to put into a single connected narrative one of the most singular and sensational crimes of modern times."[51] He objects instead to the logic of discovery that Watson's plots imply. Watson resolutely refuses to tell merely a bare reconstructed chain of events, "the severe reasoning from cause to effect which is really the only notable feature about the thing," and he earns Holmes's scientific scorn for his refusal. His stories of practical reasoning from effect to cause are rather accounts of the application of a great fund of knowledge to unsorted and puzzling circumstance. Their narrative of the diagnostic process customarily contains, like the medical case history, a minimalist retelling of the victim's story as a part of the expert's educated and meticulous reconstruction of the crime. Dr. Watson's case history is neither the story of a crime nor its victim but an account of the crime's reconstruction and explication, and like the medical case history, it celebrates the craft of hand and eye and intellect, the application of practical knowledge to a human ill.

The great age of diagnosis is now long past. The scientific medical case history and the detective story were almost simultaneously "invented" in the 1830s, when the early advances of human biology were beginning to enable the scientific physician to identify disease and accurately describe its workings in the body. Today medicine's very success has meant that most of us now die of long-term illness rather than infection, and as a result, medicine's focus has shifted from infectious to chronic disease. Yet clinical mysteries still exist. Nature and human contrivance produce new diseases to discover or discriminate, and the task of discovering what afflicts each patient remains fundamental to clinical practice and to medical education. The diagnostic skills of Sherlock Holmes are not outdated. Medical mysteries must still be solved by emplotting the clues discerned in the sufferer's tale and in the malfunctioning body. But now, when illness merges with the life of the patient and the physician goes on caring for the patient long after the disease has been diagnosed, the detective metaphor for the work of the physician is insufficient. In the cases Watson presents, Sherlock Holmes has no responsibility for the victims or their survivors. Once the crime is solved, his job is over. He is, after all, a "consulting detective." There is no expectation that he will assist them in their return to a normal life. Until lately we might not have seen this as a limitation, but today attention has shifted to puzzles of therapy and of "management"—much subtler and more subjective matters. They require of case histories "data" that are fuller and more attentive to the life circumstances of patients and to the subtleties of their values and motivation. This knowledge, even more than the diagnostic conundrums, must be the theme of a new case history.

Can the case history be expanded to accommodate all that must concern a physician in an era of chronic illness? Physicians quite reasonably resist the full scope of the duties imposed on them by the World Health Organization's idealistic definition of health as social and psychological as well as physical well-being. Medicine need not save the world. Thoreau trims the individual's obligations to more manageable proportions in his essay, "Civil Disobedience": "It is not a man's duty, as a matter of course, to devote himself to the eradication of any, even the most enormous wrong; he may still properly have other concerns to engage him; but it is his duty, at least, to wash his hands of it, and, if he gives it no thought longer, not to give it practically his support."[52] Thoreau's words fit well with medicine's oldest injunction: first do no harm. Although they must sometimes cause physical pain, physicians ought not contribute to the suffering and loneliness of the patients. The recognition of the patient's life story as distinct from the case history and a renewed and careful attention to its nuanced meaning are part of the therapeutic interaction. Human understanding is inevitably imperfect, but a physician's attention to patients' narratives acknowledges to them that those circumstances exist and are important. It is a small but rational and often effective therapeutic tool. To accomplish the therapeutic work that is properly theirs, physicians need to acknowledge those ills as they are manifested in the lives of their patients—especially the pain that medicine cannot touch.

Not to do so will ultimately require medicine to retreat to emergency rooms, operating theaters, and quick-stop offices, relinquishing the real care of the ill to other professions.

Attention to the patient's life story is a not a nostalgic return to an idealized pretechnological time when social and personal details were entered into the medical record. On the contrary, this recognition of the patient's story is a new requirement of a mobile, urban, fragile society that lacks a binding communal religious belief and has come to expect much more of physicians, haloed by their technology and the large sums of money they are paid. The medicine of neighbors that once augmented the physician's knowledge in a small or stable community now must be the object of special, reconstructive attention.

Case history adequate to this task requires a narrative self-consciousness. It depends upon a good grasp of both the diagnostic and the human possibilities in each particular case and is aided by a critical sense of medical narrative. Medical education supplies the diagnostic plots; fiction about illness can supply the human variables, both through wider reading and, for those who have the inclination and talent, through writing in forms that go beyond case reports and the patient's chart. The success of a new case history will require an appreciation of its difference from fiction and pathography, an awareness of its construction according to traditional but not inalterable rules, and the adoption of strategies for enrichment that fit its stringent form. In complaining that Watson adds "colour and life" to his case histories, adding circumstantial detail to the strict chain of cause and effect, Holmes is shortsighted. Because he does not understand his method, even as he practices it superbly, he compares it only to the method of the physical sciences, at which he also excels. Medicine must begin where Watson does, with the circumstances of the case—colorful, lively, and sometimes painful though they may be. Only by proceeding retrospectively to work out the plot can we know which of these details may turn out to belong to the investigator's deductive chain. Only by working backward along that chain can clinical detectives determine which of those details are the operative ones, which will be decisive for diagnosis and for a suitable and effective plan of treatment. With the advances of science, medicine has moved from a diagnostic exercise to the construction of pathophysiological plots. It needs now to go further, urging contemporary detectives to learn more about motivation and meaning in the lives of those whose cases, at the physical level at least, are now so quickly solved.

Sherlock Holmes very likely would have been equal to such a challenge. As a detective must be, he is first and always concerned with simple causation: "Who done it?" Yet, given an interesting case, he readily grants the power of circumstance to shape character and criminal act, and more than once this knowledge is useful to him in bringing a case to a close. Master of the open-ended interview, he exercises his skill on the motivation as well as the deeds of criminals and their victims. And although he discounts its importance, he recognizes that, scientific though his work may often be, narrative is a part of his method. Could he—can medicine today—take the further step of recognizing in the construction of that narrative that the facts uncovered are not the only facts, the diagnostic story not the only story that could truthfully be told? The challenges and rewards of the traditional Watsonian case history are not lost thereby. A new case history must preserve the detective story's careful attention to minute detail in a legible universe, its exercise of rational intellect, and the pleasure of bringing skill, diligence, and a fund of narratively organized information to bear on a human ill. Holmes need only make fuller use of Watson's awareness that the lives of those who consult them are far more richly detailed than their misfortune suggests. Likewise, physicians need first to imagine and then to acknowledge the life stories out of which their patients come and to which, well or ill, they must return.

NOTES

NOTES TO PREFACE

1. Abraham Flexner, *Medical Education in the United States and Canada* (New York: Carnegie Foundation for the Advancement of Teaching, 1910).
2. Association of American Medical Colleges Project on the General Professional Education of the Physician, "Physicians for the Twenty-First Century," *Journal of Medical Education* 59 (1984), no. 11, part 2.
3. Kathryn M. Hunter and Diana Axelsen, "The Morehouse Human Values in Medicine Program, 1978–1980: Reinforcing a Commitment to Primary Care," *Journal of Medical Education* 57 (1982), 121–23.
4. In using "malady" as a generic term, I follow the suggestion of Charles Culver, Bernard Gert, K. Danner Clouser, "Malady: A Treatment of Disease," *Hastings Center Report* 11 (1981), 29–37. "Illness" I take to designate the patient's experience, "disease" the clinical entity.

NOTES TO INTRODUCTION
INTERPRETING MEDICINE

1. Thomas McKeown, *The Role of Medicine: Dream, Mirage or Nemesis?* 2d ed. (Oxford: Blackwell, 1979).
2. Ivan Illich is the exception; see his *Medical Nemesis: The Expropriation of Health* (New York: Pantheon, 1976).
3. Phenomenologists, pragmatists, and deconstructionists as well as some late twentieth-century philosophers of science in the analytic tradition hold that all knowledge, as much in the physical sciences as elsewhere, is inevitably subjective and contextual. The distinction between the physical sciences and the human sciences is nevertheless a useful one. It marks the difference between relatively context-free knowledge that is replicable and predictive and knowledge that is inextricably context-dependent and imperfectly predictive. Granting the subjective nature of all knowledge does not alter our experience that chemistry and physics and much of human biology are more replicable and rule-governed than social sciences such as economics and political science and, a fortiori, humanities such as philosophy and literary studies. Not surprisingly the view of science as "hard" and certain continues to prevail in medicine as it does in the culture generally. While the best scientific minds are likely to be familiar with work in the philosophy of science, good minds in medicine find it irrelevant to their practical concerns and threatening to the rational ideals of scientific practice.
4. A number of recent essays have made this hermeneutical point. Steven L. Daniel likens the temporal sequence in the explication of a patient's illness—history, diagnosis, treatment, prognosis—to the medieval scheme of fourfold interpretation: literal, allegorical, moral, and anagogical in "The Patient as Text: A Model of Clinical Hermeneutics," *Theoretical Medicine* 7 (1986), 195–210. Ed-

ward L. Gogel and James S. Terry review several theories and weigh their advantages in "Medicine as Interpretation: The Uses of Literary Metaphors and Methods," *Journal of Medicine and Philosophy* 12 (1987), 205–17.

Per Sundstrom's critique of the ontological status of disease, *Icons of Disease: A Philosophical Inquiry into the Semantics, Phenomenology and Ontology of the Clinical Conceptions of Disease*, is based in clinical hermeneutics; Linkoping Studies in Arts and Science, vol. 14 (Linkoping, Sweden: Linkoping University, 1987). Rita Charon argues that it is the patient, not the illness, that is the text in "Doctor-Patient/Reader-Writer: Learning to Find the Text," *Soundings* 72 (1989), 137–52. Drew Leder, in a paper entitled "Clinical Interpretation: The Hermeneutics of Medicine," delivered at the annual meeting of the Society for Health and Human Values, Washington, D.C., October 28, 1989, distinguishes four "texts": the patient's experiential text, the medical narrative, the physical text of the body, and the instrumental text constructed by diagnostic machinery. See also my "The Physician as Textual Critic," *The Connecticut Scholar: Humanities and the Health Professions* 8 (1986), 27–37.

5. Martin S. Staum, *Cabanis: Enlightenment and Medical Philosophy in the French Revolution* (Princeton, N.J.: Princeton University Press, 1980), pp. 103–105.

6. Paul Starr supplies their history in *The Social Transformation of American Medicine* (New York: Basic Books, 1982). An elegant recent description is Leon Kass's "The Doctor-Patient Relationship: What Does It Mean?" delivered to the seminar of the Interdivisional Research Project on the Doctor-Patient Relationship at the University of Chicago, October 23, 1989.

7. Stanley Joel Reiser, *Medicine and the Reign of Technology* (Cambridge, Eng.: Cambridge University Press, 1978).

8. Marcia Angell, "Disease as a Reflection of the Psyche," *New England Journal of Medicine* 313 (1985), 1570–72.

NOTES TO CHAPTER ONE
KNOWLEDGE IN MEDICINE

1. Association of American Medical Colleges Project on the General Professional Education of the Physician, "Physicians for the Twenty-First Century," *Journal of Medical Education* 59 (1984), no. 11, part 2.

2. Jack McCue, "The Effects of Stress on Physicians and Their Medical Practice," *New England Journal of Medicine* 306 (1981), 458–63.

3. Plato, *Gorgias*, 464.

4. In the past two decades the proper model for the physician-patient relationship has been vigorously debated. Clearly it must allow for change over the duration of the relationship and for the negotiated needs and requests of patients. See Robert M. Veatch, "The Medical Model: Its Nature and Problems," *Hastings Center Studies* 1 (1973), 59–76. William F. May has argued that the relationship between physician and patient is a convenantal one in *The Physician's Covenant: Images of the Healer in Medical Ethics* (Philadelphia: Westminster, 1983).

5. Lewis Thomas, *The Youngest Science: Notes of a Medicine-Watcher* (New York: Viking, 1983).

6. I am indebted to Sylvia Foster Price for this reminder.

7. The exception is obstetrical departments, where some or all of the daily schedule is shifted and sign-out rounds are held in the early morning.

8. Larry W. Churchill and Sandra W. Churchill, "Storytelling in Medical Arenas: The Art of Self-Determination," *Literature and Medicine* 1 (1982), 73–79.

9. William L. Morgan, Jr., and George L. Engel recommend "as few notes as possible" observing that "in most instances, careful preparation eliminates the need for notes": "The Presentation of the Patient," in *The Clinical Approach to the Patient* (Philadelphia: W. B. Saunders, 1969), p. 233. In practice, almost two decades later, both had strong preferences for presentation without notes—"an unusual number of tests" (WLM) authorizing the exceptions.

10. Wilhelm Dilthey, "The Rise of Hermeneutics," trans. Fredric Jameson, *New Literary History* 3 (1972), 229–44.

11. Maladies such as myopia or a healthy twenty-year-old's broken arm may be exceptions. These, however, are not what in ordinary language we mean by "diseases." Even so, some would hold that their therapy—perhaps a prescription for contacts for a teenager or an immersible cast for a swimmer— will profit from a wider knowledge of the body and being in whom they are diagnosed.

12. Alan Harwood, "The Hot-Cold Theory of Disease: Implications for Treatment of Puerto Rican Patients," *Journal of the American Medical Association* 216 (1971), 1153–55. See also Arthur Kleinman, *Patients and Healers in the Context of Culture: An Exploration of the Borderland between Anthropology, Medicine, and Psychiatry,* Comparative Studies of Health Systems and Medical Care, no. 3 (Berkeley: University of California Press, 1980).

13. See Claude Steiner on the life and death of his teacher, Eric Berne, in "Introduction," in *Scripts People Live: Transactional Analysis of Life Scripts* (New York: Grove Press, 1974).

14. Cecile A. Carson, *The Hidden Language of Medicine: Seeing What Patients Don't Say,* forthcoming.

15. Michael Balint, *The Doctor, His Patient, and the Illness* (New York: International University Press, 1957).

16. There is a sense in which no one is the sole author of his or her life narrative. Alasdair MacIntyre takes note of this in *After Virtue: A Study in Moral Theory* (South Bend, Ind.: Notre Dame University Press, 1981), pp. 199–200. He distinguishes his view of coauthorship from Marx's often quoted, determinist account in *The Eighteenth Brumaire of Louis Bonaparte.* History, MacIntyre believes, is "an enacted dramatic narrative in which the characters are also the authors" and narrative structure of human life, far from being deterministic, entails overlapping roles, collision, unpredictability.

17. Patrick Irvine wrote, "Most of all, the funeral helps in bringing 'living' and 'medicine' into proper perspective. In a specific way it gives me perhaps my best understanding of how that person fits into his or her community—and how medical care fits into that life—on the patient's own ground": "The Attending at the Funeral," *New England Journal of Medicine* 312 (1985), 1705.

18. See, for example, W.J.T. Mitchell, ed., *The Politics of Interpretation* (Chicago: University of Chicago Press, 1983).

19. The term is from Stanley Fish, *Is There a Text in This Class? The Authority of Interpretive Communities* (Cambridge, Mass.: Harvard University Press, 1980).

20. Barney G. Glaser and Anselm L. Strauss, *The Discovery of Grounded Theory: Strategies for Qualitative Research* (Chicago: Aldine, 1967). Although describing their method as a radical, phenomenological departure from current sociological practice, they cite no philosophical antecedents.

21. John Ladd has described medicine as differing from science in the following ways: the logic of discovery in medicine is inseparable from the logic of justification; it possesses no covering laws and therefore is essentially explanatory and not predictive; and, above all, medicine is not value free. See his "Philosophy and Medicine," in *Changing Values in Medicine*, ed. Eric J. Cassell and Mark Siegler ([Frederick, Md.]: University Publications, n.d., [1985]), p. 213.

22. Arthur Conan Doyle, *A Study in Scarlet*, in *The Complete Sherlock Holmes* (New York: Doubleday, 1930, reprinted 1985), p. 49. All subsequent page references are to this edition.

23. Alvan R. Feinstein, *Clinical Judgment* (Baltimore: Williams and Wilkins, 1967).

24. Arthur Danto, *Analytical Philosophy of History* (Cambridge, Eng.: Cambridge University Press, 1965), p. 132.

25. George Steiner, *New Yorker*, May 26, 1986.

26. E. H. Gombrich, *Art and Illusion: A Study in the Psychology of Pictorial Representation*, 2d ed., Bollingen Series, no. 35 (New York: Pantheon Books, 1960).

27. Thomas S. Kuhn, *The Structure of Scientific Revolutions*, 2nd ed. (Chicago: University of Chicago Press, 1970).

28. Feinstein, *Clinical Judgment*, p. 4.

29. Otto E. Guttentag, "On the Clinical Entity," *Annals of Internal Medicine* 31 (1949), 484–96.

30. W. Scott Richardson told me this story of a medical student's discovery.

31. Sidney Feingold, "Legionnaires' Disease—Still With Us," *New England Journal of Medicine* 318 (1988), 471–73.

32. Mary Hesse, "Texts without Types and Lumps without Laws," *New Literary History* 17 (1985), 31–48.

33. Louis Pasteur, cited in Maurice B. Strauss, ed., *Familiar Medical Quotations* (Boston: Little, Brown, 1968), p. 519.

34. Edwin T. Layton, "Theory and Application in Science and the Humanities," in *Applying the Humanities*, ed. Daniel Callahan, Arthur L. Caplan, and Bruce Jennings. Hastings Center Series in Ethics, vol. 2 (New York: Plenum Press, 1985), p. 61.

35. Stephen Toulmin argues that humanists often adopt the logical-positivists' myth of "pure" science as a straw man to serve as foil for their hermeneutical views. He claims that Gadamer and Habermas, following Heidegger, "have not . . . fully recognized either the plurality or the historical variability of the interpretive modes adopted in one or another of the natural sciences for different intellectual purposes and at different stages in their historical development." See "The Construal of Reality: Criticism in Modern and Post-Modern Science," in *The Politics of Interpretation*, ed. Mitchell, pp. 99, 116.

36. Kenneth F. Schaffner, "Modeling Clinical Medicine: A Commentary on Mark Siegler," in *Changing Values in Medicine,* ed. Cassell and Siegler, pp. 43–58.

37. George L. Engel, "The Need for a New Biomedical Model: A Challenge for Biomedicine," *Science* 196 (1977), 129–36. His "The Clinical Application of the Biopsychosocial Model," *American Journal of Psychiatry* 137 (1980), 535–44, illustrates the clinical importance of the effect of medical observation upon the observed. See also Ludwig von Bertallanfy, *General Systems Theory* (New York: Braziller, 1968).

38. Schaffner points out that Engel, failing to disentangle himself from medicine's positivist view of science, exaggerates the contrast between medicine and a "universalist and unilevel" science (see the work cited in n. 36). Per Sundstrom denies that anyone practices according to the biomedical model: *Icons of Disease: A Philosophical Inquiry into the Semantics, Phenomenology and Ontology of the Clinical Conceptions of Disease,* Linkoping Studies in Arts and Science, vol. 14 (Linkoping, Sweden: Linkoping University, 1987).

39. Michael Alan Schwartz and Osborne Wiggins, "Science, Humanism, and the Nature of Medical Practice: A Phenomenological View," *Perspectives in Biology and Medicine* 28 (1985), 334. This essay with Engel's reply is appended to Charles Odegaard, *Dear Doctor* (Menlo Park, Calif.: The Henry J. Kaiser Family Foundation, 1986), 115–65.

40. Lawrence Rothfield, *Vital Signs* (Princeton, N.J.: Princeton University Press, forthcoming).

41. Harold E. Jones, "The Original of Sherlock Holmes," *Colliers* 32 (1904), no. 15, p. 14; cited by Ely Liebow, *Dr. Joe Bell: Model for Sherlock Holmes* (Bowling Green, Ohio: Bowling Green University Popular Press, 1982), p. 132.

42. Arthur Conan Doyle, *A Study in Scarlet* in *The Complete Sherlock Holmes* (New York: Doubleday, 1930; reprinted 1985), p. 17.

43. This is true even in the novel-length *A Study in Scarlet,* which is doubled in length by its inclusion of "The Country of the Saints," an omnisciently narrated section of history and etiology set in Utah fifty years earlier. This "flashback" is uncharacteristic of subsequent Sherlock Holmes stories, and in this it resembles a first, long, elaborately detailed case write-up by a medical student beginning to learn the craft. Watson was subsequently chided for "romanticism" by Holmes, who, like a chief resident, was always impatient with even the minimal circumstantiality of Watson's subsequent, well trimmed case presentations; see *The Sign of Four,* p. 90.

44. On narrative theory, see Wayne C. Booth, *The Rhetoric of Fiction* (Chicago: University of Chicago Press, 1961), and Seymour Chatman, *Story and Discourse: Narrative Structure in Fiction and Film* (Ithaca, N.Y.: Cornell University Press, 1978).

45. Peter Brooks, "Reading for the Plot," in *Reading for the Plot: Design and Intention in Narrative* (New York: Vintage, 1984), pp. 3–36.

46. These denials and "unremarkable details" are essential to diagnostic reasoning. In considering the wide range of possible illnesses that might fit the patient's symptoms, the clinician draws questions from the mental catalogue of "disease pictures" and begins to establish "pertinent negatives": "Have you had any

bowel changes with this? Any nausea or vomiting?" Both "findings" and "non-findings" (i.e., normalities) are reported as the investigator sculpts away the bits and pieces that are not part of this particular puzzle. Whole organs and regions of the body are declared to be irrelevant. Remarking on an abdominal examination that turned up nothing unusual, a physician will say, "Her liver and spleen were unremarkable." These "pertinent negatives" are not an empty category. If the report is reliable, a number of theoretically possible diseases are thereby ruled out. A patient's history of good health thus becomes a litany of denial: "No history of diabetes or hypertension, no recent surgery, only the usual childhood diseases." A tone of investigative skepticism is established by the practice; no uncorroborated fact is to be entirely trusted. Thus what seems to be a useless, perhaps absurd and misleading locution—"He denies pain"—may become skeptically suggestive: "She denies alcohol use." The physician Tolstoy gives to Ivan Ilych could have been no more like an examining magistrate than this.

47. The presenting problem can be altered. An antibiotic is often given for a fever "empirically," without testing for the presence of bacteria, and, when it works, the conclusion may be drawn that bacteria were present. But this is therapy, not investigative work.

48. Holmes's method is not, however, "deduction." On C. S. Peirce's "abduction" see Umberto Eco and Thomas A. Sebeok, eds., *The Sign of Three: Dupin, Holmes, Peirce* (Bloomington: Indiana University Press, 1983).

49. Stanley Jeyaraja Tambiah, "The Limits of Rationality and the Issue of the Translation of Cultures," Lewis Henry Morgan Lectures, University of Rochester, March 22, 1984. In the published version, Tambiah alters the metaphor to a potentially dysfunctional "spill-over" of science into other disciplines and Western culture generally; *Magic, Science, Religion and the Scope of Rationality* (Cambridge, Eng.: Cambridge University Press, 1990), pp. 140–52.

50. Michel Foucault, *The Birth of the Clinic: An Archeology of Medical Perception*, trans. A. M. Sheridan Smith (New York: Vintage, 1975), pp. 196–98.

NOTES TO CHAPTER TWO
A SCIENCE OF INDIVIDUALS

1. Sir William Osler, "On the Need of a Radical Reform in Our Methods of Teaching Medical Students," *Medical News* 82 (1904), 49–53.

2. Kenneth M. Ludmerer points out the proto-Deweyian character of the nineteenth-century revolution in American medical education in *Learning to Heal: The Development of American Medical Education* (New York: Basic Books, 1985), pp. 64–68.

3. On the alteration of disease taxonomy see Knud Faber, *Nosography in Modern Internal Medicine* (New York: Hoeber, 1923); and Michel Foucault, *The Birth of the Clinic: An Archeology of Perception*, trans. A. M. Sheridan Smith (New York: Vintage, 1975).

4. William Thayer, "Teaching and Practice," in *Osler and Other Papers* (Baltimore: Johns Hopkins University Press, 1931), p. 131; cited by Ludmerer, *Learning to Heal*, p. 66.

5. Aristotle, "Science and Its Objects," *Metaphysics*, Book 6.

6. Meteorology enjoys a degree of public understanding concerning the role of error in its practice that medicine does not share. However, in 1985 when the consequences of meteorologists' error involved loss of life, a "malpractice" case was brought against the U.S. Weather Bureau for its failure to accurately predict a storm.

7. A series of essays in the *Journal of Medicine and Philosophy* on the problem of error as an inevitable consequence of medicine as an applied science begins with Samuel Gorovitz and Alasdair MacIntyre, "Toward a Theory of Medical Fallibility," *Journal of Medicine and Philosophy* 1 (1976), 51–71. Particularly useful is Howard Brody's distinction among the sources of error, "Commentary on 'Error, Malpractice, and the Problem of Universals,'" *Journal of Medicine and Philosophy* 7 (1982), 251–57.

8. Renée C. Fox, "Training for Uncertainty," in *The Student-Physician: Introductory Studies in the Sociology of Medical Education*, ed. Robert K. Merton, George G. Reader, and Patricia L. Kendall (Cambridge, Mass.: Harvard University Press, 1957), pp. 207–41. In an eloquent chapter based on the controversy over the treatment for breast cancer, Jay Katz argues that, as an aspect of their silence, contemporary physicians claim an unwarranted certainty; see *The Silent World of Doctor and Patient* (New York: Free Press, 1984).

9. See Albert R. Jonsen and Stephen Toulmin's *The Abuse of Casuistry* (Berkeley: University of California Press, 1988). The English novel has tackled such problems from its beginnings; see George A. Starr, *Defoe and Casuistry* (Princeton, N.J.: Princeton University Press, 1971).

10. Case 31, *The Edwin Smith Surgical Papyrus*, trans. James Henry Bearsted, vol. 1 (Chicago: University of Chicago Press, 1930), p. 327.

11. Ross J. Simpson and Thomas R. Griggs, "Case Reports and Medical Progress," *Perspectives in Biology and Medicine* 28 (1985), 402–406.

12. *The Surgical Clinics of John B. Murphy, M.D., at Mercy Hospital, Chicago* 2 (1913), 819. I am indebted to W. Scott Richardson for this observation.

13. Charles L. Bosk, "Occupational Rituals in Patient Management," *New England Journal of Medicine* 303 (1980), 71–76.

14. Mark L. Cohen, "Uncertainty Rounds," *Journal of the American Medical Association* 250 (1983), 1689.

15. Kathryn Montgomery Hunter, "Limiting Treatment in a Social Vacuum: A Greek Chorus for William T.," *Archives of Internal Medicine* 145 (1985), 716–19.

16. Richard Rorty, *Philosophy and the Mirror of Nature* (Princeton, N.J.: Princeton University Press, 1979).

17. Lewis Thomas, "The Technology of Medicine," in *Lives of a Cell* (New York: Bantam, 1974), pp. 35–42.

18. See Richard K. Riegelman, *Studying a Study and Testing a Test: How to Read the Medical Literature* (Boston: Little, Brown, 1981), and Stephen H. Gehlbach, *Interpreting the Medical Literature: A Clinician's Guide* (Lexington, Mass.: Collamore Press, 1982). Although much larger in scope, David L. Sackett, R. Brian Haynes, and Peter Tugwell, *Clinical Epidemiology: A Basic Science of Clinical Medicine* (Boston: Little, Brown, 1985), is valued for the pocket-sized

cards inside its front cover, which enable their bearer to evaluate reported research on diagnosis and therapy at the drop of a reference.

19. Peter Winch, "The Universalizability of Moral Judgments," in *Ethics and Action* (London: Routledge and Kegan Paul, 1972), pp. 151–70.

20. "Quandary ethics" is William F. May's phrase in *The Physician's Covenant: Images of the Healer in Medical Ethics* (Philadelphia: Westminster, 1983).

21. See Hans-Georg Gadamer's discussion of Helmholtz's account of the tact essential to the human sciences: *Truth and Method*, 2d ed. (New York: Crossroad Publishing, 1984), pp. 16–17.

22. Louis Lasagna, "Historical Controls: The Practitioner's Clinical Trials," *New England Journal of Medicine* 307 (1983), 1339–40.

23. Alvan R. Feinstein, *Clinical Judgment* (Baltimore: Williams and Wilkins, 1967).

24. Feinstein, "An Additional Basic Science for Clinical Medicine, I–IV," *Annals of Internal Medicine* 99 (1983), 393–97, 554–60, 705–12, 843–48.

25. Jerome P. Kassirer, "The Principles of Clinical Decision Making: An Introduction to Decision Analysis," *Yale Journal of Biology and Medicine* 49 (1976), 149–64.

26. Barbara J. McNeill and Stephen G. Pauker, "Impact of Patient Preferences on the Selection of Therapy," *Journal of Chronic Disease* 34 (1981), 77–86.

27. Donald Bordley, Alvin I. Mushlin, James G. Dolan, W. Scott Richardson, Michael Berry, John Polio, and Paul F. Griner, "Early Clinical Signs Predict Good Outcome in Acute Upper Gastrointestinal Hemorrhage," *Journal of the American Medical Association* 253 (1985), 3282–85.

28. Susanna E. Bedell, Thomas L. Delbanco, E. Francis Cook, and Franklin H. Epstein, "Survival after Cardiopulmonary Resuscitation in the Hospital," *New England Journal of Medicine* 309 (1983), 569–76.

29. William A. Knaus, Jack E. Zimmerman, Douglas P. Wagner, Elizabeth A. Draper, and Diane Lawrence, "APACHE—Acute Physiology and Chronic Health Evaluation: A Physiologically Based Classification System," *Critical Care Medicine* 9 (1981), 591–97.

30. Erwin H. Ackernecht, *A Short History of Medicine*, rev. ed. (New York: Ronald, 1968), pp. 170–74. The ongoing tension between these "two lines of thought" is the argument of Faber's *Nosography*.

31. That people in other times and other places have practiced a medicine shaped by their culture has always been acknowledged; our progressive prejudice is that now these misconceptions have been set aside in favor of not just better medicine but conceptions that are the naked, asocial truth. See Arthur Kleinman, *Patients and Healers in the Context of Culture* (Berkeley: University of California Press, 1980), and Peter Wright and Andrew Treacher, eds., *The Problem of Medical Knowledge: Examining the Social Construction of Medicine* (Edinburgh: Edinburgh University Press, 1982). For a description of the clinical application of an anthropological understanding of medicine, see Eric J. Cassell, *The Healer's Art: A New Approach to the Doctor-Patient Relationship* (New York: Penguin, 1976).

32. Roger C. Schank and Robert P. Abelson, *Scripts, Plans, Goals and Understanding: An Inquiry into Human Knowledge* (Hillsdale, N.J.: Erlbaum,1981). I am indebted to Ellen Key Harris for bringing this work to my attention.

33. As INTERNIST, this program was originally described in R. A. Miller, H. E. Pople, Jr., and J. D. Myers, "INTERNIST–I, an Experimental Computer-Based Diagnostic Consultant for General Internal Medicine," *New England Journal of Medicine* 307 (1982), 468–76. Its success is reported in *Science*, April 15, 1983, pp. 261 ff.

This and other medical information systems, along with the role of computers in medicine generally, are lucidly described by Marsden S. Blois in *Information and Medicine* (Berkeley: University of California Press, 1984).

34. Carl Gustav Hempel, *Aspects of Scientific Explanation* (New York: Free Press, 1965).

35. Dennis J. McShane, Alison Harlow, R. Guy Kraines, and James F. Fries, "TOD: A Software System for the ARAMIS Data Bank," *Computer* 12 (1979), 34–40.

36. Perri Klass, "Classroom Ethics on the Job," *Harvard Medical Alumni Bulletin* 60 (1986), 36. I take it that her "written descriptions" means a simple list; for, of course, the narrative arrangement of these signs, their clustering and the timing of their appearance, are primary discriminators of a malady.

NOTES TO CHAPTER THREE
THE REPRESENTATION OF THE PATIENT

1. William L. Morgan, Jr., and George L. Engel, *The Clinical Approach to the Patient* (Philadelphia: Saunders, 1969).

2. This custom is no longer universally observed. Not only has scientific medicine become our society's folk medicine, but the prevalence of chronic disease has created expert patients. A patient's chief complaint today is likely to omit physical details in favor of an interpretive, diagnostic, statement: "My gall bladder's giving me trouble." "I've got heart failure." For this reason as long ago as 1957 Simon S. Leopold advised, "If the patient's description is suitable, use it; if he says he has 'gallbladder trouble,' ignore the time-worn exhortation to 'use the patient's own words.' Give the symptoms: 'Belching and pain in the stomach whenever I eat fried stuff'"; *The Principles and Methods of Physical Diagnosis: Correlation of Physical Signs with Certain Physiological and Pathological Changes in Disease*, 2d ed. (Philadelphia: Saunders, 1957), p. 9. Morgan and Engel silently omit discussion of the chief complaint in *The Clinical Approach to the Patient*. More recent introductions to physical diagnosis follow suit, but the oral tradition persists.

3. Although lists, diagrams, and flow charts are increasingly the rule, students are advised to record the history of the present illness narratively in the chart. See Morgan and Engel, *The Clinical Approach*, pp. 177–85.

4. John D. Stoeckle, Christopher Seiberling, and Andrew Dodds, *Richard Clark Cabot: Medical Reform in the Progressive Era* (Boston: Massachusetts General Hospital/Harvard Medical School, 1983).

5. Pierre-C.-A. Louis, *An Essay on Clinical Observation* (Paris, 1834). Case histories, of course, were written long before this time. Indeed, the diagnostic case method might be said to have been invented by Henry Fielding, one of the patriarchs of the English novel, who in his work as a London magistrate assembled evidence for narratively constructed indictments in criminal cases. See John

Bender, *Imagining the Penitentiary: Fiction and the Architecture of Mind in Eighteenth-Century England* (Chicago: University of Chicago Press, 1986), p. 145.

6. Henry I. Bowditch, "Louis and His Contemporaries," *Bulletin of Medicine and Surgery* 87 (1872), 292–95.

7. Edward C. Atwater, "Touching the Patient: The Teaching of Internal Medicine in America," in *Sickness and Health in America: Readings in the History of Medicine and Public Health,* 2d ed., ed. Judith Walzer Leavitt and Ronald L. Numbers (Madison: University of Wisconsin Press, 1985), pp. 129–47.

8. The intransitive form of "present" is also found in primatology, where it is used for primates who turn their rumps defenselessly to another to initiate grooming behavior or sexual intercourse or as a sign of conciliation.

9. This is statistical medical folklore: widely believed, probably true, but unproven. See Mark Siegler, "The Nature and Limits of Clinical Medicine," in *Changing Values in Medicine,* ed. Eric J. Cassell and Mark Siegler ([Frederick, Md.]: University Publications of America, n.d. [1985]), p. 27.

10. Marsden S. Blois, *Information and Medicine: The Nature of Medical Descriptions* (Berkeley: University of California Press, 1984), p. 165.

11. This shortsightedness is not peculiar to medicine, although it may be most cruel there. My professor grandfather cautioned me about the academic variant as I took my first college position, advising me to remember that I would be teaching not literature but students. Some time passed before I understood him.

12. R. J. Havey, "A Piece of My Mind: Classic Case," *Journal of the American Medical Association* 242 (1984), 2886.

13. I owe this view to Bertrand Bronson, who in a formalist era insisted on reading Boswell's *Johnson* inside out.

14. The recent addition of a previous diagnosis to the opening statement of the case presentation—"Mr. Jefferson is a 61-year-old black man with a history of angina"— violates this convention. No doubt hurry and overwork play their part in this shortcut, but primarily it reflects the prevalence of chronic disease and the frequency with which physicians must address not only its progression but problems of treatment and iatrogenic complications.

15. See Paul Ricoeur, *Time and Narrative,* 3 vols., trans. Kathleen McLaughlin Blamey and David Pellauer (Chicago: University of Chicago Press, 1984–88).

16. Georg Lukács, *Writer and Critic* (New York: Grosset and Dunlap, 1971), quoted by D. G. Marshall, "Plot as Trap, Plot as Mediation," in *The Horizon of Literature,* ed. Paul Hernadi (Lincoln: University of Nebraska Press, 1982), p. 80.

17. Arthur Conan Doyle, "Silver Blaze," in *The Complete Sherlock Holmes* (New York: Doubleday, 1930; reprinted 1985), p. 336.

NOTES TO CHAPTER FOUR
"THERE WAS THIS ONE GUY . . ."

1. D. A. Miller discusses the relation between an initiating, narratable event and closure in the nineteenth-century novel in *The Novel and Its Discontents* (Princeton, N.J.: Princeton University Press, 1981). In *Before Novels,* J. Paul Hunter describes the appetite for novelty as one of the productive circumstances for the emergence of the English novel (New York: W. W. Norton, 1990).

2. Anecdotes share this quality with the placebo effect; see Howard Brody, *Placebos and the Philosophy of Medicine* (Chicago: University of Chicago Press, 1980).

3. Stanley Joel Reiser, *Medicine and the Reign of Technology* (Cambridge, Eng.: Cambridge University Press, 1978).

4. The first locution, "I had. . .," is common among surgeons, perhaps a reflection of their rather more carnal knowledge of their patients. Other specialists tend toward the latter form—or even the more impersonal, "There was a patient on 7-14 last winter . . . ."

5. Ross J. Simpson and Thomas R. Griggs, "Case Reports and Medical Progress," *Perspectives in Biology and Medicine* 28 (1985), 402–406.

6. Lawrence K. Altman, "Doctor's World: How Safe Are Prescriptions Drugs?" *New York Times,* March 22, 1983. See the letter based on a single case, Steven A. Samuel, "Apparent Anaphylactic Reaction to Zomepirac (Zomax)," *New England Journal of Medicine* 304 (1981), 978.

7. Steven B. Abramson, Chrystia M. Odajnyk, Anthony J. Greico, Gerald Weissmann, and Elliot Rosenstein, "Hyperalgesic Pseudothrombophlebitis: New Syndrome in Male Homosexuals," *American Journal of Medicine* 78 (1985), 317–20. I am indebted to Gerald Weissmann for this story.

8. Ludwig Fleck, *The Growth and Development of a Scientific Fact: Introduction to the Study of Thoughtstyle and Thoughtcollective* [1935], ed. T. J. Trenn and R. Merton (Chicago: University of Chicago Press, 1979).

9. Helen B. Taussig, "A Study of the German Outbreak of Phocomelia," *Journal of the American Medical Association* 180 (1962), 1106–14.

10. David Hilfiker, "Facing Our Mistakes," *New England Journal of Medicine* 310 (1984), 118–22, collected in *Healing the Wounds: A Physician Looks at His Work* (New York: Pantheon, 1985).

11. Charles L. Bosk, *Forgive and Remember: Managing Medical Failure* (Chicago: University of Chicago Press, 1979).

NOTES TO CHAPTER FIVE
WRITING UP THE CASE

1. "Charting privileges," the right to write about the patient in the chart, are carefully measured out to medical and paramedical staff in every office and hospital. Hospital social workers have gained the privilege as their institutions have come to depend on them for two vital functions: establishing patients' Medicaid eligibility and "placement," the movement of patients to nursing homes. Chaplains have gained charting privileges in a number of hospitals. The location of these "other" notes in relation to physicians' notes is a matter of some interest. In some hospitals there are two sets; in others they are integrated. In at least one hospital they are divided by a vertical line down the page; the narrower left column is labeled "Non-Physicians Write Here."

2. "Progress" notes might seem an invariantly optimistic category, but diseases are described from a natural-history viewpoint as progressing when medical therapy does not otherwise produce "progress." "SOAPing" is part of L. L. Weed's problem-oriented medical record; see *Medical Records, Medical Education and Patient Care* (Cleveland: Case Western Reserve University Press, 1970).

3. Gerald Weissmann, "The Chart of the Novel," in *The Woods Hole Cantata: Essays on Science and Society* (Boston: Houghton Mifflin, 1985), pp. 101–108. Like Lawrence Rothfield, he finds a touchstone for both the nineteenth-century novel's narrative realism and the modern scientific case study in Claude Bernard's *An Introduction to the Study of Experimental Medicine* (1865); see "Discursive Intertextuality: The Case of Mme Bovary," *Novel* 19 (1985), 57–81.

4. Rita Charon, "To Listen, To Recognize," *The Pharos* 49 (1986), 10–13.

5. Following E. M. Forster's remarks in *Aspects of the Novel*, Hayden White distinguishes among annals, chronicle, and narrative. Annals typically list "events" without interpretation or conclusion: "Interval 1: The king died. Interval 2: Crops failed. Interval 3: The Queen died." A chronicle introduces selectivity and sequence, the germ of a story, but still lacks closure: "The King died, then the Queen died." Narrative implies causality or the operation of a moral principle: "The King died; then the Queen died of grief." See Hayden White, "The Value of Narrativity in the Representation of Reality," *Critical Inquiry* 7 (1980), 5–27.

6. Linda Orr in "The Revenge of Literature: A History of History," *New Literary History* 18 (1986), 1–22, imagines the possibility of capturing the process of historical knowing: "It might be interesting to see a historical narrative that raveled a series of questions concerning what it would be necessary to know in order to pose the main question, which itself would have to be postponed, as would the answer; or that would detail what is always eliminated; or the back and forth between question and document which rephrases the question which requires a rereading of the documents, and so forth, allowing that figure of zigzag to act as the history itself. Would such stories be remarketed as novels?"

They might instead be mistaken for a medical chart, its plot deferred by multiple authors, by slow lapse of time, reexaminations, the use of tests to rule out possibilities, and, above all, by illness's frequent refusal to be corralled and understood.

7. Suzanne Poirier and Daniel J. Brauner, "Voices of the Medical Record," *Theoretical Medicine* 11 (1990), 29–39.

8. J. W. Mold and Howard F. Stein, "The Cascade Effect in the Clinical Care of Patients," *New England Journal of Medicine* 314 (1986), 512. See also Jerome P. Kassirer, "Our Stubborn Quest for Diagnostic Certainty: A Cause of Excessive Testing," *New England Journal of Medicine* 320 (1989), 1489–91.

9. Eliot Freidson describes the beginning of the chart's alteration from a "natural precipitate" of everyday work to a "response to the administrative requirements of some announced review procedure." It is a shift from an indigenous professional control to a broader societal one; see "The Threat of the Medical Record," in *Doctoring Together: A Study of Professional Social Control* (New York: Elsevier, 1975), pp. 167–85. See also Constance A. Nathanson and Marshall H. Becker, "Doctors, Nurses, and Clinical Records," *Medical Care* 11 (1973), 214–23.

10. Weissmann, "The Chart of the Novel," p. 102.

11. Lawrence L. Weed, *Medical Records, Medical Education and Patient Care.*

12. Peter Brooks, *Reading for the Plot: Design and Intention in Narrative* (New York: Vintage, 1984), p. 10.

13. Louis Lasagna, "Historical Controls: The Practitioner's Clinical Trials," *New England Journal of Medicine* 307 (1983), 1339–40.

14. Edward J. Huth, *How to Write and Publish Papers in the Medical Sciences* (Philadelphia: Institute for Scientific Information Press, 1982), p. 58. The italics are mine.

15. Myra W. Wiener, Laura J. Vondoenhoff, and Jules Cohen, "Aortic Regurgitation First Appearing 12 Years after Successful Septal Myectomy for Hypertrophic Obstructive Cardiomyopathy," *American Journal of Medicine* 72 (1982), 157–60. Subsequent citations are from this case report.

16. Cf. Arthur Conan Doyle, "The Adventure of the Dancing Men [sic]," in *The Complete Sherlock Holmes* (New York: Doubleday, 1930; reprinted 1985), pp. 511–26.

17. Editorial reply to Kevin Leehey, Alayne Yates, and Catherine M. Shisslak, "Alteration of Case Reports in Running—An Analogue of Anorexia?" *New England Journal of Medicine* 310 (1984), 600.

18. Myra W. Wiener, Laura J. Vondoenhoff, and Jules Cohen, "Aortic Regurgitation," pp. 157–58.

19. The customs of case reportage in internal medicine, which in Erik Erikson's terms are more "generative" than those of other specialties, suggest that the first-named author is likely to be a resident who did the primary work of hospital care and the last-named will be a professor. In my example, Myra W. Wiener, at the time a fourth-year medical student, had responsibility for the records in the patient's chart and drafted the report; Laura J. Vondoenhoff, then a fellow in cardiology, served as a consultant while the patient was in the hospital and provided the echocardiographical data for the report; Jules Cohen, a cardiologist and professor of medicine, was the attending physician, oversaw the patient's care, and contributed to the manuscript.

20. Dewitt Stettin, Jr., "Coping with Blindness," *New England Journal of Medicine* 305 (1981), 458–60.

NOTES TO CHAPTER SIX
AN *N* OF 1

1. For a discussion of clinical virtues, see Rudolph J. Napodano, *Values in Medical Practice* (New York: Human Sciences Press, 1986).

2. Lance R. Peterson, LoAnn C. Peterson, and Anja K. Peterson, "French Vanilla Frostbite," *New England Journal of Medicine* 307 (1982), 1028. Subsequent references in this chapter are to this journal unless otherwise noted.

3. Paul Dudley White, "The Tight-Girdle Syndrome," 288 (1973), 584.

4. Robert J. Joynt, "Foam Filling Faints Feigning Fits," 288 (1973), 219; and Max Deutch and Ralph C. Parker, Jr., "Edgar Lee Masters and Satchel Page on Ski-Boot Syncope" [2 letters], 288 (1973), 742.

5. Shirley Blotnick Moskow, ed., *Hunan Hand and Other Ailments: Letters to the New England Journal of Medicine* (Boston: Little, Brown, 1987).

6. The prevalence of left-handed baseball players in the major leagues, reported in a study complete with chi-square analysis, requires no therapeutic attention (whatever a right-handed pitcher might say). The study of neuroscience has

simply given the physician-authors some insight into the sensitivity and specificity of certain methods of batting and throwing: John M. McLean and Francis M. Ciurczak, "Bimanual Dexterity in Major League Baseball Players: A Statistical Study," 307 (1982), 1278–79.

7. Whether because readers of syndrome letters tend to be physicians with a literary bent or because literary physicians (after exercising their clinical skills on what seem more stable, written texts) are strongly predisposed to rush into print, there have been a number of epistolary flurries on the ailments of literary characters and such ancillary topics as the importance of contemporary knowledge of the Eustachian tube in *Hamlet*. See Avrim R. Eden and Jeff Opland, "Bartolommeo Eustachio's *De Auditus Organis* and the Unique Murder Plot in Shakespeare's *Hamlet*," 307 (1982), 259–61; and Edward Tabot and Edward Shapiro, "Eerie Murder in Shakespeare's *Hamlet*," [2 letters] 307 (1982), 1531. The etiology of Falstaff's quirks is debated in Jack J. Adler, "Did Falstaff Have the Sleep-Apnea Syndrome?" 308 (1983), 404; and R. P. Junghans, "Falstaff Was Drunker than He Was Fat," 308 (1983), 1483.

8. Ahud Sternberg, Alexander A. Deutsch, and Rafael Reiss, "Scarpa's Fascia Hernia," 307 (1982), 561.

9. William B. Cobb, Charles M. Helms, and Pope L. Moseley, "Toxic-Shock Syndrome in a Young Man with a Pilonidal Abscess," 306 (1982), 1422–23.

10. J. L. Trotter, D. B. Clifford, C. B. Anderson, R. C. Van der Veen, B. C. Hicks, and G. Banks, "Elevated Serum Interleukin-2 Levels in Chronic Progressive Multiple Sclerosis," 318 (1988), 1206.

11. A. M. Lerner, D. P. Levine, and M. P. Reyes, "Two Cases of Herpes Simplex Virus Encephalitis in the Same Family," 308 (1983), 1481.

12. M. Tobi, M. Garretto, M. O. Blackstone, and A. L. Baker, "Periumbilical Hemorrhage Complicating Percutaneous Liver Biopsy," 308 (1983), 1541–42.

13. John A. Dutro and Lloyd G. Phillips, "Ipsilateral Horner's Syndrome as a Rare Complication of Tube Thoracostomy," 313 (1985), 121.

14. Robert W. Lyons, "Orange Contact Lenses from Rifampin," 300 (1979), 372–73.

15. Elaine German and Nurul Siddiqui, "Atropine Toxicity from Eyedrops," 282 (1970), 689.

16. Julie V. Hoff, Peter A. Beatty, and James L. Wade, "Dermal Necrosis from Dobutamine," 300 (1979), 1280.

17. M. A. Gertz, J. P. Garton, and W. H. Jennings, "Aplastic Anemia Due to Tocainide," 314 (1986), 583–84.

18. Carl E. Dettman, "Suppression of Salivation in Wind-Instrument Players with Scopolamine," 310 (1984), 1396.

19. W. R. Hudgins, "The Crossed-Straight-Leg-Raising Test," 297 (1977), 1127.

20. Kenneth B. Desser and Alberto Benchimol, "Click in the Neck—Unusual Presentation of Mitral-Valve Prolapse," 297 (1977), 619.

21. R. D. Andersen and A. H. Johnson, "Frigid Headache," 291 (1974), 1259.

22. Stephen J. Peroutka and Laura A. Peroutka, "Autosomal Dominant Transmission of the 'Photic Sneeze Reflex,'" 310 (1984), 599–600.

23. Marc B. Garnick, "Hot-Watch Syndrome," 294 (1976), 54.

24. Michael F. Roizen, Barry Engelstad, and Robert Hattner, "Gaussian Carditis," 307 (1982), 448.

25. J. D. Battle, Jr., "Credit-Carditis," 274 (1966), 467.

26. Walley J. Temple and Doreen H. Farley Temple, "The Succussion Splash as an Infant 'Burp' Sign," 308 (1983), 1604.

27. Joan Zidulka and Arnold Zidulka, "Tympany in Traube's Space as an Infant 'Burp' Sign," 309 (1983), 859.

28. Arthur J. Siegel and David H. Serfas, "The 'Cloret' Sign," 299 (1978), 102.

29. M. P. O'Meara, "Another 'Cloret' Sign," 299 (1978), 780.

30. Brad Evans, "The Greening of Urine: Still Another 'Cloret Sign,'" 300 (1979), 202.

31. Shiro Tanaka, Alexander B. Smith, William Halperin, and Roger Jensen, "Carpet-Layer's Knee," 307 (1982), 1276–77.

32. Thomas H. Bracken, "'Genu Genuflectorum,'" 308 (1983), 1107.

33. Minerva, "Views," British Medical Journal 286 (1983), 1654.

34. William E. Griffiths, "Genu Genuflectorum Revisited," 309 (1983), 561.

35. Gerald Y. Minuk, Jeanne G. Waggoner, Jay A. Hoofnagle, Reginald G. Hansen, and S. Chris Pappas, "Pipetter's Thumb," 306 (1982), 751.

36. E. Roullet and P. Castaigne, "Pipetter's Thumb, Type II," 307 (1982), 502.

37. Jacqueline J. Wertsch, "Pricer Palsy," 312 (1985), 1645.

38. Michael A. Kron and Jerrold J. Ellner, "Buffer's Belly," 318 (1988), 584.

39. Franz von Lichtenberg, "Lawn Mower's Arm," 307 (1982), 1029.

40. Nathaniel Gould, "Back-Pocket Sciatica," 290 (1974), 633.

41. Eulogio H. Rectra, Jr., and Warren C. Litts, Jr., "Grocery Bag Neuropathy," 291 (1974), 742.

42. David F. Smail, "Handlebar Palsy," 292 (1975), 322.

43. Alexander R. MacKay, "Back-Pack Meralgia," 293 (1975), 702.

44. W. King Engel, "Ponderous-Purse Disease," 299 (1978), 557.

45. Joel M. Geiderman, "Pumpkin Carver's Palm," 298 (1978), 348.

46. Melvin Hershkowitz, "Penile Frostbite: An Unforeseen Hazard of Jogging," 296 (1977), 178.

47. Halley S. Faust and Mark L. Dembert, "Frisbee Finger," 293 (1975), 304.

48. David H. Wegman, John M. Peters, and B. S. Levy, "Frisbee Finger (cont.)," 293 (1975), 725–26.

49. Mutaz B. Habal, Michael M. Meguid, and Joseph E. Murray, "The Long-Scarf Syndrome—A New Health Hazard," 284 (1971), 734.

50. P. Itin, A. Haenel, and H. Stalder, "From the Heavens, Revenge on Joggers," 311 (1984), 1703.

51. Colm O'Herlihy, "Jogging and Suppression of Ovulation," 306 (1982), 50–51.

52. Mark Sherman, "Are Exercise Ailments Cyclical?" 309 (1983), 858–59.

53. Reported in Rectra and Litts, "Grocery Bag Neuropathy."

54. Duncan W. McBride, Lawrence P. Lehman, and John R. Mangiardi, "Break-Dancing Neck," 312 (1985), 186.

55. Frederick W. Walker, Keith D. Lillemoe, and Robert R. Farquharson, "Disco Felon," 301 (1979), 166–67.

56. Susan V. Lawrence, "'Disco Felon' Not Felonious: 'Disco Digit' Better?" 301 (1979), 947–48.

57. G. M. Todd, "Side Effects from Dietetic Candy," 275 (1966), 1384.

58. Ervin H. Epstein, Jr., and Mark D. Oren, "Popsicle Panniculitis," 282 (1970), 966–67.

59. Stephen Sulkes, "'Hydrox Fecalis,'" 310 (1984), 52.

60. Lawrence K. Altman, *Who Goes First? The Story of Self-Experimentation in Medicine* (New York: Random House, 1988).

61. Timothy C. McCervan, "Space-Invaders Wrist," 304 (1981), 1368.

62. Robert D. Powers, Geoffrey C. Lamb, Robert C. Matyasz, Michael T. Spilane, and Robert A. Van Iyn, "Urban-Cowboy Rhabdomyolysis," 304 (1981), 427.

63. Robert Graebner, "Fondue Folly," 284 (1971), 162; Helene S. Thorpe, "Fondue Rendue," 284 (1971), 796; and Leslie Fisher, "Dangers of Fondue Pots," 285 (1971), 1381.

64. John Ladd, "Philosophy and Medicine," in *Changing Values in Medicine*, ed. Eric J. Cassell and Mark Siegler ([Frederick, Md.]: University Publications, [1985]), p. 213. See also Marsden S. Blois, "Medicine and the Nature of Vertical Reasoning," 318 (1988), 847–51.

65. Steven A. Samuel, "Apparent Anaphylactic Reaction to Zomepirac (Zomax)," 304 (1981), 978.

66. J. A. Robinson and A. Barnett, "*Jaws* Neurosis," 293 (1975), 1154.

67. J. B. Peter, "Pigmenturia from 'Loving Care' Hair Dye," 293 (1975), 458.

68. Allan R. Glass, "Should Letters Be Reviewed?" 308 (1983), 1232.

69. Arnold S. Relman, "How Reliable Are Letters?" 308 (1983), 1219–20.

70. Stephen G. Pauker, "Grand-Rounds Whiplash," 283 (1970), 600–601.

71. H. C. Gilman, "Grand-Rounds Whiplash: Predisposing Cause," 283 (1970), 1235.

72. David Bateman, "Syndrome-Reader's Scowl," 305 (1981), 1595.

73. In Michel Foucault's terms, we expect medical narrative to be an "author-free" discourse, when in fact it is characterized by the "author-function"; Michel Foucault, "What Is an Author?" in *Textual Strategies*, ed. J. V. Harari (Ithaca, N.Y.: Cornell University Press, 1979), p. 150.

NOTES TO CHAPTER SEVEN
PATIENTS, PHYSICIANS, AND RED PARAKEETS

1. The sociologist Everett Cherrington Hughes characterized the different worldviews of professional and client: "To the layman the technique . . . should be pure instrument . . . while to the people who practice it, every occupation tends to become an art." See especially his "Mistakes at Work," which focuses on medicine: *Men and Their Work* (Glencoe, Ill.: Free Press, 1958), pp. 88–101. The manifestations of incommensurability have been studied by Eliot Freidson in *Doctoring Together: A Study of Professional Social Control* (New York: Elsevier,

1975). See also the collection of essays edited by Freidson and Judith Lorber, *Medical Men and Their Work* (New York: Atherton, 1972).

2. Jonathan Z. Smith, "I Am a Parakeet—Red," *History of Religion* 11 (1972), 391–413. His history of the Western concept of "primitive mentality" begins with Karl von den Steinen's ambiguous report of Bororo statements in *Unter den Naturvölkern Zentral-Brasiliens* (Berlin, 1891), pp. 352–53. See also Stanley Jeyaraja Tambiah, *Magic, Science, Religion, and the Scope of Rationality* (Cambridge, Eng.: Cambridge University Press, 1990).

3. Arthur Kleinman, himself both anthropologist and psychiatrist, recommends the physician's conscious adoption of the anthropologist's role in his *The Illness Narratives: Suffering, Healing and the Human Condition* (New York: Basic Books, 1988); see especially chapter 15, pp. 227–51. His emphasis is on understanding the cultural world of the patient. I differ from him, if at all, in believing that an awareness of narrative is a more useful vehicle for the recognition of the patient's reality. The physician need not necessarily understand the patient's culture in its detail but must be able to hear the patient's account of his or her life in that world as a narrative construction, accepting it on its own terms as something other than the medical narrative that will be abstracted from it. Even if patient and physician share a culture and a social class, there will not be a perfect fit between their phenomenal worlds: there is a subculture of illness to which the patient gains a lonely admission.

4. Barney G. Glaser and Anselm L. Strauss, *The Discovery of Grounded Theory: Strategies for Qualitative Research* (Chicago: Aldine, 1967).

5. Walter L. Peterson, Richard A.L. Sturdevant, Howard D. Frankl, et al., "Healing of Duodenal Ulcer with an Antacid Regimen," *New England Journal of Medicine* 297 (1977), 341–45.

6. Candace West analyzes communication between patients and physicians as an expression of their differing roles and status, finding that the frequency of interruption in the opening interview embodies the social control exercised by physicians, especially white male physicians with female patients; see *Routine Complications: Troubles with Talk between Doctors and Patients* (Bloomington: Indiana University Press, 1984).

7. Leo Tolstoy, "The Death of Ivan Ilych," in *The Death of Ivan Ilych and Other Stories*, trans. Aylmer Maude (New York: Signet, 1960).

8. Franz Ingelfinger, "Arrogance," *New England Journal of Medicine* 303 (1980), 1507–11.

9. Once hiking with friends, I conducted an ad hoc experiment in the matter of satisfactory closure. The five of us had come upon a young man with a swollen, unworkable, injured knee and reported his location to a park ranger. We watched as he was brought out of a canyon by an experienced rescue team. We waited on and on, although the sun was going down and the spring air was getting colder, to see him delivered to the ambulance. "What do we need in order to leave?" I asked. One of us wanted to know why he had moved so far from the place we left him. Had he not trusted us to get help? Another wanted to know what had happened to the friend who, long before we found him, had gone for help; would the friend be with him now? A third wondered whether his family had arrived and

192 NOTES TO CHAPTER SEVEN

what they looked like. The physician among us agreed these were all interesting questions; after a pause she added, almost as if it belonged to a new conversation, "I'd really like to know what was wrong with his knee."

10. Surgery and extended treatment like chemotherapy have a variant plot: the trial by torture. Uncle Henry will begin the otherwise chronological story of his operation *in medias res* by declaring the procedure he has undergone: "When I had my appendix out last fall . . .." Like the audiences of Peter Falk's "Columbo" mysteries, we know the solution first. The story concerns the construction of a sustained flashback. If Uncle Henry has had straightforward diagnosis and a prompt recovery, then in the months that follow, as he tells his story and hears others like it in exchange, its abnormality—and thus its narratability—will begin to fade. Only if there was something unusual about his diagnosis and treatment—especially a long delay or a mistake—will it stay a tellable story for long.

11. Michael Balint, *The Doctor, His Patient, and the Illness* (New York: International University Press, 1957).

12. Sigmund Freud, *Dora: An Analysis of a Case of Hysteria* (New York: Collier, 1963), p. 32.

13. Stanley Joel Reiser, *Medicine and the Reign of Technology* (Cambridge, Eng.: Cambridge University Press, 1978).

14. Sir William Osler, "Books and Men," in *Aequanimitas, with Other Addresses to Medical Students, Nurses and Practitioners of Medicine*, 2d ed. (Philadelphia: Blakiston, 1906), p. 220.

15. This biblical interpretation is the original sense of hermeneutics.

16. Sir William Osler's "Aequanimitas" is the locus classicus for this view. See also Talcott Parsons, "Social Structure and Dynamic Process: The Case of Modern Medical Practice," in *The Social System* (Glencoe, Ill.: Free Press, 1951), pp. 428–79. Renée Fox describes the medical student's cultivation of "detached concern" in "Training for Uncertainty," in *The Student-Physician: Introductory Studies in the Sociology of Medical Education*, ed. Robert K. Merton, George G. Reader, and Patricia L. Kendall (Cambridge, Mass.: Harvard University Press, 1957), pp. 207–41.

17. "The Wound Dresser," ll. 53–58, in Walt Whitman, *Complete Poetry and Collected Prose*, ed. Justin Kaplan (New York: Library of America, 1982), p. 443.

18. See Lester King, *Medical Thinking: A Historical Preface* (Princeton, N.J.: Princeton University Press, 1982). Judith Wilson Ross writes about the military metaphor in "The Militarization of Disease: Do We Really Want a War on AIDS?" *Soundings* 72 (1989), 39–58.

19. Lewis Thomas, "Germs," in *The Lives of a Cell: Notes of a Biology Watcher* (New York: Bantam, 1974), pp. 88–94.

20. The view is expressed by Donald W. Seldin in "Presidential Address: The Boundaries of Medicine," *Transactions of the Association of American Physicians* 94 (1981), 73–84; cited in Charles E. Odegaard, *Dear Doctor: A Personal Letter to a Physician* (Palo Alto, Calif.: Kaiser Family Foundation, 1986).

21. William T. Branch and Anthony Suchman address this loss in "Meaningful Experiences in Medicine," *American Journal of Medicine* 88 (1990), 56–59.

22. Julia E. Connelly, "The Whole Story," *Literature and Medicine* 9 (1990), 151.

23. Clifford Geertz, "Thick Description: Toward an Interpretive Theory of Culture," in *The Interpretation of Cultures* (New York: Basic Books, 1973), pp. 3–30. Geertz compares the distinction between "description" and "explanation" with the distinction between " 'inscription' ('thick description') and 'specification' ('diagnosis')," p. 27.

24. Lester S. King expertly sorts through the concepts of causality in medicine in *Medical Thinking: A Historical Preface*, pp. 187–223.

25. Francis W. Peabody, "The Care of the Patient," *Journal of the American Medical Association* 88 (1927), 877–82.

26. L. J. Henderson, "The Practice of Medicine as Applied Sociology," *Transactions of the Association of American Physicians* 51 (1936), 17, 20. See also "The Physician and Patient as Social System," *New England Journal of Medicine* 212 (1938), 819–23.

27. Alan Harwood, "The Hot-Cold Theory of Disease: Implications for Treatment of Puerto Rican Patients," *Journal of the American Medical Association* 216 (1971), 1153–55.

28. Loudell Snow, "Folk Medical Beliefs and Their Implications for Care of Patients: A Review Based on Studies among Black Americans," *Annals of Internal Medicine* 81 (1974), 82–96.

29. Lyle Saunders, "Healing Ways in the Spanish Southwest," in *Patients, Physicians and Illness*, ed. E. G. Jaco (Glencoe, Ill.: Free Press, 1958), pp. 189–206.

30. Muriel R. Gullick, "Common-Sense Models of Health and Disease," *New England Journal of Medicine* 313 (1985), 700–703.

31. Eric J. Cassell, *The Healer's Art: A New Approach to the Doctor-Patient Relationship* (New York: Lippincott, 1976).

32. Fred Davis describes intentionally deceptive communication in Eliot Freidson and Judith Lorber, *Medical Men and Their Work* (New York: Atherton, 1972).

33. Glaser and Strauss, *The Discovery of Grounded Theory*; see also chapter 1, pp. 15–16.

34. Georg Lukács, *Writer and Critic* (New York: Grosset and Dunlap, 1971), quoted by D. G. Marshall, "Plot as Trap, Plot as Mediation," in *The Horizon of Literature*, ed. Paul Hernadi (Lincoln: University of Nebraska Press, 1982), p. 80.

35. Leon Eisenberg, "What Makes Persons 'Patients' and Patients 'Well'?" *American Journal of Medicine* 69 (1980), 277–86.

36. Grace Gredys Harris, "Mechanism and Morality in Patients' Views of Illness and Injury," *Medical Anthropology Quarterly* 3 [NS] (1989), 3–21.

37. George L. Engel, "The Clinical Application of the Biopsychosocial Model," *American Journal of Psychiatry* 137 (1980), 535–44.

38. Cassell, *The Healer's Art*, pp. 149–63.

39. Edmund D. Pellegrino and David C. Thomasma, *A Philosophical Basis of Medical Practice* (New York: Oxford University Press, 1981).

40. "Each human life will . . . embody a story whose shape and form will

depend upon what is counted as a harm and danger and upon how success and failure, progress and its opposite, are understood and evaluated." Alasdair Mac-Intyre, *After Virtue* (South Bend, Ind.: Notre Dame University Press, 1981), p. 135.

41. Leon Eisenberg, "Science in Medicine: Too Much or Too Little and Too Limited in Scope?" Also in Ker L. White, ed., *The Task of Medicine: Dialogue at Wickenburg* (Palo Alto, Calif.: Kaiser Family Foundation, 1988).

42. Pedro Lain Entralgo, *The Therapy of the Word in Classical Antiquity*, ed. and trans. L. J. Rather and John M. Sharp (New Haven: Yale University Press, 1970).

43. Jay Katz, *The Silent World of Doctor and Patient* (New York: Free Press, 1984). Both Katz and Lain Entralgo are psychiatrists.

44. Albert Murray, "Train Whistle Guitar," in *American Negro Short Stories*, ed. John Henrik Clarke (New York: Hill and Wang, 1966). The novel that grew out of this story is *Train Whistle Guitar* (New York: McGraw-Hill, 1980).

NOTES TO CHAPTER EIGHT
A CASE FOR NARRATIVE

1. Leo Tolstoy, "The Death of Ivan Ilych," *The Death of Ivan Ilych and Other Stories*, trans. Aylmer Maude (New York: Signet, 1960), p. 121.

2. Albert R. Jonsen and Stephen Toulmin, *The Abuses of Casuistry* (Berkeley: University of California Press, 1988), was preceded by Toulmin's "The Tyranny of Principles," *Hastings Center Report* 11 (1981), 30–39, and Jonsen's "Casuistry in Clinical Ethics," *Theoretical Medicine* 7 (1986), 65–74.

See also Warren Thomas Reich, "Caring for Life in the First of It: Moral Paradigms for Perinatal and Neonatal Ethics," *Seminars in Perinatology* 11 (1987), 279–87, and Howard Brody, *Stories of Sickness* (New Haven: Yale University Press, 1988). All are on the faculty of a medical school; Brody is also a physician. In a new preface to his first book, *The Place of Reason in Ethics* [1950] (Chicago: University of Chicago Press, 1986), Stephen Toulmin describes the influences that drew him away from analytical philosophy's way of conducting moral philosophy toward a more historical, contextual protocasuist method.

3. Leon Kass, *Toward a More Natural Science: Biology and Human Affairs* (New York: Free Press, 1985), p. 12.

4. The term "pathography" is Anne Hunsaker Hawkins's; see "Two Pathographies: A Study in Illness and Literature," *Journal of Medicine and Philosophy* 9 (1984), 231–52.

5. Brian Clark, *Whose Life Is It Anyway?* (Derbyshire, Eng.: Amber Lane Press, 1978).

6. Robert B. White and H. Tristram Engelhardt, Jr., "A Demand to Die," *Hastings Center Report* 5 (1975), 9–10.

7. Larry Kramer, *The Normal Heart* (New York: New American Library, 1985).

8. William M. Hoffman, *As Is* (New York: Vintage, 1985).

9. Eric J. Cassell, "The Nature of Suffering and the Goals of Medicine," *New England Journal of Medicine* 306 (1982), 639–45.

10. Terry Mizrahi, *Getting Rid of Patients: Contradictions in the Socialization of Physicians* (New Brunswick, N.J.: Rutgers University Press, 1986).

11. John Berger, *A Fortunate Man*, with photographs by Jean Mohr (New York: Holt, 1967), p. 103.

12. William Carlos Williams, "The Autobiography" (1951), in *The William Carlos Williams Reader*, ed. M. L. Rosenthal (New York: New Directions Press, 1966), p. 307.

13. A. C. Dornhurst argues for a pragmatic approach to medical education in "Information Overload: Why Medical Education Needs a Shake-up," *Lancet* 2 [8245] (1981), 513–14.

14. Association of American Medical Colleges Project on the General Professional Education of the Physician, "Physicians for the Twenty-First Century," *Journal of Medical Education* 59 (1984), no. 11, part 2.

15. Robert Coles, *The Call of Stories: Teaching and the Moral Imagination* (Boston: Houghton Mifflin, 1989); "Medical Ethics and Living a Life," *New England Journal of Medicine* 301 (1979), 444–46.

16. Howard Brody, *Stories of Sickness* (New Haven: Yale University Press, 1988).

17. Arthur Kleinman, *The Illness Narratives: Suffering, Healing, and the Human Condition* (New York: Basic Books, 1988).

18. Marcel Proust, *Remembrance of Things Past: Swann's Way*, trans. C. K. Scott Moncrief and Terence Kilmartin (New York: Vintage, 1982).

19. Howard Brody, "Hope," *Journal of the American Medical Association* 246 (1981), 1411–12.

20. See Daniel Callahan, *Setting Limits: Medical Goals in an Aging Society* (New York: Simon and Schuster, 1987), and Brody, "The Physician-Patient Relationship as a Narrative," in *Stories of Sickness*, pp. 171–81.

21. David Burrell and Stanley Hauerwas, "From System to Story: An Alternative Pattern for Rationality in Ethics," *Knowledge, Value and Belief*, vol. 2: *The Foundations of Ethics and Its Relationship to Science*, ed. H. Tristram Engelhardt, Jr., and Daniel Callahan (Hastings-on-Hudson, N.Y.: The Hastings Center, 1977), pp. 111–52.

22. William Carlos Williams, "Asphodel, That Greeny Flower," in *Reader*, pp. 73–74.

23. Kathryn Montgomery Hunter, "Remaking the Case," *Literature and Medicine* 11 (1992), in press.

24. Alvan R. Feinstein, *Clinical Judgment* (Baltimore: Williams and Wilkins, 1967).

25. Feinstein, "An Additional Basic Science for Clinical Medicine, I–IV," *Annals of Internal Medicine* 99 (1983), 393–97, 554–60, 705–12, 843–48.

26. Lawrence L. Weed, "Medical Records That Guide and Teach," *New England Journal of Medicine* 278 (1968), 593–600, 652–57. See also Weed, *Medical Records, Medical Education and Patient Care* (Cleveland: Case Western Reserve University Press, 1970).

27. George L. Engel, "The Need for a New Biomedical Model: The Challenge for Biomedicine," *Science* 196 (1977), 129–36.

28. Mack Lipkin, Jr., Timothy E. Quill, and Rudolph J. Napodano, "The

Medical Interview: A Core Curriculum for Residency in Internal Medicine," *Annals of Internal Medicine* 100 (1984), 277–84. See, too, its valuable list of references.

29. For history, see Hayden White, "The Value of Narrativity in the Representation of Reality," *Critical Inquiry* 7 (1980), 5–27; and Dominick LaCapra, *History, Politics, and the Novel* (Ithaca, N.Y.: Cornell University Press, 1987). For anthropology, see Clifford Geertz, *The Interpretation of Culture*, and Renato Rosaldo, *Culture and Truth: The Remaking of Social Analysis* (Boston: Beacon Press, 1989).

30. Larry W. Churchill and Sandra W. Churchill, "Storytelling in Medical Arenas: The Art of Self-Determination," *Literature and Medicine* 1 (1982), 73–79.

31. Eric J. Cassell describes this as a problem of clinical language in "An Everyday Language of Description," in *Talking with Patients*, vol. 1: *The Theory of Doctor-Patient Communication* (Cambridge, Mass.: MIT Press, 1985), 194–207.

32. David Hilfiker, *Healing the Wounds: A Physician Looks at His Work* (New York: Pantheon, 1985).

33. Richard E. Peschell and Enid Rhodes Peschell, *When a Doctor Hates a Patient and Other Chapters in a Young Physician's Life* (Berkeley: University of California Press, 1986).

34. Julia E. Connelly, "The Right Moment," *Journal of the American Medical Association* 258 (1987), 832.

35. Among others, there are Charles LeBaron, *Gentle Vengeance* (New York: Penguin, 1982); David Hellerstein, *Battles of Life and Death* (Boston: Houghton Mifflin, 1986); Perri Klass, *A Not Entirely Benign Procedure: Four Years as a Medical Student* (New York: Putnam, 1987); Melvin Konner, *Becoming a Doctor: A Journey of Initiation in Medical School* (New York: Viking, 1987).

36. Their most accessible American editions are entitled *Dora: An Analysis of a Case of Hysteria* and *Three Case Histories: The "Wolf Man," the "Rat Man," and the Psychotic Doctor Schreber*, both with an introduction by Philip Rieff (New York: Collier, 1963).

37. Thanks to Sacks's advocacy, these "clinical biographies" have been recently reprinted: A. R. Luria, *The Man with a Shattered World: The History of a Brain Wound*, and *The Mind of a Mnemonist: A Little Book about a Vast Memory* (Cambridge, Mass.: Harvard University Press, 1987).

38. Oliver Sacks, *The Man Who Mistook His Wife for a Hat and Other Clinical Tales* (New York: Summit Books, 1986).

39. Oliver Sacks, *A Leg to Stand On* (New York: Summit Books, 1984).

40. Exactly this has happened with "Fragment of an Analysis of a Case of Hysteria." Dora's abuse by the adults in her life and Freud's acceptance of their values has been vividly argued by feminists and revisioned in Hélène Cixous's play "Portrait of Dora," *Diacritics* 13 (1983), pp. 2–32.

41. Roy Schafer, *Language and Insight* (New Haven: Yale University Press, 1978).

42. Donald Spence, *Narrative Truth, Historical Truth: Meaning and Interpretation in Psychoanalysis* (New York: Norton, 1982).

43. James Hillman, "The Fiction of Case History: A Round with Freud," in *Healing Fiction* (Barrytown, N.Y.: Station Hill, 1983), pp. 1–49. This essay first appeared in *Religion as Story*, ed. James B. Wiggins (New York: Harper and Row, 1975), pp. 123–73.

44. Howard F. Stein, *The Psycho-Dynamics of Medical Practice: Unconscious Factors in Patient Care* (Berkeley: University of California Press, 1985).

45. Rosaldo, *Culture and Truth*, pp. 2ff. Geertz's "thick description" is an example of complexity.

46. Anatole Broyard, "Critically Ill," University of Chicago, April 9, 1990. His forthcoming book about his illness will have the same title.

47. Cecile A. Carson, *The Hidden Language of Medicine: Seeing What Patients Don't Say*, forthcoming.

48. Eric J. Cassell, *Talking with Patients*, 2 vols. (Cambridge, Mass.: MIT Press, 1985).

49. William Donnelly, "From Chronicle to Story," *Journal of the American Medical Association* 260 (1988), 823–25.

50. "The Country of the Saints," the etiology of the crime that delays the denouement of *A Study in Scarlet*, is unique in the canon both for its intrusive length and for its lack of a documented source. There is no evidence that Watson is its narrator. It is the apparent villain's "past medical history" told at great length by a beginner. By the time Watson, the new intern, writes a second story, he has streamlined his case presentation. He and Arthur Conan Doyle ventured into the long form three more times. In the rest of Holmes's numerous adventures, the explanatory circumstances are economically, even parsimoniously, presented.

51. Arthur Conan Doyle, *The Hound of the Baskervilles*, in *The Complete Sherlock Holmes* (New York: Doubleday, 1930; reprinted 1985), p. 753.

52. Henry David Thoreau, "Civil Disobedience" [1849], in *Walden and Civil Disobedience*, ed. Sherman Paul (Boston: Houghton Mifflin, 1960).

INDEX

Abelson, Robert P., 182 n.32
Abramson, S. B., 185 n.7
Abse, Dannie, 163
academic medicine, xxi, 5, 8, 51, 52, 81, 105, 137; hierarchy in, 28, 32–34, 72–79, 187 n.19
Ackernecht, Erwin H., 182 n.30
Adams, Alice, *Second Chances*, 158
Adler, Jack J., 188 n.7
Altman, Lawrence K., 185 n.6, 190 n.60
Andersen, R. D., 188 n.21
Anderson, C. B., 188 n.10
anecdotes, xiii, xxii, 70–82, 166
Angell, Marcia, 176 n.8
Aristotle, 28, 181 n.5
Association of American Medical Colleges, *Physicians for the Twenty-first Century* (the GPEP Report), xi, 156, 175 n.2, 176 n.1, 195 n.14
Atwater, Edward C., 184 n.7
Axelsen, Diana, 175 n.3

Baker, A. L., 188 n.12
Balint, Michael, 128, 167, 177 n.15, 192 n.11
Banks, G., 188 n.10
Barnett, A., 190 n.66
Barth, John, *Letters*, 87
Bateman, David, 120–21, 190 n.72
Battle, J. D., Jr., 189 n.25
Beatty, Peter A., 188 n.16
Becker, Marshall, 186 n.9
Bedell, Suzanna, 41, 182 n.28
Bell, Joe, 22
Benchimol, Alberto, 188 n.20
Bender, John, 184 n.5
Berger, John, and Jean Mohr, *A Fortunate Man*, 155, 195 n.11
Bernard, Claude, 186 n.3
Berry, Michael, 182 n.27
Bertallanfy, Ludwig von, 21, 179 n.37
Blackstone, M. O., 188 n.12
Blois, Marsden S., 59, 183 n.33, 184 n.10, 190 n.64
Booth, Wayne, 179 n.44
Bordley, Donald, 41, 182 n.27

Bororos, 123–25, 128, 131, 145
Bosk, Charles L., 33, 181 n.13, 185 n.11
Boswell, James, *Life of Samuel Johnson*, 64
Bowditch, Henry I., 184 n.6
Bracken, Thomas H., 189 n.32
Branch, William T., 192 n.21
Brauner, Daniel J., 88, 186 n.7
Brody, Howard, 181 n.7, 185 n.2, 195 nn.19–20; *Stories of Sickness*, 157, 194 n.2, 195 n.16
Bronson, Bertrand, 184 n.13
Brooks, Peter, 24, 92, 179 n.45, 186 n.12
Burrell, David, 195 n.21

Cabanis, Pierre-Jean-George, xix
Cabot, Richard, 21, 56
Callahan, Daniel, 178 n.34, 195 nn.20–21
Caplan, Arthur L., 178 n.34
Carson, Cecile A., 177 n.14, 197 n.47
case history. *See* medicine, narrative in
case presentation, xxii, 6–7, 51–68, 69, 76, 86, 94, 98, 127, 167, 169
case report, xxii, 69, 81, 83, 93–102, 106
Cassell, Eric J.: *Changing Values in Medicine* (ed. with Mark Siegler), 178 n.21, 179 n.36, 184 n.9, 190 n.64; *The Healer's Art*, 140, 182 n.31, 193 n.31, 193 n.38; *Talking to Patients*, 168, 196 n.31, 197 n.48; "The Nature of Suffering and the Goals of Medicine," 154, 194 n.9
Castaigne, P., 189 n.36
casuistry. *See* clinical casuistry
causality, xxi, 84, 102–106, 139, 186 n.5, 197 n.50
Charon, Rita, 86–87, 176 n.4, 186 n.4
chart, xxii, 6, 69, 83–93, 101, 186 n.6. *See also* problem-oriented medical record
Chatman, Seymour, 179 n.44
Churchill, Larry W., 177 n.8, 196 n.30
Churchill, Sandra W., 177 n.8, 196 n.30
Ciurczak, Francis M., 188 n.6
Cixous, Hélène, 196 n.40
Clark, Brian, *Whose Life Is It Anyway?*, 154, 194 n.5